HOW TO SAVE
CORPORATE AMERICA

VICTOR O. OKOCHA

Copyright © 2022 Victor O. Okocha.

All rights reserved. No part of this book may be reproduced, stored, or transmitted by any means—whether auditory, graphic, mechanical, or electronic—without written permission of both publisher and author, except in the case of brief excerpts used in critical articles and reviews. Unauthorized reproduction of any part of this work is illegal and is punishable by law.

ISBN: 979-8-88640-403-6 (sc)
ISBN: 979-8-88640-404-3 (hc)
ISBN: 979-8-88640-405-0 (e)

Because of the dynamic nature of the Internet, any web addresses or links contained in this book may have changed since publication and may no longer be valid. The views expressed in this work are solely those of the author and do not necessarily reflect the views of the publisher, and the publisher hereby disclaims any responsibility for them.

One Galleria Blvd., Suite 1900, Metairie, LA 70001
1-888-421-2397

CONTENTS

Introduction 1

Chapter 1   Organizations are Extensions of Individuals 51

Chapter 2   Organizations Have Foundations 94

Chapter 3   Organizations Come in Different Forms 120

Chapter 4   Organizations are Very Important to the Society 164

Chapter 5   Organizations Do Grow 178

Chapter 6   Organizations Do Die 203

Chapter 7   Organizations Can Be Transformed 227

Conclusions 291

End Notes 303

Acknowledgments 305

INTRODUCTION

Corporate America is all about American corporations and how they influence the American society both economically and politically. The number of American corporations runs into millions and there are tens of hundreds of these that make annual revenues in billions of dollars. There are at least three hundred of the Fortune 500 corporations that run global operations and influence international affairs by implication. American corporations reflect the image and strength of America. The bravery of Americans is reflected in all the scientific discoveries, technological inventions, process innovations, and entrepreneurial exploits which are deployed to provide both local solutions and global interventions. That America is great is due to the greatness of its corporations. American corporations provide solutions to various human needs, create the jobs that sustain the middle class, and ensure economic empowerment for individuals and households that guarantees personal freedom and promotes national democracy. American corporations also contribute to the income of the government through payment of corporate taxes. They also add great value to the overall development of the American society. As a result, we can boldly say that America is not run by the politicians in Washington DC but by powerful corporations which corporate offices tower into the city skylines across the fifty states of the United States. Corporations promote capitalism which sustains our democracy. We cannot have true democracy without practicing capitalism. As the American economist, Walter E. Williams[1] rightly puts it: "Capitalism is relatively new in human history. Prior to capitalism, the way people amassed great wealth was by looting, plundering, and enslaving their fellow man. Capitalism made it possible to become wealthy by serving your fellow man."

According to Investopedia website, 'a corporation is a legal entity that is separate and distinct from its owners. Under the law, corporations possess many of the same rights and responsibilities as individuals. They can enter contracts, loan and borrow money, sue and be sued, hire employees, own assets, and pay taxes.'[2] A corporation is created when it is incorporated by a group of shareholders who share ownership of the corporation, represented by their holding of stock or shares, and pursuit of a common goal. The vast majority of corporations have a goal of returning a profit for their shareholders. However, some corporations, such as charities or fraternal organizations, are nonprofit or not-for-profit. A corporation can be described as follows: Corporation = Space + Objective + Leadership + Unity of purpose + Technology + Idea + Optimism + Needs (SOLUTION). The idea for a corporation is usually conceived by an individual or group of individuals. A corporation is formed to create a solution. Every corporation is established to meet a specific need or group of needs. Some provide retail services while some manufacture products. Some provide media services while others construct homes. Some provide financial services while others are into telecommunications. Some provide transportation services while others engage in agricultural production. Some are into fashion designing while others are involved in industrial processing. No matter the nature of the corporation, it takes ordinary individuals to establish it.

The ultimate aim of every corporation is to make reasonable returns to its investors or shareholders by ensuring that the total revenue it generates is greater than the total cost of its operations in a given period. For several decades, however, there has been a clarion call for corporations to extend their bottom line beyond the financial gains towards social benefits as well. Following the resolution of the G8 summit in 2013[3], the Social Impact Investment Task-force was created to help develop an impact-focused marketplace. This ultimately led to the promotion of benefit corporations here in the United States. As at 2015, over 1,500 of these B corporations have been established including Warby Parker and Etsy. The goal here is to ensure that corporations contribute reasonably to the overall development of the society in which they operate so that there is a balance between economic gains and social impact. American corporations continue to lead global advancements in technology, health care, aerospace, defense, media, entertainment, telecommunications, retail services, etc.

At the turn of the 20th century, two major events changed the world: The First and the Second Word Wars which took place in 1914 to 1918 and 1939 to 1944, respectively. The prominent role played by the United States in the course of the Second World War made America emerge as the world power and the most influential nation in the United Nations. The United Nations is a world organization formed after the Second World War to promote peace and forestall a future global war. Thereafter, the American dollar became the international currency and an acceptable medium of exchange in all international trade and global financial transactions. All these gave a further boost to the already-booming American economy, which was based on its industrial dominance and commercial relevance. The whole world looked up to America's high-quality products based on American scientific ingenuity and technological expertise. If any nation needed military jets as well as sophisticated arms and ammunition, it went to the United States. Educational institutions around the world looked up to the United States for quality books and research materials. Medical facilities from around the world copied from hospitals in the United States. Individuals who needed quality automobiles, electronics, clothing, furniture, medicine, office equipment, building materials, etc., preferred made-in-America products. As American exports soared, government revenue multiplied through corporate and personal income taxes, leading to an increase in infrastructural developments, more funding for technological, medical, and other research and greater arming of the US military. As demand for American products increased, employment opportunities doubled and working as well as living conditions improved, creating a thriving middle class. The best brains from around the world were attracted and they started migrating to the United States in search of better life and to be a part of the 'American dream.'

However, towards the end of the 20th century and at the beginning of the 21st century, the American environment was bedeviled by high rate of unemployment as well as under-employment. This resulted from massive factory closures and relocation overseas. Some CEOs of American corporations argue that the price of made-in-America products was no longer competitive in comparison with imported products. The cost of domestic production was rising astronomically. Other nations had developed their industrial sectors and were producing competing products at a cheaper rate than those produced here in the United States. Consequently, imports into the United States increased while exports dropped resulting to a drop in employment as well as in government revenue. As a result of this new reality, the American industrialist, immediately propelled by the global competition but remotely fueled by greed, started shutting down production facilities in the United States and relocating to areas where there is abundance of cheap but largely unskilled labor such as in China and Mexico. Little did they realize at that time that these seeming harmless activities were going to hurt the American economy, create socio-economic inequality among Americans and impact America's influence around the world. Those corporations that relocated their factories outside of the United States now import and sell to the American people without creating employment and a source of income for them. Those corporations that failed to relocate have been devising and executing various anti-labor strategies to intimidate the American workers and make life miserable for them. The average American worker is now made to work more for less pay. American corporations are becoming more and more powerful and are influencing public policies in their favor. Labor unions have been sidelined and employees discouraged from joining unions. Should the American democracy, which is usually interpreted as 'government of the people for the people by the people' encourage the intimidation of the masses by a few? Is today's capitalism in conflict with democracy?

INTRODUCTION

Why are corporations becoming richer and stronger while American people are becoming poorer and weaker?

The huge influence of corporate organizations and wealthy individuals on the economic spectrum of the United States is being used to shape and reshape political decisions and government actions that continue to make those organizations and individuals more influential over the socio-political landscape. Both campaign contributions and lobbying funds are often used to determine the direction of government policies, programs and projects which indirectly help to promote the donors' interest as well as protect their investments at the expense of the masses, provide more opportunities for amassing wealth, and ultimately position them for greater influence on the larger society. What made America great a few decades ago is now making Americans to regret. Can American corporations be transformed to provide the much-needed succor to the American people or are things going to continue this downward trend?

This book seeks to explore and explain the origin, benefits, achievements, and difficulties of American organizations and how they can be transformed and re-positioned to address today's challenges and remain tomorrow's giants. The greatness of America lies on the robustness of its private-sector-driven economy which results in job and income creation for the American people and revenue generation for the government. Failure of the private sector to achieve these two scenarios, simultaneously, portends danger to the American nation. We must find a way to redistribute the huge revenue generated by the private sector without necessarily resorting to socialism or communism. Government must continue to act as the unbiased umpire in the private-sector-driven economy so that every stakeholder can fully enjoy the fruits of our collective labor.

In the course of my business management career, I have come across numerous books written about organizations and how best to manage them. I have also seen hundreds, if not thousands, of organizations struggle and then disappear, especially startups. In all these, one thing has always remained remarkable; when an organization goes down, many people go down with it. Individuals, families, communities as well as entire nations, are constantly affected when once-a-blossoming organization suddenly goes into extinction. Looking around, I have also seen a good number of organizations that have lasted for several decades and handed down from one generation to another. What then is the secret behind the success or failure of organizations and what can we do to help more organizations emerge, survive, and thrive amid daunting challenges?

Organizations are as old as the human race

Organizations are human institutions established for specific reasons. The existence of a problem that cannot be solved by an individual often calls for the establishment of an organization. So, we can conclude that an organization is an organized setup that involves more than one person for the purpose of solving a problem that cannot be handled by one individual. We can also say that an organization is a group of two or more persons coming together to solve a particular problem or set of problems. Many, sometimes conflicting and confusing, definitions have been advanced for the word 'organization' but the rallying point remains one and the same; that organizations are formed for specific purposes - to meet specific needs that will be difficult for an individual to achieve alone. But an organization is usually the idea of an individual. So, the saying that an organization is an extension of an individual is a truth that cannot be denied but rather validated with solid facts.

The main objective of this book is to highlight those intrinsic human values that enable an individual to conceive, establish, manage, grow, and sustain organizations and then hand them down from one generation to another. As stated earlier, organizations are formed to solve problems, meet needs, proffer solutions, and attain goals that would have been extremely difficult or nearly impossible for an individual alone. This means that organizations create some kind of synergy where the product of a team supersedes the summation of the products from individual efforts. This is the whole essence of an organization - to help create solutions and results that would have been impossible for people to obtain individually. We can, therefore, say that a family is an organization, a community is an organization, a city, state, region, nation, The United Nations, businesses, nonprofits, Churches, schools, colleges, clubs, hospitals, universities, research institutes, political parties, sports teams, music groups, labor unions, military formations, religious bodies, terrorist groups, etc. The differentiating factor between one organization and another is the objective. Most organizations have good intentions but a few, unfortunately, have bad intentions. Some organizations are established to create value and provide solutions whereas others are formed to destroy value and to create confusion and insecurity.

The family is the first organization to ever exist. The family institution was established by God to provide companionship, assistance, protection, and procreation. In case you are wondering why I am talking about God in a management book, just relax and let me explain. I have come to realize that God is the source of humanity and that the Bible has the most comprehensive and authentic account of the origin of man (creation), his potentials (talents), and his purpose on the earth (destiny). It is in pursuant of his or her destiny that an individual establishes an organization. That is the link! After creating him, God saw that Adam needed help to carry out his responsibility of being fruitful, multiplying, replenishing the earth, subduing the earth, and having dominion over it (Genesis 1:28; 2:18,21-24)[4]. The condition of the family is significant because experience has shown that once the family system is distorted, the society is devastated. Most of the problems we have around the world today are as a result of broken family values; a situation where kids are raised under certain conditions that can hardly be referred to as family - the father has left the home to be alone, the mother is hardly at home to fill the gap, and the kids are left alone to play the role of mom and dad, which they can't. Now the society is left with men and women who know little or nothing about family values. And when men and women that know nothing about family values find themselves in the community, at schools, in work areas and other public places, they simply exhibit their deficiencies and inefficiencies, which tend to make the society worse off.

When the family system is destroyed the social structure is decapitated. The rising rates of single parenthood as well as separation and divorce among married couples do lead to the total collapse of the family system which results in the raising of delinquent children, leading to child abandonment and endangerment, increased rate of crime, drug addiction, alcoholism, pornography, indiscriminate sex, teenage pregnancy, and abortion, etc. There is also the issue of bullying, sexual harassment, rape, racial discrimination, selfishness, arrogance, total disrespect for law and order, and little or no regard for one another. Available statistics show that most children raised without the father and the mother under the same roof, end up dropping out of school, committing crime, going to jail, and dying prematurely. The news media is awash daily with news about street gangs, revenge killings, drug overdoses, mass shootings, and suicide. There is little or no regard for human life in our society anymore. Our Police Departments are getting overwhelmed by the spate of crime and rate of violence while the government has run out of options to tackle the problem as well as the budget to provide for the incarceration of those we consider social miscreants. But the entire problem started from the neglect of the family unit! When we create conditions that make it easier for men to be excused from taking up their responsibility as fathers or establish policies that make it an offense for parents to discipline their children at home, we will experience nothing but social implosion. We should understand that there is a significant difference between child discipline and child abuse. Any society that cannot identify this difference is jeopardizing its future. Our children need parental guidance to be able to make right decisions, take right actions, lead positive lifestyles, and contribute meaningfully to societal development. When parental discipline and guidance are absent, youth decadence takes over. Unfortunately, this is the reality in most modern societies!

INTRODUCTION

We cannot overemphasize the fact that most of the challenges we face in our society today are as a result of the breakdown in our family system. Take for example the housing sector. What determines the cost of homes is the interplay between demand and supply. When the demand for homes rises beyond the supply of houses, the cost of houses will rise. And when the demand for homes falls below the supply of houses, the cost of houses with fall. You will recall that the cost of housing has a ripple effect on the general economy as it did in the 2008/2009 economic crisis. The main factors that lead to an increase in the number of homes demanded are (1) parents sending their teenage kids to go get a job and start their own life, (2) new couples moving to their first homes, (3) old couples moving into bigger homes, and (4) people moving to new locations. The other one is couples separating/divorcing and moving into separate homes. Let us assume that most of the separated/divorced men and women who are still single get married and move into one home with their spouses, and most of the single moms and dads get married and move into one home with their spouses, we will immediately have more houses on the supply side than on the demand side, and the cost of homes will drop drastically. Therefore, the state of the family unit determines the way most things happen in the larger society. And unless the family is fixed, the rest of the society cannot be completely fixed.

Communities are also a form of organization. Communities are geographic expressions of families and individuals living in the same location and having shared values on relationships, security, tradition, education, means of livelihood, property ownership, and continuity, etc. Most times, people are selected or elected to enforce common rules and policies based on those shared values. This gave rise to the formation of cities, states, regions and nations; establishing governments to enforce common laws based on the shared values that guide various interactions among citizens.

The other organizations are established as an extension of individuals' ideas, services, products, properties, discoveries, inventions, innovations, skills, and experience in such a way as to provide greater solution to a greater number of people in different locations. For example, a political organization is a group of individuals with similar political ideology who come together to streamline their ideas, sell it to the electorate, present their candidates for election, and then ensure that their elected party men and women use the party ideology or manifesto to add value to the society by providing solutions, giving directions, and maintaining conditions that make the citizens better off. If citizens are not better off, then the political organization has failed to reach its objective or deliver on its promises. The main reason why citizens clamor for a change in national leadership is as a result of the failure of the ruling political party to live up to its campaign promises and make things better for the citizenry.

This book was conceived to address the seven hard facts about organizations and to reveal how individuals can conceive, establish, and grow successful organizations which can be passed on from generation to generation. Human beings were not created to exist independently but to operate as inter-dependent individuals. No single individual possesses all that he or she needs to excel in life hence the need to interact and co-operate with other individuals to get what you need on one hand, and to share what you have on the other hand. Some regions of the world are warm most of the year (tropical region) while other regions are cold most of the year (temperate region). Certain types of food can grow well in certain parts of the world while they cannot do the same in other parts. What is scarce in some parts of the world is in abundance in other parts in order to necessitate exchange, which is the whole essence of international trade.

In fact, the only thing that provides the need for relationship among individuals, and by extension nations, is that there is something one needs that the other has. Trade by barter was the first form of economic exchange among human beings. If an individual has everything he needs, he may never relate with another. In the same vein, if any nation has everything it needs, it may never relate with another. So, the scarcity or deficiency we have in our lives is a natural reason for us to relate with other people for completeness. Selfishness, therefore, is a sign of deep-seated inferiority complex based on nothing else than ignorance. The fear that every other person wants to harm you is the greatest challenge of the human society. Fear breeds suspicion and creates disharmony in the society. If you are afraid of your neighbor, when you actually need him to survive, then you are already dead while still alive. Bad neighbors must, however, be avoided or confronted. Organizations cannot be established in the presence of fear. Communities cannot be created in the midst of fear. Nations cannot be built in the presence of fear. And the world cannot survive in the midst of fear. Fear demoralizes people and polarizes nations.

Natural resources are comparatively dispersed so that what one nation lacks, another has in order to facilitate healthy exchange between one and another and not wanton exploitation of one by the other. Natural talents are also relatively dispersed so that what one individual lacks, another has in order to necessitate sharing and not slaving. There are no inferior human beings but people with diverse talents, competencies, and capabilities in different shades of skin so that we can complement and complete each other and make the world a better place for us all. Superiority complex is the bane of human co-existence and the reason for most social dysfunction and economic disparity. If every individual has everything he needs, there would be no need for organizations. So, organizations are established to cater for individual deficiencies on one hand and to provide for human needs on the other. The proper understanding of this fact paves way for further discussions on the operations of organizations throughout this book.

The book has been laid out in seven chapters, each depicting a unique characteristic of organizations. Chapter one confirms that organizations are extensions of individuals. It is someone's idea that gives birth to an organization. So, if an organization undermines the importance of individuals in its operation, it jeopardizes the very foundation on which it stands. The organization is not the buildings, the machines, the computers, the desks, chairs, cars, trucks, telephones, and the management information system, etc. The organization is not even the office space or cash in the bank. The organization is those human beings who have come together to meet a need, provide a solution, or attain an objective. All other things help to facilitate their work and enhance the result. That is why when individual members of the organization go home at the end of each day's activities, the organization is shut down; when the people are on vacation, the organization is out of operation.

The second chapter focuses on the foundations or basic principles of the organization. It lays out the foundation on which the organization stands and discusses the various factors that strengthen the organization. Chapter three considers the various forms of organizations. All organizations are not the same because they are not formed by the same people or for the same purpose. This chapter highlights what makes one organization different from another and provides an extensive discussion about these differences so that the reader can appreciate as well as apply them in his or her day to day life as a student, teacher, worker, researcher, or regulator. The fourth chapter makes it very clear that organizations are very important to the society. The importance of organizations cannot be overemphasized especially based on the backdrop that once there is a need that requires two or more people to come together to solve, an organization is formed. Over the centuries of human existence, the organization has achieved so much ranging from the construction of Egyptian pyramids, formation of the Roman army, establishment of the Greek government, landing of the first man in the moon, mounting of the first satellite in the space, to fighting against global hunger, disease and terror. There is no limit to what can be achieved once human beings come together in search of solution. The only challenge is usually the ability to come together.

Chapters five and six discuss the facts that organizations grow and die, respectively. Just as every other living organism, organizations do grow. Chapter five focuses on the factors that contribute to the growth, development, and sustainability of organizations while chapter six concentrates on the factors that lead to the demise of organizations. Do organizations actually die just as all other living organisms? How long are organizations expected to live before they go into extinction? Finally, can organizations be transformed? If yes, what actions can be taken to make this possible? That is the focus of Chapter 7, the last chapter of the book. This chapter explores the challenges and opportunities of 21st century organizations. In the face of the globalization challenge, and all the benefits it offers, what chances do organizations have to strive, survive, and thrive in an era of increasing uncertainties?

It has been long discovered that business, that is, the profitable production and distribution of goods and services for consumption, is at the center of everything we do in the world hence the huge influence of business organizations on the society. This book gives details of the role of business in shaping the world. Business entails commerce and industry. It has also been referred to by some as trade and investments. Business exists as a result of the need for exchange. No individual possesses, or produces, all that he needs by himself. In the same vein, no nation possesses, or produces, all it needs by itself. As a result, individuals must exchange what they have for what they need; nations must also exchange what they produce for what they need. For example, a nation that produces steel materials will need leather materials. Business organizations come into the equation to facilitate these exchanges in a smooth and effective manner so that each nation is able to get what it needs by giving out a part of what it has. This is the whole idea behind global business.

How are individual goods produced and how are commercial services provided? These are critical questions aimed at determining the nature of technology available at every stage of human existence. The set of people that utilize better means of production are said to be more developed than those who use lesser methods because they are getting the most results from their environment. The fact also remains that the knowledge available to one set of people usually flows to another set of people to enable them improve their own method of production of goods and provision of services. This happens through improved information systems. So, the means of information dissemination available at a certain period of time determines the rate at which the method of production available in one location is also available in other locations. Does this situation negatively affect economic exchange at the international stage? To a large extent it does not. The simple reason is that there are other things needed for production to take place apart from information about technology. Raw materials, right equipment, and skilled labor have to be there as well for production to take place.

Information is becoming a major resource in production even though the factors of production traditionally remained land, labor, capital, and entrepreneurship. Organizations can no longer do without having the right information for their day-to-day operations. The speed at which information flows is, therefore, pivotal to the success or failure of organizations. At a time, the discovery of the printing press altered the nature of global development because the information available in one location became readily available in another location through printed books. The research results, discoveries, inventions, and innovations taking place in one part of the globe became available in another part so that development in production became almost evenly distributed. These days, the introduction of the computer and the internet has made information dissemination much faster than ever in the history of mankind. With a click of the button, the information available in Miami, Florida can become accessible to someone in faraway Mumbai, India. This has brought a whole lot of changes in the process of production. The parts of a product assembled in USA can now be manufactured in China, India, Mexico, Canada, Japan, or Brazil so that it is no longer logical to say that the product is 'made in America.' Products can now be designed in America, manufactured in Africa, and sent back to America for sale. This is the globalization of production with its far-reaching implication on the nature of business operations around the world.

The last part of the book has been devoted to the discussion on the challenges and opportunities of 21st century organizations. How are current changes in information dissemination affecting the success of 21st century businesses and other organizations, and what should be done to take advantage of the opportunities these changes offer and curtail the threat they pose? Those who wish to start, operate, and grow organizations, especially business organizations, must have a deep understanding of today's environment and the opportunities it offers as well as the threats it poses. Knowledge, they say, is power, and without it, failure is inevitable!

Organizations are created by ordinary individuals

To further buttress the fact that organizations are extensions of individuals, below is a compendium of a few notable corporations, the individuals that founded them, the dates they were founded, and how small they started. Their current location, financial status, and operational scope have also been added for greater understanding. (Source: www.wikipedia.org)[5]

Table 0.1

Name of Corporation, founder(s), year and location of founding, and original size.	Current location, financial status, and scope of operation.
1. Procter & Gamble Procter & Gamble was founded by William Procter and James Gamble in 1837 at Cincinnati, Ohio. William and James had married from the same family and it was their father in-law who persuaded them to become business partners. The company made its first $1 million sales revenue in 1859.	A multinational consumer goods company with headquarters at Cincinnati, Ohio, and subsidiaries around the world. It is specialized in cleaning agents, Personal care products, Beauty Care Products, Personal Healthcare Products, etc. In 2019, its total assets stood at $115 billion with 97 thousand employees and $67.7 billion in sales revenue.
2. J.C. Penney J.C. Penney was founded by James Cash Penney & William Henry McManus in 1902 at Kemmerer, Wyoming as a retail store. The company grew over the years by acquiring other retail shops. The 500th store was opened in 1924 while the 1000th store was opened in 1928 with sales revenue of $190 million.	By 2017, J.C. Penney had a total asset of $9 billion, recorded a sales revenue of $12.5 billion, and had 106 thousand employees working in 1013 stores nationwide. However, in May 2020, JCPenney filed for Chapter 11 bankruptcy protection due to the effects of the COVID-19 pandemic and in September 2020, Brookfield Property Partners and Simon Property Group agreed to purchase JCPenney for around "$300 million in cash".
3. General Electric General Electric was founded by Charles A. Coffin, Elihu Thomson, Edwin J. Houston, Thomas Edison, and J.P. Morgan through a merger on April 15, 1892 in Schenectady, New York as a manufacturer of electrical products. Over the years, GE acquired several companies to become a global conglomerate operating in the areas of aircraft engines, electrical distribution, electric motors, energy, finance, health care, software, and wind turbines.	With headquarters in Boston, Massachusetts, GE currently has worldwide operations with a total number of 307,000 employees and a total revenue of $113.245 billion and a total asset base of $656.56 billion in 2013. From 2020 records, with subsidiaries such as GE Additive, GE Aviation, GE Capital, GE Global, GE Hitachi Nuclear Energy, GE Healthcare, GE Power, GE Renewable Energy, and GE Ventures, General Electric now has a total of 205,000 employees, a total revenue of $75.619 billion and a total asset base of $253.452 billion.
4. Walt-Disney World Also known as Walt Disney World Resort, it is an entertainment resort complex in Bay Lake and Lake Buena Vista in Florida designed by Walt Disney. At the death of Walt Disney in 1966, his elder brother, Roy Disney, completed the project, which opened for business in 1971. The complex covers nearly 25,000 acres of land with 4 theme parks, 2 water parks, 31 themed resort hotels, 9 non-Disney hotels, several golf courses, a camping resort, and other entertainment venues, including the outdoor shopping center, Disney Springs.	In 2018, Walt Disney World was the most visited vacation resort in the world, with an average annual attendance of more than 58 million. Due to COVID-19, the attendance dropped to 19 million in 2020. The resort is the flagship destination of Disney's worldwide corporate enterprise and has become a popular staple in American culture. In 2020, Walt Disney World was chosen to host the NBA Bubble for play of the 2019-2020 season of the National Basketball Association to resume at the ESPN Wide World of Sports Complex. On October 1, 2021, Walt Disney World honored its 50th anniversary with 'The World's Most Magical Celebration.'

5. Walmart Walmart Inc. is an American multi-national retail corporation that operates a chain of hypermarkets, also called super-centers, discount department stores, and grocery stores headquartered in Bentonville, Arkansas. The company was founded by Sam Walton in nearby Rogers, Arkansas in 1962 and incorporated under Delaware General Corporation Law on October 31, 1969. It also owns and operates Sam's Club retail warehouses. Within its first five years, the company expanded to 18 stores in Arkansas and reached $9 million in sales. In 1968, it opened its first stores outside Arkansas in Sikeston, Missouri and Claremore, Oklahoma.	As of January 31, 2022, Walmart has 10,593 stores and clubs in 24 countries, operating under 48 different names. The company operates under the name Walmart in the United States and Canada. Walmart is the world's largest company by revenue, with US$548.743 billion, according to the Fortune Global 500 list in 2020. It is also the largest private employer in the world with 2.2 million employees. It is a publicly traded family-owned business, as the company is controlled by the Walton family. Sam Walton's heirs own over 50 percent of Walmart through both their holding company, Walton Enterprises, and their individual holdings. Walmart was the largest United States grocery retailer in 2019, and 65 percent of Walmart's US$510.329 billion sales came from U.S. operations.
6. Warner Media Warner Media was an American multinational mass media and entertainment conglomerate corporation. It was headquartered at the 30 Hudson Yards complex in New York City, United States. It was originally established in 1972 by Steve Ross as Warner Commu-nications, and Time Warner was created in 1990, following a merger between Time Inc. and the original Warner Communications. The company has film, television and cable operations, with its assets including Warner Media Studios & Networks (consisting of the entertainment assets of Turner Broadcasting, HBO, and Cinemax as well as Warner Bros., which itself consists of the film, animation, television studios, the company's home entertainment division and Studio Distribution Services, its joint venture with Universal Pictures Home Entertainment, DC Comics, New Line Cinema, and, together with CBS Entertainment Group, through its Warner Bros. Entertainment subsidiary, a 50% interest in The CW television network); Warner Media News & Sports (consisting of the news and sports assets of Turner Broadcasting, including CNN, Turner Sports, and AT&T SportsNet); WarnerMedia Sales & Distribution (consisting of digital media company Otter Media); and Warner Media Direct (consisting of the HBO Max streaming service).	Despite spinning off Time Inc. in 2014, the company retained the Time Warner name until AT&T's acquisition in 2018, after which it became Warner Media. On October 22, 2016, AT&T officially announced that they intended on acquiring Time Warner for $85.4 billion (including assumed Time Warner debt), valuing the company at $107.50 per share. The proposed merger was confirmed on June 12, 2018, after AT&T won an antitrust lawsuit that the U.S. Justice Department filed in 2017 to attempt to block the acquisition. The merger closed two days later, with the company becoming a subsidiary of AT&T. The company's current name was adopted a day later. Under AT&T, the company moved to launch a streaming service built around the company's content, known as HBO Max. Warner Media refolded Turner's entertain-ment-based networks under a singular umbrella unit on August 10, 2020, through a consolidation of the Warner Media Entertain-ment and Warner Bros. Entertainment assets into a new unit, Warner Media Studios & Networks Group. On May 17, 2021, nearly three years after the acquisition, AT&T decided to leave the entertainment business and announced that it had proposed to relinquish its ownership of Warner Media and merge it with Discovery, Inc. to form a new publicly traded company, Warner Bros. Discovery, under Discovery Inc.'s CEO David Zaslav. The deal was closed on April 8, 2022.

7. HP Inc.

HP Inc. was formerly known as Hewlett-Packard. Hewlett-Packard was founded in 1939 by Bill Hewlett and David Packard, who both graduated with degrees in electrical engi-neering from Stanford University in 1935. The company started off in the HP Garage in Palo Alto, California. On November 1, 2015, Hewlett-Packard was renamed to HP Inc. and the company enterprise business were spun off and renamed to Hewlett Packard Enterprise. HP is listed on the New York Stock Exchange and is a constituent of the S&P 500 Index. It is the world's 2nd largest personal computer vendor by unit sales as of January 2021, after Lenovo. In the 2018 Fortune 500 list, HP is ranked 58th largest United States corporation by total revenue.

HP Inc. is an American multinational infor-mation technology company headquartered in Palo Alto, California, that develops personal computers (PCs), printers and related supplies, as well as 3D printing solutions. It was formed on November 1, 2015, renamed from the personal computer and printer divisions of the original Hewlett-Packard Company, with that company's enterprise product and business services divisions becoming Hewlett Packard Enterprise. The split was structured so that Hewlett-Packard changed its name to HP Inc. and spun off Hewlett Packard Enterprise as a new publicly traded company. HP Inc. retains Hewlett-Packard's pre-2015 stock price history and its former stock ticker symbol, HPQ, while Hewlett Packard Enterprise trades under its own symbol, HPE.

8. Wells Fargo & Company

Wells Fargo & Company is an American multinational financial services company with corporate headquarters in San Francisco, California, operational headquarters in Manhattan, and managerial offices throughout the United States and internationally. The company has operations in 35 countries with over 70 million customers globally. It is considered a systemically important financial institution by the Financial Stability Board. The firm's primary subsidiary is Wells Fargo Bank, N.A., a national bank chartered in Wilmington, Delaware, which designates its main office in Sioux Falls, South Dakota. It is the fourth largest bank in the United States by total assets and is one of the largest as ranked by bank deposits and market capitalization. Along with JPMorgan Chase, Bank of America, and Citigroup, Wells Fargo is one of the "Big Four Banks" of the United States. It has 8,050 branches and 13,000 ATMs. It is one of the most valuable bank brands.

Wells Fargo in its present form is a result of a merger between the original Wells Fargo & Company and Minneapolis-based Norwest Cor-poration in 1998. While Norwest was the nominal survivor, the merged company took the better-known Wells Fargo name and moved to Wells Fargo's hub in San Francisco, while its banking subsidiary merged with Wells Fargo's Sioux Falls-based banking subsidiary. With the 2008 acquisition of Charlotte-based Wachovia, Wells Fargo became a coast-to-coast bank. Wells Fargo is ranked 37th on the Fortune 500 list of the largest companies in the US. The company has been the subject of several investigations by regulators; on February 2, 2018, account fraud by the bank resulted in the Federal Reserve barring Wells Fargo from growing its nearly $2 trillion-asset base any further until the company fixed its internal problems to the satisfaction of the Federal Reserve. In September 2021, Wells Fargo incurred further fines from the United States Justice Department charging fraudulent behavior by the bank against foreign-exchange currency trading customers.

9. J.P. Morgan Chase & Co.

JPMorgan Chase & Co. is an American multinational investment bank and financial services holding company headquartered in New York City and incorporated in Delaware. As of December 31, 2021, JPMorgan Chase is the largest bank in the United States, the world's largest bank by market capitalization, and the fifth-largest bank in the world in terms of total assets, with total assets totaling to US$3.831 trillion. As a "Bulge Bracket" bank, it is a major provider of various investment banking and financial services. It is one of America's Big Four banks, along with Bank of America, Citigroup, and Wells Fargo. JPMorgan Chase is considered to be a universal bank and a custodian bank. The J.P. Morgan brand is used by the investment banking, asset management, private banking, private wealth management, and treasury services divisions. Fiduciary activity within private banking and private wealth management is done under the aegis of JPMorgan Chase Bank, N.A.—the actual trustee. The Chase brand is used for credit card services in the United States and Canada, the bank's retail banking activities in the United States and United Kingdom, and commercial banking. Both the retail and commercial bank and the bank's corporate headquarters are currently located at 383 Madison Avenue in Midtown Manhattan, New York City, since the prior headquarters building directly across the street, 270 Park Avenue, was demolished and a larger replacement headquarters is being built on the same site. It is considered a systemically important bank by the Financial Stability Board.

The current company was originally known as Chemical Bank, which acquired Chase Manhattan and assumed that company's name. The present company was formed in 2000, when Chase Manhattan Corporation merged with J.P. Morgan & Co. JPMorgan Chase, in its current structure, is the result of the combination of several large U.S. banking companies since 1996, including Chase Manhattan Bank, J.P. Morgan & Co., Bank One, Bear Stearns and Washington Mutual. Going back further, its predecessors include major banking firms among which are Chemical Bank, Manufacturers Hanover, First Chicago Bank, National Bank of Detroit, Texas Commerce Bank, Providian Financial and Great Western Bank. The company's oldest predecessor institution, The Bank of the Manhattan Company, was the third oldest banking corporation in the United States, and the 31st oldest bank in the world, having been established on September 1, 1799, by Aaron Burr. The Chase Manhattan Bank was formed upon the 1955 purchase of Chase National Bank (established in 1877) by The Bank of the Manhattan Company (established in 1799), the company's oldest predecessor institution. The Bank of the Manhattan Company was the creation of Aaron Burr, who transformed the company from a water carrier into a bank. Led by David Rockefeller during the 1970s and 1980s, Chase Manhattan emerged as one of the largest and most prestigious banking concerns, with leadership positions in syndicated lending, treasury and securities services, credit cards, mortgages, and retail financial services. Weakened by the real estate collapse in the early 1990s, it was acquired by Chemical Bank in 1996, retaining the Chase name.

10. Amazon.com, Inc.

Amazon.com, Inc. is an American multinational technology company which focuses on e-commerce, cloud computing, digital streaming, and artificial intelligence. It has been referred to as "one of the most influential economic and cultural forces in the world", and is one of the world's most valuable brands. It is one of the Big Five American information technology companies, alongside Alphabet, Apple, Meta, and Microsoft. Amazon was founded by Jeff Bezos from his garage in Bellevue, Washington, on July 5, 1994. Initially an online marketplace for books, it has expanded into a multitude of product categories: a strategy that has earned it the moniker The Everything Store. It has multiple subsidiaries including Amazon Web Services (cloud computing), Zoox (autonomous vehicles), Kuiper Systems (satellite Internet), Amazon Lab126 (computer hardware R&D). Its other subsidiaries include Ring, Twitch, IMDb, and Whole Foods Market. Its acquisition of Whole Foods in August 2017 for US$13.4 billion substantially increased its footprint as a physical retailer.

Amazon has earned a reputation as a disruptor of well-established industries through technological innovation and mass scale. As of 2021, it is the world's largest online retailer and marketplace, smart speaker provider, cloud computing service through AWS, live-streaming service through Twitch, and Internet company as measured by revenue and market share. In 2021, it surpassed Walmart as the world's largest retailer outside of China, driven in large part by its paid subscription plan, Amazon Prime, which has over 200 million subscribers worldwide. It is the second-largest private employer in the United States. Amazon also distributes a variety of downloadable and streaming content through its Amazon Prime Video, Amazon Music, Twitch, and Audible units. It publishes books through its publishing arm, Amazon Publishing, film and television content through Amazon Studios, and has been the owner of film and television studio Metro-Goldwyn-Mayer since March 2022. It also produces consumer electronics—most notably, Kindle e-readers, Echo devices, Fire tablets, and Fire TVs.

11. Ford Motor Company

Ford Motor Company (commonly known as Ford) is an American multinational automobile manufacturer headquartered in Dearborn, Michigan, United States. It was founded by Henry Ford and incorporated on June 16, 1903. The company sells automobiles and commercial vehicles under the Ford brand, and luxury cars under its Lincoln luxury brand. Ford also owns Brazilian SUV manufacturer Troller, an 8% stake in Aston Martin of the United Kingdom and a 32% stake in China's Jiangling Motors. It also has joint ventures in China (Changan Ford), Taiwan (Ford Lio Ho), Thailand (AutoAlliance Thailand), Turkey (Ford Otosan), and Russia (Ford Sollers). The company is listed on the New York Stock Exchange and is controlled by the Ford family; they have minority ownership but the majority of the voting power. Ford introduced methods for large-scale manufacturing of cars and large-scale management of an industrial workforce using elaborately engineered manufacturing sequences typified by moving assembly lines; by 1914, these methods were known around the world as Fordism. Ford's former UK subsidiaries Jaguar and Land Rover, acquired in 1989 and 2000 respectively, were sold to the Indian automaker Tata Motors in March 2008. Ford owned the Swedish automaker Volvo from 1999 to 2010. In 2011, Ford discontinued the Mercury brand, under which it had marketed entry-level luxury cars in the United States, Canada, Mexico, and the Middle East since 1938.

Ford is the second-largest U.S.-based auto-maker (behind General Motors) and the fifth-largest in the world (behind Toyota, Volks-wagen, Hyundai and General Motors) based on 2015 vehicle production. At the end of 2010, Ford was the fifth-largest automaker in Europe. The company went public in 1956 but the Ford family, through special Class B shares, still retain 40 percent of the voting rights. During the financial crisis of 2007–08 the company struggled financially but did not have to be rescued by the federal government, unlike the other two major US automakers. Ford Motors has since returned to profitability, and was the eleventh-ranked overall American-based company in the 2018 Fortune 500 list, based on global revenues in 2017 of $156.7 billion. In 2008, Ford produced 5.532 million automobiles and employed about 213,000 employees at around 90 plants and facilities worldwide. The Henry Ford Company was Henry Ford's first attempt at a car manufacturing company and was established on November 3, 1901. This became the Cadillac Motor Company on August 22, 1902, after Ford left with the rights to his name. The Ford Motor Company was launched in a converted factory in 1903 with $28,000 (equivalent to $844,000 in 2021) in cash from twelve investors, most notably John and Horace Dodge (who would later found their own car company). The first president was not Ford, but local banker John S. Gray, who was chosen in order to assuage investors' fears that Ford would leave the new company the way he had left its predecessor.

12. Standard Oil Company

Standard Oil Co. was an American oil production, transportation, refining, and marketing company that operated from 1870 to 1911. At its height, Standard Oil was the largest petroleum company in the world, and its success made its co-founder and chairman, John D. Rockefeller, the wealthiest American of all time and the richest person in modern history. Its history as one of the world's first and largest multinational corporations ended in 1911, when the U.S. Supreme Court ruled that it was an illegal monopoly. The company was founded in 1863 by Rockefeller and Henry Flagler, and was incorporated in 1870. Standard Oil dominated the oil products market initially through horizontal integration in the refining sector, then, in later years vertical integration; the company was an innovator in the development of the business trust. The Standard Oil trust streamlined production and logistics, lowered costs, and undercut competitors. "Trust-busting" critics accused it of using aggressive pricing to destroy competitors and form a monopoly that threatened other businesses. Rockefeller ran the company as its chairman, until his retirement in 1897. He remained the major shareholder, and in 1911, with the dissolution of the trust into 34 smaller companies, Rockefeller became the richest person in modern history, as the initial income of these individual enterprises proved to be much bigger than that of a single larger company. Its successors such as Chevron, ExxonMobil Amoco, and Marathon Petroleum, are still among the companies with the largest revenues in the world. By 1882, Rockefeller's top aide was John Dustin Archbold, whom he left in control after disengaging from business to concentrate on philanthropy after 1896. Other notable principals of the company include Henry Flagler, developer of the Florida East Coast Railway and resort cities, and Henry H. Rogers, who built the Virginian Railway.

By 1911 the Supreme Court of the United States ruled, in Standard Oil Co. of New Jersey v. United States, that Standard Oil of New Jersey must be dissolved under the Sherman Antitrust Act and split into 34 companies. Two of these companies were Standard Oil of New Jersey (Jersey Standard or Esso), which eventually became Exxon, and Standard Oil of New York (Socony), which eventually became Mobil; those two companies later merged into ExxonMobil. Over the next few decades, both companies grew significantly. Jersey Standard, led by Walter C. Teagle, became the largest oil producer in the world. It acquired a 50 percent share in Humble Oil & Refining Co., a Texas oil producer. Socony purchased a 45 percent interest in Magnolia Petroleum Co., a major refiner, marketer, and pipeline transporter. In 1931, Socony merged with Vacuum Oil Co., an industry pioneer dating back to 1866, and a growing Standard Oil spin-off in its own right. In the Asia-Pacific region, Jersey Standard had oil production and refineries in Indonesia but no marketing network. Socony-Vacuum had Asian marketing outlets supplied remotely from California. In 1933, Jersey Standard and Socony-Vacuum merged their interests in the region into a 50–50 joint venture. Standard-Vacuum Oil Co., or "Stanvac", operated in 50 countries, from East Africa to New Zealand, before it was dissolved in 1962. Rockefeller's original company, Standard Oil Company of Ohio (Sohio), effectively ceased to exist when it was purchased by BP in 1987. BP continued to sell gasoline under the Sohio brand until 1991. Other Standard oil entities include "Standard Oil of Indiana" which became Amoco after other mergers and a name change in the 1980s, and "Standard Oil of California" which became the Chevron Corp. As of 2021, six states that have the Standard Oil name rights are not being actively used by the companies that own them. Chevron withdrew from Kentucky in 2010, while BP gradually withdrew from five Great Plains and Rocky Mountain states since the initial conversion of Amoco sites to BP.

13. U.S. Steel Corporation

United States Steel Corporation, more commonly known as U.S. Steel, is an American integrated steel producer headquartered in Pittsburgh, Pennsylvania, with production operations in the United States and Central Europe. It was the 8th largest steel producer in the world in 2008. By 2018, the company was the world's 38th-largest steel producer and the second-largest in the US, trailing only Nucor Corporation. Though renamed USX Corporation in 1986, the company was renamed United States Steel in 2001 after spinning off its energy business, including Marathon Oil, and other assets from its core steel concern. J. P. Morgan formed U.S. Steel on March 2, 1901 (incorporated on February 25), by financing the merger of Andrew Carnegie's Carnegie Steel Company with Elbert H. Gary's Federal Steel Company and William Henry "Judge" Moore's National Steel Company for $492 million ($16.03 billion today). At one time, U.S. Steel was the largest steel producer and largest corporation in the world. It was capitalized at $1.4 billion ($45.6 billion today), making it the world's first billion-dollar corporation. The company established its headquarters in the Empire Building at 71 Broadway in New York City; it remained a major tenant in the building for 75 years. Charles M. Schwab, the Carnegie Steel executive who originally suggested the merger to Morgan, ultimately emerged as the new corporation's first President.

At the end of the twentieth century, the corporation was deriving much of its revenue and net income from its energy operations. Led by CEO Thomas Usher, U.S. Steel spun off Marathon and other non-steel assets (except railroad company Transtar) in October 2001. It expanded internationally for the first time by purchasing operations in Slovakia and Serbia. In the early 2010s, U.S. Steel began investing to upgrade software programs throughout their manufacturing facilities. In January 2012, U.S. Steel sold its Serbian mills outside Belgrade to the Serbian government, as their operations had been running at an economic loss. On May 2, 2014, U.S. Steel announced an undisclosed number of layoffs affecting employees worldwide. On July 2, 2014, U.S. Steel was removed from S&P 500 index and placed in the S&P MidCap 400 Index, in light of its declining market capitalization. U.S. Steel's largest domestic facility is Gary Works, in Gary, Indiana, on the shore of Lake Michigan. For many years, the Gary Works Plant was the world-largest steel mill and it remains the largest integrated mill in North America. It was built in 1906 and has been operating since June 28, 1908. Gary is also home to the U.S. Steel Yard baseball stadium. U.S. Steel operates a tin mill in East Chicago now known as East Chicago Tin. The mill was idled in 2015, but reopened shortly after. The mill was then 'permanently idled' in 2019, however the facility remains in possession of the corporation as of early 2020.

14. Tesla Inc.

Tesla, Inc. is an American automotive and clean energy company based in Austin, Texas. Tesla designs and manufactures electric vehicles (electric cars and trucks), battery energy storage from home to grid-scale, solar panels and solar roof tiles, and related products and services. Tesla is one of the world's most valuable companies and remains the world's most valuable automaker with a market capitalization of more than US $1 trillion. The company had the most worldwide sales of battery electric vehicles and plug-in electric vehicles, capturing 23% of the battery-electric (purely electric) market and 16% of the plug-in market (which includes plug-in hybrids) in 2020. Through its subsidiary Tesla Energy, the company develops and is a major installer of photovoltaic systems in the United States. Tesla Energy is also one of the largest global suppliers of battery energy storage systems, with 3.99 gigawatt-hours (GWh) installed in 2021. Founded in July 2003 by Martin Eberhard and Marc Tarpenning as Tesla Motors, the company's name is a tribute to inventor and electrical engineer Nikola Tesla. In February 2004, via a $6.5 million investment, Elon Musk became the largest shareholder of the company. He has served as CEO since 2008. According to Musk, the purpose of Tesla is to help expedite the move to sustainable transport and energy, obtained through electric vehicles and solar power. Tesla began production of its first car model, the Roadster sports car, in 2009. This was followed by the Model S sedan in 2012, the Model X SUV in 2015, the Model 3 sedan in 2017, and the Model Y crossover in 2020. The Model 3 is the all-time best-selling plug-in electric car worldwide, and, in June 2021, became the first electric car to sell 1 million units globally. Tesla's global sales were 936,222 cars in 2021, an 87% increase over the previous year, and cumulative sales totaled 2.3 million cars at the end of 2021. In October 2021, Tesla's market capitalization reached $1 trillion, the sixth company to do so in U.S. history. Tesla was founded in San Carlos, California. In 2010, Tesla moved its corporate headquarters and opened a powertrain development facility in Palo Alto.

Tesla's first retail store was opened in 2008 in Los Angeles, followed by others in major U.S. cities. As of September 2020, Tesla operates 130 stores and galleries in the United States, has stores and galleries in 34 other countries, and has 466 service centers globally. Tesla's first assembly plant occupies the former NUMMI plant in Fremont, California, known as the Tesla Factory. The factory was originally opened by General Motors in 1962, and then operated by a joint venture of GM and Toyota from 1984. The original factory was closed in 2010, and was acquired by Tesla the same year. By 2015, Tesla also occupied a second factory in Fremont a few miles from the original Fremont plant. In 2020, Tesla ranked as the world's best-selling plug-in and battery electric passenger car manufacturer, with a market share of 16% of the plug-in segment and 23% of the battery electric segment 2020 sales. Tesla reported 2021 vehicle deliveries of 936,222 units, up 87% from 2020. At the end of 2021, Tesla's global sales since 2012 totaled 2.3 million units. For the fiscal (and calendar) year 2021, Tesla reported a net income of $5.52 billion. The annual revenue was $53.8 billion, an increase of 71% over the previous fiscal year. Tesla ended 2020 with over $19 billion of cash on hand after having raised approximately $12 billion in stock sales. At the end of 2019 it had $6.3 billion cash on hand. Of the revenue number in 2021, $314 million came from selling regulatory credits to other automakers to meet government pollution standards. That number has been a smaller percentage of revenue for multiple quarters. In Q1 2022, Tesla sold $679 million of regulatory carbon credits. In February 2021, a 10-K filing revealed that Tesla had invested some $1.5 billion in the cryptocurrency Bitcoin, and the company indicated it would soon accept Bitcoin as a form of payment. Critics then pointed out how investing in cryptocurrency can run counter to Tesla's environmental goals. Tesla made more profit from the 2021 investment than the profit from selling cars in 2020, due to the Bitcoin price increase after the investment was announced. The quarter ending June 2021 was the first time Tesla made a profit independent of Bitcoin and regulatory credits. In May 2020, after Alameda County had refused to let the Tesla factory reopen after a COVID-19 lockdown, Elon Musk threatened that he would move the company's headquarters from California to Texas or Nevada. On December 1, 2021, Tesla officially relocated its headquarters to the Gigafactory site in Austin, Texas.

15. Du Pont Corp

E. I. du Pont de Nemours and Company, commonly referred to as DuPont was an American company that was founded in July 1802 in Wilmington, Delaware, as a gunpowder mill by French-American chemist and industrialist Éleuthère Irénée du Pont de Nemours. In the 20th century, DuPont developed many polymers such as Vespel, neoprene, nylon, Corian, Teflon, Mylar, Kapton, Kevlar, Zemdrain, M5 fiber, Nomex, Tyvek, Sorona, Corfam and Lycra. DuPont developed Freon (chlorofluorocarbons) for the refrigerant industry, and later other refrigerants. It also developed synthetic pigments and paints including ChromaFlair. DuPont was founded in 1802 by Éleuthère Irénée du Pont, using capital raised in France and gunpowder machinery imported from France. He started the company at the Eleutherian Mills, on the Brandywine Creek, near Wilmington, Delaware, two years after du Pont and his family left France to escape the French Revolution and religious persecution against Huguenot Protestants. The company began as a manufacturer of gunpowder, as du Pont noticed that the industry in North America was lagging behind Europe. The company grew quickly, and by the mid-19th century had become the largest supplier of gunpowder to the United States military, supplying one-third to one-half the powder used by the Union Army during the American Civil War. The Eleutherian Mills site is now a museum and a National Historic Landmark. In 2011, DuPont was the largest producer of titanium dioxide in the world, primarily provided as a white pigment used in the paper industry. DuPont has 150 research and development facilities located in China, Brazil, India, Germany, and Switzerland, with an average investment of $2 billion annually in a diverse range of technologies for many markets including agriculture, genetic traits, biofuels, automotive, construction, electronics, chemicals, and industrial materials. DuPont employs more than 10,000 scientists and engineers around the world. On January 9, 2011, DuPont announced that it had reached an agreement to buy Danish company Danisco for US$6.3 billion. On May 16, 2011, DuPont announced that its tender offer for Danisco had been successful and that it would proceed to redeem the remaining shares and delist the company. On May 1, 2012, DuPont announced that it had acquired from Bunge full ownership of the Solae joint venture, a soy-based ingredients company. DuPont previously owned 72 percent of the joint venture while Bunge owned the remaining 28 percent. In February 2013, DuPont Performance Coatings was sold to the Carlyle Group and rebranded as Axalta Coating Systems. In October 2015, DuPont sold the Neoprene chloroprene rubber business to Denka Performance Elastomers, a joint venture of Denka and Mitsui. In 2014, DuPont was the world's fourth-largest chemical company based on market capita-lization and eighth-largest based on revenue. On August 31, 2017, it merged with the Dow Chemical Company to create DowDuPont.

16. Apple Inc.

Apple was founded as Apple Computer Company on April 1, 1976, by Steve Jobs, Steve Wozniak and Ronald Wayne to develop and sell Wozniak's Apple I personal computer. It was incorporated by Jobs and Wozniak as Apple Computer, Inc. in 1977 and the company's next computer, the Apple II became a best seller. Apple went public in 1980, to instant financial success. The company developed computers featuring innovative graphical user interfaces, including the original Macintosh, announced in a critically acclaimed advertisement, "1984," directed by Ridley Scott. By 1985, the high cost of its products and power struggles between executives caused problems. Wozniak stepped back from Apple amicably, while Jobs resigned to found NeXT, taking some Apple employees with him. As the market for personal computers expanded and evolved throughout the 1990s, Apple lost considerable market share to the lower-priced duopoly of the Microsoft Windows operating system on Intel-powered PC clones (also known as "Wintel"). In 1997, weeks away from bankruptcy, the company bought NeXT to resolve Apple's unsuccessful operating system strategy and entice Jobs back to the company. Over the next decade, Jobs guided Apple back to profitability through a number of tactics including introducing the iMac, iPod, iPhone and iPad to critical acclaim, launching memorable advertising campaigns, opening the Apple Store retail chain, and acquiring numerous companies to broaden the company's product portfolio. Jobs resigned in 2011 for health reasons, and died two months later. He was succeeded as CEO by Tim Cook.

Apple Inc. is an American multinational technology company that specializes in consumer electronics, software and online services. Apple is the largest information technology company by revenue, totaling US$365.8 billion in 2021) and, as of January 2021, it is the world's most valuable company, the fourth-largest personal computer vendor by unit sales and second-largest mobile phone manufacturer. It is one of the Big Five American information technology companies, alongside Alphabet, Amazon, Meta, and Microsoft. Apple became the first publicly traded U.S. company to be valued at over $1 trillion in August 2018, then $2 trillion in August 2020, and most recently $3 trillion in January 2022. The company sometimes receives criticism regarding the labor practices of its contractors, its environmental practices, and its business ethics, including anti-competitive practices and materials sourcing. Nevertheless, the company enjoys a high level of brand loyalty, and is ranked as one of the world's most valuable brands. On August 19, 2020, Apple's share price briefly topped $467.77, making Apple the first US company with a market capitalization of $2 trillion. During its annual WWDC keynote speech on June 22, 2020, Apple announced it would move away from Intel processors, and the Mac would transition to processors developed in-house. The announcement was expected by industry analysts, and it has been noted that Macs featuring Apple's processors would allow for big increases in performance over current Intel-based models. On November 10, 2020, the MacBook Air, MacBook Pro, and the Mac Mini became the first Mac devices powered by an Apple-designed processor, the Apple.

17. Berkshire Hathaway Inc.

Berkshire Hathaway Inc. is an American multinational conglomerate holding company headquartered in Omaha, Nebraska, United States. The company wholly owns GEICO, Duracell, Dairy Queen, BNSF Railway, Lubrizol, Fruit of the Loom, Helzberg Diamonds, Long & Foster, FlightSafety International, Shaw Industries, Pampered Chef, Forest River, and NetJets, and also owns 38.6% of Pilot Flying J; and significant minority holdings in public companies Kraft Heinz Company (26.7%), American Express (18.8%), The Coca-Cola Company (9.32%), Bank of America (11.9%), and Apple (6.3%). The company is known for its control and leadership by Warren Buffett, who serves as chairman and chief executive, and Charlie Munger, the company's vice chairman. In the early part of his career at Berkshire, Buffett focused on long-term investments in publicly traded companies, but more recently he has more frequently bought whole companies. Berkshire now owns a diverse range of businesses including confectionery, retail, railroads, home furnishings, encyclopedias, manufacturers of vacuum cleaners, jewelry sales, manufacture and distribution of uniforms, and several regional electric and gas utilities.

From 2016, the company acquired large holdings in the major US airlines United Airlines, Delta Air Lines, Southwest Airlines, and American Airlines, but these were sold early in 2020 in the wake of the COVID-19 pandemic. Berkshire Hathaway has averaged an annual growth in book value of 19.0% to its shareholders since 1965 (compared to 9.7% from the S&P 500 with dividends included for the same period), while employing large amounts of capital, and minimal debt. According to the Forbes Global 2000 list and formula, Berkshire Hathaway is the eighth-largest public company in the world, the tenth-largest conglomerate by revenue and the largest financial services company by revenue in the world. As of August 2020, Berkshire's Class B stock is the seventh-largest component of the S&P 500 Index (which is based on free-float market capitalization) and the company is famous for having the most expensive share price in history with Class A shares costing around $500,000 each. This is because there has never been a stock split in its Class A shares and Buffett stated in a 1984 letter to shareholders that he does not intend to split the stock. On 16 March 2022, Berkshire Hathaway Class A shares closed above record $500,000 a share, resulting in company's market cap above $730 billion.

18. Meta Platforms, Inc.

Meta Platforms, Inc., doing business as **Meta** and formerly known as **Facebook, Inc.**, and **TheFacebook, Inc.**, is an American multinational technology conglomerate based in Menlo Park, California. The company is the parent organization of Facebook, Instagram, and WhatsApp, among other subsidiaries. Meta is one of the world's most valuable companies. It is considered one of the Big Five American information technology companies, alongside Google, Amazon, Apple, and Microsoft. Meta products and services include Facebook, Messenger, Facebook Watch, and Facebook Portal. It has also acquired Oculus, Giphy, Mapillary, Kustomer, Presize and has a 9.99% stake in Jio Platforms. In 2021, the company generated 97.5% of its revenue from the sale of advertisement placements to marketers. Facebook filed for an initial public offering (IPO) on January 1, 2012. The preliminary prospectus stated that the company sought to raise $5 billion, had 845 million monthly active users, and a website accruing 2.7 billion likes and comments daily. After the IPO, Zuckerberg would retain a 22% ownership share in Facebook and would own 57% of the voting shares. Throughout its existence, Facebook, Inc./Meta has acquired multiple companies (often identified as talent acquisitions). One of its first major acquisitions was in April 2012, when it acquired Instagram for approximately US$1 billion in cash and stock. In October 2013, Facebook, Inc. acquired Onavo, an Israeli mobile web analytics company. In February 2014, Facebook, Inc. announced it would buy mobile messaging company WhatsApp for US$19 billion in cash and stock.

In October 2021, media outlets reported that the parent company of Facebook planned to change its name to "reflect its focus on building [what it refers to as] the metaverse". According to Meta, the "metaverse" refers to the integrated environment that links all of the company's products and services. It was rebranded as Meta later that month on October 28. Soon after the rebranding of the company, in early February 2022, Meta reported a greater-than-expected decline in profits in the fourth quarter of 2021. The company reported no growth in monthly users, and indicated it expected revenue growth to stall. The company also expected measures taken by Apple, Inc. to protect user privacy to cost it some $10 billion in advertisement revenue, an amount equal to roughly 8% of its revenue for 2021. In meeting with Meta staff the day after earnings were reported, Zuckerberg blamed competition for user attention, particularly from video-based apps like TikTok, for the poor financial performance. The 27% reduction in the company's share price which occurred in reaction to the news eliminated some $230 billion of value from Meta's market capitalization. Bloomberg referred to the decline as "... an epic rout that, in its sheer scale, is unlike anything Wall Street or Silicon Valley has ever seen". Mark Zuckerberg's net worth fell by as much as $31 billion due to the decline. Zuckerberg controls 13% of Meta, and the holding makes up the bulk of his wealth. In November 2020, Facebook, Inc. announced that it planned to purchase the customer-service platform and chatbot specialist startup Kustomer to promote companies to use their platform for business. It has been reported that Kustomer is valued at slightly over $1 billion. The deal was closed in February 2022 after regulatory approval.

19. Microsoft Corp.

Microsoft Corporation is an American multinational technology corporation which produces computer software, consumer electronics, personal computers, and related services. Its best-known software products are the Microsoft Windows line of operating systems, the Microsoft Office suite, and the Internet Explorer and Edge web browsers. Its flagship hardware products are the Xbox video game consoles and the Microsoft Surface lineup of touchscreen personal computers. Microsoft ranked No. 21 in the 2020 Fortune 500 rankings of the largest United States corporations by total revenue; it was the world's largest software maker by revenue as of 2016. It is one of the Big Five American information technology companies, alongside Google, Amazon, Apple, and Meta. Microsoft (the word being a portmanteau of "microcomputer software" was founded by Bill Gates and Paul Allen on April 4, 1975, to develop and sell BASIC interpreters for the Altair 8800. It rose to dominate the personal computer operating system market with MS-DOS in the mid-1980s, followed by Microsoft Windows. The company's 1986 initial public offering (IPO), and subsequent rise in its share price, created three billionaires and an estimated 12,000 millionaires among Microsoft employees. Since the 1990s, it has increasingly diversified from the operating system market and has made a number of corporate acquisitions, their largest being the acquisition of LinkedIn for $26.2 billion in December 2016, followed by their acquisition of Skype Technologies for $8.5 billion in May 2011.

As of 2015, Microsoft is market-dominant in the IBM PC compatible operating system market and the office software suite market, although it has lost the majority of the overall operating system market to Android. The company also produces a wide range of other consumer and enterprise software for desktops, laptops, tabs, gadgets, and servers, including Internet search (with Bing), the digital services market (through MSN), mixed reality (HoloLens), cloud computing (Azure), and software development (Visual Studio). Steve Ballmer replaced Gates as CEO in 2000, and later envisioned a "devices and services" strategy. This unfolded with Microsoft acquiring Danger Inc. in 2008, entering the personal computer production market for the first time in June 2012 with the launch of the Microsoft Surface line of tablet computers, and later forming Microsoft Mobile through the acquisition of Nokia's devices and services division. Since Satya Nadella took over as CEO in 2014, the company has scaled back on hardware and has instead focused on cloud computing, a move that helped the company's shares reach its highest value since December 1999. Earlier dethroned by Apple in 2010, in 2018 Microsoft reclaimed its position as the most valuable publicly traded company in the world. In April 2019, Microsoft reached the trillion-dollar market cap, becoming the third U.S. public company to be valued at over $1 trillion after Apple and Amazon respectively. As of 2020, Microsoft has the third-highest global brand valuation.

20. Walgreens

Walgreen Company, or Walgreens, is an American company that operates the second-largest pharmacy store chain in the United States behind CVS Health. It specializes in filling prescriptions, health and wellness products, health information, and photo services. Walgreens began in 1901, with a small food front store on the corner of Bowen and Cottage Grove Avenues in Chicago, owned by Dixon, Illinois native Charles R. Walgreen. By 1913, Walgreens had grown to four stores on Chicago's South Side. It opened its fifth in 1915 and four more in 1916. By 1919, there were 20 stores in the chain. In 2010, Walgreens acquired New York City-area chain Duane Reade for $1.075 billion, including debt, and continued to use the Duane Reade name on some stores in the New York City metropolitan area. In March 2011, Walgreens acquired Drugstore.com for $409 million. On June 19, 2012: Walgreens paid $6.7 billion for a 45% interest in Alliance Boots. That year, Walgreens acquired Mid-South drug store chain operating under the USA Drug, Super D Drug, May's Drug, Med-X, and Drug Warehouse banners. Walgreens has its corporate headquarters in Deerfield, Illinois. Walgreens has had a technology office located in Chicago since 2010. The location serves as their digital hub. In November 2010 Walgreens filed a trademark infringement lawsuit against the Wegmans supermarket chain, claiming the "W" in the Wegman's logo is too similar to Walgreens'. The lawsuit was settled in April 2011, with Wegmans agreeing to discontinue use of its "W" logo by June 2012, although the supermarket retained the right to use the "Wegmans" name in script. According to Jo Natale, Wegmans director of media relations, "The cost of making relatively minor changes to a limited number of products was much less than the cost of litigating this case to the end." In the summer of 2014, a corporate relocation to Switzerland was considered as part of a merger with Alliance Boots, a European drugstore chain. This drew controversy as many consumers felt that it was an attempt at tax inversion. On August 5, 2014, Walgreens announced that it would not be relocating its headquarters. As of August 31, 2019, the company operated 9,277 stores in the United States.

21. Boeing

The Boeing Company is an American multinational corporation that designs, manufactures, and sells airplanes, rotorcraft, rockets, satellites, telecommunications equipment, and missiles worldwide. The company also provides leasing and product support services. Boeing is among the largest global aerospace manufacturers; it is the third-largest defense contractor in the world based on 2020 revenue, and is the largest exporter in the United States by dollar value. Boeing stock is included in the Dow Jones Industrial Average. Boeing is incorporated in Delaware. Boeing was founded by William Boeing in Seattle, Washington, on July 15, 1916. The present corporation is the result of the merger of Boeing with McDonnell Douglas on August 1, 1997. Then chairman and CEO of Boeing, Philip M. Condit, assumed those roles in the combined company, while Harry Stonecipher, former CEO of McDonnell Douglas, became president and COO. The Boeing Company has its corporate headquarters in Chicago, Illinois. Boeing is organized into four primary divisions: Boeing Commercial Airplanes (BCA); Boeing Defense, Space & Security (BDS); Boeing Global Services; and Boeing Capital. In 2019, Boeing recorded US$76.6 billion in sales. Boeing is ranked 54th on the Fortune magazine "Fortune 500" list (2020), and ranked 121st on the "Fortune Global 500" list (2020). In 2019, Boeing's global reputation, commercial business, and financial rating suffered after the 737 MAX was grounded worldwide following two fatal crashes in late 2018 and early 2019.

The corporate headquarters were moved from Seattle to Chicago in 2001. In 2018, Boeing opened its first factory in Europe at Sheffield, UK, reinforced by a research partnership with The University of Sheffield. In May 2020, the company cut over 12,000 jobs due to the drop in air travel during the COVID-19 pandemic with plans for a total 10% cut of its workforce or approximately 16,000 positions. In July 2020, Boeing reported a loss of $2.4 billion as a result of the pandemic and the grounding of its 737 MAX aircraft, and that it was in response planning to make more job and production cuts. On August 18, 2020, CEO Dave Calhoun announced further job cuts; on October 28, 2020 nearly 30,000 employees were laid off, as the airplane manufacturer was increasingly losing money due to the COVID-19 pandemic. The Boeing 777X, the largest capacity twinjet, made its maiden flight on January 25, 2020. Following an incident during flight testing, estimated first delivery of the aircraft was delayed until 2024. For the fiscal year 2017, Boeing reported earnings of US$8.191 billion, with an annual revenue of US$93.392 billion, a 1.25% decline over the previous fiscal cycle. Boeing's shares traded at over $209 per share, and its market capitalization was valued at over US$206.6 billion. From 2013 to 2019, Boeing spent over $60 billion on dividends and stock buybacks, twice as much as the development costs of the 787. In 2020, Boeing's revenue was $11.8 billion as a result of the pandemic slump. Due to higher sales in other divisions and an influx in deliveries of commercial jetliners in 2021, revenue increased 44%, reaching nearly $17 billion.

22. Deere & Company

John Deere is the brand name of Deere & Company, an American corporation that manufactures agricultural machinery, heavy equipment, forestry machinery, diesel engines, drivetrains (axles, transmissions, gearboxes) used in heavy equipment, and lawn care equipment. In 2019, it was listed as 87th in the Fortune 500 America's ranking and was ranked 329th in the global ranking. The company also provides financial services and other related activities. Deere & Company began when John Deere, born in Rutland, Vermont, United States on February 7, 1804, moved to Grand Detour, Illinois in 1836 to escape bankruptcy in Vermont. Already an established blacksmith, Deere opened a 1,378-square-foot (128 m2) shop in Grand Detour in 1837, which allowed him to serve as a general repairman in the village, as well as a manufacturer of tools such as pitchforks and shovels.

Deere & Company is listed on the New York Stock Exchange under the symbol DE. The company's slogan is "Nothing Runs Like a Deere", and its logo is a leaping deer, with the words 'JOHN DEERE' under it. Various logos incorporating a leaping deer have been used by the company for over 155 years. Deere & Company is headquartered in Moline, Illinois. Deere & Company ranked No. 84 in the 2020 Fortune 500 list of the largest United States corporations. Their different tractor series include D series, E series, Speciality Tractors, Super Heavy Duty Tractors, and JDLink. John Deere manufactures a range of forestry machinery, among others, harvesters, forwarders, skidders, feller bunchers and log loaders. Timberjack was a subsidiary of John Deere from 2000 to 2006. Other products the company manufactures include consumer and commercial equipment such as lawn mowers, compact utility tractors, snow throwers, snowmobiles, all-terrain vehicles, and StarFire (a wide-area differential GPS).

23. Burger King

Burger King (BK) is an American multinational chain of hamburger fast food restaurants. Headquartered in Miami-Dade County, Florida, the company was founded in 1953 as Insta-Burger King, a Jacksonville, Florida–based restaurant chain. After Insta-Burger King ran into financial difficulties in 1954, its two Miami-based franchisees David Edgerton and James McLamore purchased the company and renamed it "Burger King". Over the next half-century, the company changed hands four times, with its third set of owners, a partnership of TPG Capital, Bain Capital, and Goldman Sachs Capital Partners, taking it public in 2002. In late 2010, 3G Capital of Brazil acquired a majority stake in the company, in a deal valued at US$3.26 billion. The new owners promptly initiated a restructuring of the company to reverse its fortunes. 3G, along with partner Berkshire Hathaway, eventually merged the company with the Canadian-based doughnut chain Tim Hortons, under the auspices of a new Canadian-based parent company named Restaurant Brands International. The predecessor to Burger King was founded in 1953 in Jacksonville, Florida, as Insta-Burger King. After visiting the McDonald brothers' original store location in San Bernardino, California, the founders and owners (Keith J. Kramer and his wife's uncle Matthew Burns), who had purchased the rights to two pieces of equipment called "Insta-machines", opened their first restaurants. Their production model was based on one of the machines they had acquired, an oven called the "Insta-Broiler". This strategy proved to be so successful that they later required all of their franchises to use the device.

In recent years, Burger King has turned to trolling fast food rival McDonald›s with their advertising strategy. The company›s tactics have included LOLA MullenLowe›s "Scary Clown Night" which offered a free Whopper to anyone dressed as a clown (McDonald's mascot) on Halloween; FCB New York's Whopper Detour initiative, which encouraged mobile app users to go to a nearby McDonald's in order to unlock a 1-center Whopper; and Ingo's "The Not Big Macs" menu, which poked fun at McDonald's recent loss of the Big Mac trademark in the EU. In February 2019, the company launched an advertising campaign called "Eat Like Andy". The television spot which premiered during the Super Bowl LIII features archival documentary film footage from "66 Scenes from America" by Jørgen Leth of the pop artist Andy Warhol (1928–1987) unwrapping and eating a Whopper. The footage was approved for use by the fast food giant courtesy of the Andy Warhol Foundation. Meanwhile, prior to the game, the mass market hamburger chain made available to viewers who ordered it in advance via DoorDash an "Andy Warhol Mystery Box" which contains among other items a plastic bottle of ketchup and a platinum wig so one can "Eat Like Andy." In 2019, Burger King reported that it planned to close up to 250 low-volume locations per year, with closures coming into effect in 2020. In February 2021, Burger King began testing a customer loyalty rewards program called "Royal Perks" in Los Angeles, Miami, New York City, New Jersey and Long Island. In March 2022, Burger King suspended all its corporate support in Russia in response to the 2022 Russian invasion of Ukraine, including the more than 800 fully franchised restaurant chains in Russia managed by a local master franchisee.

24. Coca-Cola Company The Coca-Cola Company is a multinational beverage corporation incorporated under Delaware's General Corporation Law and headquartered in Atlanta, Georgia. The Coca-Cola Company has interests in the manufacturing, retailing, and marketing of non-alcoholic beverage concentrates and syrups, and alcoholic beverages. The company produces Coca-Cola, the sugary drink it is best known for, invented in 1886 by pharmacist John Stith Pemberton. At the time, the product was made with coca leaves, which added an amount of cocaine to the drink, and with kola nuts, which added caffeine, so that the coca and the kola together provided a stimulative effect. This stimulative effect is the reason the drink was sold to the public as a healthy "tonic", and the coca and the kola are also the source of the name of the product and of the company. In 1889, the formula and brand were sold for $2,300 (roughly $71,000 in 2022) to Asa Griggs Candler, who incorporated the Coca-Cola Company in Atlanta in 1892.	Coca-Cola is the best-selling soft drink in most countries, and was recognized as the number one global brand in 2010. While the Middle East is one of the few regions in the world where Coca-Cola is not the number one soda drink, Coca-Cola nonetheless holds almost 25% market share (to Pepsi's 75%) and had double-digit growth in 2003. Similarly, in Scotland, where the locally produced Irn-Bru was once more popular, 2005 figures show that both Coca-Cola and Diet Coke now outsell Irn-Bru. In Peru, the native Inca Kola has been more popular than Coca-Cola, which prompted Coca-Cola to enter in negotiations with the soft drink's company and buy 50% of its stakes. In Japan, the best selling soft drink is not cola, as (canned) tea and coffee are more popular. As such, the Coca-Cola Company's best selling brand there is not Coca-Cola, but Georgia. In May 2016, the Coca-Cola Company temporarily halted production of its signature drink in Venezuela due to sugar shortages. Since then, the Coca-Cola Company has been using "minimum inventories of raw material" to make their signature drinks at two production plants in Venezuela.
25. Mary Kay Mary Kay Inc. is an American privately owned multi-level marketing company. According to Direct Selling News, Mary Kay was the sixth largest network marketing company in the world in 2018, with a wholesale volume of US$3.25 billion. Mary Kay is based in Addison, Texas. The company was founded by Mary Kay Ash in 1963. Richard Rogers, Ash's son, is the chairman, and David Holl is president and was named CEO in 2006. Mary Kay sells cosmetics through a multi-level marketing model. Mary Kay distributors, called beauty consultants, can potentially make income by directly selling to people in their community, and also receive a commission when they recruit others to begin selling under their distribution network. Mary Kay distributors must purchase a $100 starter kit to qualify.	The company's primary manufacturing plant is in Dallas, Texas. A second plant was opened in Hangzhou, China, to manufacture and package products for that market. A third plant was opened in 1997, in La Chaux-de-Fonds, Switzerland for the European market. The Swiss plant closed in 2003. Starting in 1963 with 318 consultants and sales of $198,154, the company exceeded $500 million in sales through 220,000 consultants by 1991. In 1995, its sales had grown to $950 million, including $25 million in Russia. As of 2017, Mary Kay's continuous multinational expansion had seen its sales grow to $3.7 billion with 2.5 million consultants, 39,000 directors and 600 national directors. Mary Kay Independent Beauty Consultants earn a 50% gross profit on products they sell at full retail price. Mary Kay releases few details about the average income of its sellers.

26. Panera Bread

Panera Bread Company is an American chain store of bakery-café fast casual restaurants with over 2,000 locations, all of which are in the United States and Canada. Its headquarters are in Sunset Hills, Missouri. Ken and Linda Rosenthal founded The St. Louis Bread Company in 1987 with the first location in Kirkwood, Missouri. The Rosenthals invested $150,000 and received a $150,000 Small Business Administration loan.[12] Au Bon Pain Co., a public company, purchased the St. Louis Bread Company in 1993 for $23 million. In 1997, Au Bon Pain changed the company name to Panera, from a word that has roots in the Latin word for "breadbasket" and is identical to the word for "breadbasket" in Spanish and Catalan. At the same time, the St. Louis Bread Company renovated its 20 bakery-cafés in the St. Louis area. In May 1999, Au Bon Pain Co. sold Au Bon Pain to the firm Bruckmann, Rosser, Sherrill & Co. for $78 million, in order to focus on the Panera Bread chain. In 2000, Panera Bread moved its headquarters to Richmond Heights, Missouri.[18] Panera Bread in 2007 purchased a 51% stake in Paradise Bakery & Café, a Phoenix metropolitan area-based concept with over 70 locations in 10 states, predominantly in the west and southwest, for $21.1 million. The company purchased the balance of Paradise in June 2009.

The company operates as **Saint Louis Bread Company** in the Greater St. Louis area, where it has over 100 locations. Offerings include bakery items, pasta, salads, sandwiches, soups, and specialty drinks. As of 2020, the menu also includes flatbread pizzas. The company, which also owns Au Bon Pain, is owned by JAB Holding Company which is, in turn, owned by the Reimann family of Germany. Panera offers a wide array of pastries and baked goods, such as bagels, brownies, cookies, croissants, muffins, and scones. These, along with Panera's artisan breads, are typically baked before dawn by an on-staff baker. Aside from the bakery section, Panera has a regular menu for dine-in or takeout including: flatbreads, panini, Panera Kids, pastas, salads, sandwiches, side choices, and soups, as well as coffee, espresso drinks, frozen drinks, fruit smoothies, hot chocolate, iced drinks, lattes, lemonade, and tea. During its final 20 years as a public company, from 1997 to 2017, it was the best performing restaurant stock, delivering an 86-fold return to shareholders. In 2005, Panera ranked 37th on Bloomberg BusinessWeek's list of "Hot Growth Companies", earning $38.6 million with a 42.9 percent increase in profits. In a 2008 Health magazine study, Panera Bread was judged North America's healthiest fast casual restaurant. In 2009 and 2012, Zagat named Panera one of the most popular restaurants for eating on the go.

27. Johnson & Johnson

Johnson & Johnson (J&J) is an American multinational corporation founded in 1886 that develops medical devices, pharma-ceuticals, and consumer packaged goods. Its common stock is a component of the Dow Jones Industrial Average and the company is ranked No. 36 on the 2021 Fortune 500 list of the largest United States corporations by total revenue. Johnson & Johnson is one of the world's most valuable companies, and is one of only two U.S.-based companies that has a prime credit rating of AAA, higher than that of the United States government. Robert Wood Johnson began his professional training at age 16 as a pharmaceutical apprentice at an apothecary run by his mother's cousin, James G. Wood, in Poughkeepsie, New York. Johnson co-founded his own company with George Seabury in 1873. The New York-based Seabury & Johnson became known for its medicated plasters. Robert Wood Johnson represented the company at the 1876 World's Fair. There he heard Joseph Lister's explanation of a new procedure: antiseptic surgery. Johnson parted ways with his business partner Seabury in 1885. Robert Wood Johnson joined his brothers, James Wood Johnson and Edward Mead Johnson, and created a line of ready-to-use sterile surgical dressings in 1886. They founded Johnson & Johnson in 1886 with 14 employees, eight women and six men. They manufactured sterile surgical supplies, household products, and medical guides. Those products initially featured a logo that resembled the signature of James Wood Johnson, very similar to the current logo. Robert Wood Johnson served as the first president of the company.

Johnson & Johnson is headquartered in New Brunswick, New Jersey, the consumer division being located in Skillman, New Jersey. The corporation includes some 250 subsidiary companies with operations in 60 countries and products sold in over 175 countries. Johnson & Johnson had worldwide sales of $82.6 billion during calendar year 2020. Johnson & Johnson's brands include numerous household names of medications and first aid supplies. Johnson & Johnson's pharmaceutical arm is Janssen Pharma-ceuticals. For the fiscal year 2018, Johnson & Johnson reported earnings of $15.3 billion, with an annual revenue of $81.6 billion, an increase of 6.7% over the previous fiscal cycle. Johnson & Johnson's shares traded at over $126 per share, and its market capitalization was valued at over $367.5 billion in September 2018. The company announced in November 2021 that it would split into two publicly traded companies: one focused on consumer products and the other on pharmaceuticals. The company's business is divided into three major business sectors: Pharmaceuticals, Medical Devices, and Consumer Health. In 2020, these segments contributed 55%, 28%, and 17%, respectively, of the company's total revenues. In April 2020, Johnson & Johnson entered a partnership with Catalent who will provide large-scale manufacturing of J&J's vaccine at Catalent's Bloomington facility. The partner-ship was expanded to include Catalent's Italian facility in July 2020. In June 2020, Johnson & Johnson and the National Institute of Allergy and Infectious Diseases (NIAID) confirmed its intention to start a clinical trials of J&J's vaccine in September 2020, with the possibility of Phase 1/2a human clinical trials starting at an accelerated pace in the second half of July.

28. Goodyear Tire & Rubber Company

The Goodyear Tire & Rubber Company is an American multinational tire manufacturing company founded in 1898 by Frank Seiberling and based in Akron, Ohio. Goodyear manufactures tires for automobiles, commercial trucks, light trucks, motorcycles, SUVs, race cars, airplanes, farm equipment and heavy earth-moving machinery. It also makes bicycle tires, having returned from a break in production between 1976 and 2015. As of 2017, Goodyear is one of the top four tire manufacturers along with Bridgestone (Japan), Michelin (France) and Continental (Germany). The company was named after American Charles Goodyear, inventor of vulcanized rubber. The first Goodyear tires became popular because they were easily detachable and required little maintenance. Though Goodyear had been manufacturing airships and balloons since the early 1900s, the first Goodyear advertising blimp flew in 1925. Today, it is one of the most recognizable advertising icons in America. The company is the most successful tire supplier in Formula One history, with more starts, wins, and constructors' championships than any other tire supplier. They pulled out of the sport after the 1998 season. It is the sole tire supplier for NASCAR series. Goodyear was the first global tire manufacturer to enter China when it invested in a tire manufacturing plant in Dalian in 1994. Goodyear was a component of the Dow Jones Industrial Average between 1930 and 1999. The company opened a new global headquarters building in Akron in 2013. The first Goodyear factory opened in Akron, Ohio, in 1898. The company originally manufactured bicycle and carriage tires, rubber horseshoe pads, and poker chips, and grew with the advent of the automobile. In 1901, Goodyear founder Frank Seiberling provided Henry Ford with racing tires. In 1903, Goodyear president, chairman and CEO Paul Weeks Litchfield was granted a patent for the first tubeless automobile tire. In 1916, Litchfield found land in the Phoenix area suitable for growing long-staple cotton, which was needed to reinforce its rubber in tires. The 36,000 acres purchased were controlled by the Southwest Cotton Company, formed with Litchfield as president. (This included land that would develop into the towns of Goodyear and Litchfield Park.)

The last major restructuring of the company took place in 1991. Goodyear hired Stanley Gault, former CEO of Rubbermaid, to expand the company into new markets. The moves resulted in 12,000 employees being laid off. In 2005, Titan Tire purchased the farm tire business of Goodyear, and manufactures Goodyear agricultural tires under license. This acquisition included the plant in Freeport, Illinois. In the summer of 2009, the company announced it would close its tire plant in the Philippines as part of a strategy to address uncompetitive manufacturing capacity globally by the end of the third quarter of that year. Goodyear announced plans to sell the assets of its Latin American off-road tire business to Titan Tire for $98.6 million, including the plant in Sao Paulo, Brazil and a licensing agreement that allows Titan to continue manufacturing under the Goodyear brand. This deal is similar to Titan's 2005 purchase of Goodyear's US farm tire assets. In 2011, more than 70 years after the dissolution of the Goodyear-Zeppelin Corporation, it is announced that Goodyear will partner with Zeppelin again (the legacy company Zeppelin Luftschifftechnik) to build more zeppelins together. In 2018, Goodyear and Bridgestone announced the creation of TireHub, a joint wholesale distribution network across the United States. At the same time, Goodyear also announced that it was ending its distribution relationship with American Tire Distributors, which used to be the largest tire wholesaler in the US. In 2018, Goodyear was ordered to pay $40.1 million to J. Walter Twidwell, who claimed he developed mesothelioma because of exposure to asbestos. After the trial, Goodyear asked the New York Supreme Court for a new trial. Goodyear attorney James Lynch said Goodyear did not receive proper consideration from the jury. Lynch said that the other side's attorneys engaged in character assassinations against expert witnesses. During closing remarks, the attorneys for Twidwell put up a slide with the heads of Goodyear's expert witnesses pasted onto "insulting caricatures." In December 2018, Goodyear ceased operations in Venezuela due a lack of materials and rising costs resulting from hyperinflation. In February 2021, Goodyear announced that it will acquire the Cooper Tire & Rubber Company for $2.5 billion. The transaction is expected to close in the second half of 2021

29. Hershey Company

The Hershey Company, commonly known as **Hershey's**, is an American multinational company and one of the largest chocolate manufacturers in the world. It also manufactures baked products, such as cookies and cakes, and sells beverages like milkshakes, and many more that are produced globally. Its headquarters are in Hershey, Pennsylvania, which is also home to Hersheypark and Hershey's Chocolate World. It was founded by Milton S. Hershey in 1894 as the Hershey Chocolate Company, a subsidiary of his Lancaster Caramel Company. The Hershey Trust Company owns a minority stake but retains a majority of the voting power within the company. In 1896, Hershey built a milk-processing plant so he could create and refine a recipe for his milk chocolate candies. In 1899, he developed the Hershey process, which is less sensitive to milk quality than traditional methods. In 1900, he began manufacturing Hershey's Milk Chocolate Bars, also known as Hershey's Bars or Hershey Bars. Hershey's chocolate is available across the United States, and in over 60 countries worldwide. It has three large distribution centers with modern labor management systems. In addition, Hershey is a member of the World Cocoa Foundation. It is also associated with the Hersheypark Stadium and the Giant Center.

In December 2011, Hershey reached an agreement to acquire Brookside Foods Ltd., a privately held confectionery company based in Abbotsford, British Columbia. In April 2015, the Hershey chocolate plant on East Chocolate Avenue in Hershey, Pennsylvania was demolished to make way for mixed-use development. In 2016, Hershey acquired barkTHINS, a New York-based chocolate snack foods company that expected to generate between $65 million and $75 million in revenue for that year, for $290 million. An August 2016 attempt to sell Hershey to Mondelez International was abandoned because of objections by the Hershey Trust. In 2017, Hershey acquired Amplify Snack Brands, Austin, Texas-based maker of SkinnyPop, in an all-cash transaction valued at approximately $1.6 billion. In September 2018, Hershey announced to buy Pirate Brands from B&G Foods for $420 million in an all-cash deal. In August 2019, Hershey announced it would purchase protein bar maker One Brands LLC for $397 million. In October 2019, Hershey announced a collaboration with Yuengling to produce a limited release collaboration beer titled Yuengling Hershey's Chocolate Porter, becoming Hershey's first licensed beer partnership. In June 2021, Hershey acquired Lily's for $425 million. In November 2021, Hershey announced plans to acquire Dot's Pretzels, and their co-packer, Pretzel INC for $1.2BN.

30. Sears, Roebuck and Co.

Sears, Roebuck and Co., commonly known as **Sears**, is an American chain of department stores founded in 1892 by Richard Warren Sears and Alvah Curtis Roebuck and reincorporated in 1906 by Richard Sears and Julius Rosenwald. What began as a mail ordering catalog company migrated to opening retail locations in 1925, the first in Chicago, Illinois. In 2005, the company was bought by the management of the American big box discount chain Kmart, which upon completion of the merger, formed Sears Holdings. Through the 1980s, Sears was the largest retailer in the United States. In 2018, it was the 31st-largest. After several years of declining sales, Sears's parent company filed for Chapter 11 bankruptcy on October 15, 2018. It announced on January 16, 2019, that it had won its bankruptcy auction, and that a reduced number of 425 stores would remain open, including 223 Sears stores. Sears was based in the Sears Tower in Chicago from 1973 until 1995, and is currently headquartered in Hoffman Estates, Illinois. Sears announced in 2021 that it would be selling its Hoffman Estates headquarters building(s). On September 24, 2018, the retailer's CEO warned that the company was "running out of time" to salvage its business. Sears Holdings filed for Chapter 11 bankruptcy on October 15, 2018, ahead of a $134 million debt payment due that day. On June 3, 2019, the company announced that Transform Holdco would acquire Sears Hometown & Outlet Stores. As per deal, it might need to divest its Sears Outlet division to gain approval. On August 6, 2019, it was announced that 26 stores, including 21 Sears stores, including the last Sears store in Alabama, at Riverchase Galleria in Hoover, and the last Sears store in West Virginia, at Huntington Mall in Barboursville, would be closing in October, with plans to "accelerate the expansion of our smaller store formats which includes opening additional Home & Life stores and adding several hundred Sears Hometown stores after the Sears Hometown and Outlet transaction closes." On August 31, 2019, it was announced that Transform would close an additional 92 stores, including 15 Sears stores, by the end of 2019. 100 more stores closed by January 2020. 51 Sears stores were closed in February 2020. More stores continued to close throughout 2020 and 2021. As of September 16, 2021 the company's website listed 35 Sears stores. Near the end of 2019, Sears sold the brand name DieHard to Advance Auto Parts for $200 million. In September 2021, Sears announced that it would close more stores, including the last Sears store in New York City. The New York City Sears closed by November 24, 2021, and will potentially be demolished for redevelopment.

31. Giant Eagle Inc

Giant Eagle, Inc. is an American supermarket chain with stores in Pennsylvania, Ohio, West Virginia, Indiana, and Maryland. The company was founded in 1918 in Pittsburgh, Pennsylvania, and incorporated on August 31, 1931. Supermarket News ranked Giant Eagle 21st on the "Top 75 North American Food Retailers" based on sales of $10 billion. In 2021, it was the 36th-largest privately held company, as determined by Forbes. Based on 2005 revenue, Giant Eagle is the 49th-largest retailer in the United States. As of Summer 2014, the company had approximately $9.9 billion in annual sales. As of Summer 2021, Giant Eagle, Inc. had 480 stores across the portfolio. 216 supermarkets (Giant Eagle, Giant Eagle Express, Market District, Market District Express) and 264 fuel station/convenience stores under the GetGo banner. The company is headquartered in an office park in the Pittsburgh suburb of O'Hara Township.

In 2004, Giant Eagle purchased nine former Big Bear stores in Columbus, Newark, and Marietta from parent company Penn Traffic. Giant Eagle has since expanded to several additional locations, acquiring other abandoned Big Bear stores and in newly constructed buildings using the current Giant Eagle prototype. Giant Eagle opened its 20th Columbus-area at New Albany Road at the Ohio Rt. 161 freeway (New Albany) in August 2007, its 21st area store at Hayden Run and Cosgray Roads (Dublin) in November 2007, its 22nd area store at Stelzer and McCutcheon Roads (Columbus) in July 2008 and its 23rd area store at South Hamilton Road and Winchester Pike (Groveport) in August 2008. A new Giant Eagle opened in Lancaster, in November 2008, and the former Big Bear located at Blacklick Crossing is undergoing an expansion and remodeling. On September 27, 2018, Giant Eagle announced it would purchase the Ricker's convenience store chain in Indiana, marking the largest acquisition for GetGo since the chain's launch. The chain has built large prototypes, and it has experimented with many departments unusual to supermarkets.

32. Dunkin' Donuts LLC

Dunkin' Donuts LLC, also known as **Dunkin'** and by the initials **DD**, is an American multinational coffee and doughnut company, as well as a quick service restaurant. It was founded by Bill Rosenberg in Quincy, Massachusetts, in 1950. Bill Rosenberg opened Open Kettle in 1948, a restaurant selling donuts and coffee in Quincy, Massachusetts (a suburb of Boston), but he changed the name in 1950 to Dunkin' Donuts after discussing with company executives. The chain was acquired by Baskin-Robbins's holding company Allied Lyons in 1990; its acquisition of the Mister Donut chain and the conversion of that chain to Dunkin' Donuts facilitated the brand's growth in North America that year. Dunkin' and Baskin-Robbins eventually became subsidiaries of Dunkin' Brands, headquartered in Canton, Massachusetts, in 2004, until being purchased by Inspire Brands on December 15, 2020. The chain began rebranding as a "beverage-led company", and was renamed Dunkin', in January 2019; while stores in the U.S. began using the new name, the rebranding will eventually be rolled out to all of its international stores. With approximately 12,900 locations in 42 countries, Dunkin' is one of the largest coffee shop and donut shop chains in the world. Its products include donuts, bagels, coffee, and "Munchkins" donut holes.

On July 11, 2018, Dave Hoffmann took over from Nigel Travis to become the CEO. He is looking to add 1,000 new locations outside of the Northeastern United States by the end of 2020 and to have a revenue increase of 3 percent for stores open a year or longer. Also late 2018, Dunkin' installed espresso machines at all possible locations and launched espresso products using a new recipe. In June 2019, Dunkin' partnered with Grubhub to begin the rollout of its new Dunkin' Delivers service. Later in July 2019, Dunkin' partnered with Beyond Meat to introduce a meatless breakfast sandwich in Manhattan, becoming the first U.S. restaurant brand to serve Beyond Sausage. The sandwich launched nationally later in 2019. In October 2020, Dunkin' Brands stated that the company was in conversation with Inspire Brands, a private equity-backed company, negotiating to sell the company. Inspire Brands announced on Saturday, October 31, 2020, that they would be acquiring Dunkin' Brands Group for $11.3 billion, which would include Dunkin' Brands' debt that Inspire Brands would be taking on. Inspire would pay $106.50 in cash for each of Dunkin' Brands' shares. On December 15, 2020, the acquisition was completed, and Dunkin' Brands ceased to exist as a separate company, with Dunkin', Baskin-Robbins, and the trademark management of Mister Donut, becoming part of Inspire Brands.

33. KFC

KFC (Kentucky Fried Chicken) is an American fast food restaurant chain headquartered in Louisville, Kentucky, that specializes in fried chicken. It is the world's second-largest restaurant chain (as measured by sales) after McDonald's, with 22,621 locations globally in 150 countries as of December 2019. The chain is a subsidiary of Yum! Brands, a restaurant company that also owns the Pizza Hut, Taco Bell and WingStreet chains. KFC was founded by Colonel Harland Sanders, an entrepreneur who began selling fried chicken from his roadside restaurant in Corbin, Kentucky, during the Great Depression. Sanders identified the potential of the restaurant franchising concept and the first "Kentucky Fried Chicken" franchise opened in Utah in 1952. KFC popularized chicken in the fast-food industry, diversifying the market by challenging the established dominance of the hamburger. By branding himself as "Colonel Sanders", Harland became a prominent figure of American cultural history and his image remains widely used in KFC advertising to this day. However, the company's rapid expansion overwhelmed the aging Sanders and he sold it to a group of investors led by John Y. Brown Jr. and Jack C. Massey in 1964.

KFC was one of the first American fast-food chains to expand internationally, opening outlets in Canada, the United Kingdom, Mexico and Jamaica by the mid-1960s. Throughout the 1970s and 1980s, it experienced mixed fortunes domestically, as it went through a series of changes in corporate ownership with little or no experience in the restaurant business. In the early 1970s, KFC was sold to the spirits distributor Heublein, which was taken over by the R. J. Reynolds food and tobacco conglomerate; that company sold the chain to PepsiCo. The chain continued to expand overseas, however, and in 1987 it became the first Western restaurant chain to open in China. It has since expanded rapidly in China, which is now the company's single largest market. PepsiCo spun off its restaurants division as Tricon Global Restaurants, which later changed its name to Yum! Brands. KFC is a subsidiary of Yum! Brands, one of the largest restaurant companies in the world. KFC had sales of $23 billion in 2013. KFC is incorporated under Delaware General Corporation Law, and has its headquarters at 1441 Gardiner Lane, Louisville, Kentucky, in a three-story colonial style building known colloquially as the "White House" due to its resemblance to the US president's home.

34. The Home Depot

The Home Depot, Inc., commonly known as **Home Depot**, is the largest home improvement retailer in the United States, supplying tools, construction products, appliances, and services. The company is headquartered in incorporated Cobb County, Georgia, with an Atlanta mailing address. It operates many big-box format stores across the United States (including the District of Columbia, Guam, Puerto Rico and the U.S. Virgin Islands); all 10 provinces of Canada; and all 32 Mexican states and Mexico City. MRO company Interline Brands (now The Home Depot Pro) is also owned by The Home Depot, with 70 distribution centers across the United States. The Home Depot was co-founded by Bernard Marcus, Arthur Blank, Ron Brill, and Pat Farrah in 1978. The Home Depot's proposition was to build home-improvement superstores, larger than any of their competitors' facilities. Investment banker Ken Langone helped Marcus and Blank to secure the necessary capital. Home Depot stores average 105,000 ft2 (9,755 m2) in size and are organized warehouse-style, stocking a large range of supplies. Home Depot's two largest stores are located in Vauxhall, New Jersey.

In 2013, The Home Depot established two large distribution centers in Atlanta and Los Angeles. On July 22, 2015, Home Depot acquired Interline Brands from P2 Capital Partners, Goldman Sachs' private equity arm, and the management of Interline Brands for $1.6 billion. Interline Brands became fully integrated with The Home Depot in August 2016 with the Interline Brands website merging with The Home Depot website. The subsidiaries of Interline Brands are now companies of The Home Depot. In 2017, Home Depot acquired the online presence of The Company Store from Hanover Direct. The Company Store was founded in 1911, operating primarily as catalog and online sales, but with five physical locations. The five physical locations were not included in the deal. For the Q2 of 2020, the company reported sales of $38.1 billion, which represented a growth of 23.4% from the same period, the previous year. The net earnings for the period of three months (ending August 2) rose 27% up to $4.3 billion. The growth in the sales was a result of Americans staying at home as a result of the COVID-19 pandemic. In the Q3 for 2020, ending November 1, Home Depot reported a revenue of $33.5 billion; it represents a year-on-year increase of 24 per cent.

35. Starbucks

Starbucks Corporation is an American multinational chain of coffeehouses and roastery reserves headquartered in Seattle, Washington. It is the world's largest coffeehouse chains. Starbucks was founded in 1971 by Jerry Baldwin, Zev Siegl, and Gordon Bowker at Seattle's Pike Place Market. During the early 1980s, they sold the company to Howard Schultz who – after a business trip to Milan, Italy – decided to convert the coffee bean store into a coffee shop serving espresso-based drinks. As chief executive officer from 1986 to 2000, Schultz's first tenure led to an aggressive expansion of the franchise, first in Seattle, then across the West Coast of the United States. As of November 2021, the company had 33,833 stores in 80 countries, 15,444 of which were located in the United States. Out of Starbucks' U.S.-based stores, over 8,900 are company-operated, while the remainder are licensed. In 2021–2022, votes to join Starbucks unions were successful at multiple Starbucks locations, including in cities such as Seattle, Buffalo, Rochester, Ithaca, Kansas City and Manhattan. The rise of the second wave of coffee culture is generally attributed to Starbucks, which introduced a wider variety of coffee experiences. Starbucks serves hot and cold drinks, whole-bean coffee, micro-ground instant coffee, espresso, caffe latte, full and loose-leaf teas, juices, Frappuccino beverages, pastries, and snacks. Some offerings are seasonal, or specific to the locality of the store.

In June 2020, during the COVID-19 pandemic in the United States, the company announced that it would close 400 of its locations in the US/Canada region over the subsequent 18 months as it moves from the coffee house concept to what it calls "convenience-led" formats with drive-through and curbside pickup. Starbucks announced that it planned to open 300 stores that will primarily focus on carryout and pickup orders. The new stores will work with the Starbucks mobile app for prepayment by the customer before arrival to pick up the order. The layout of some stores will also be modified with a separate counter for picking up mobile orders. In December 2020, Starbucks announced that it is planning to increase its store count to about 55,000 by 2030, up from roughly 33,000. Analysts have long believed that the firm's corporate governance must determine how to contend with higher materials prices and enhanced competition from lower-priced fast-food chains, including McDonald's and Dunkin' Donuts. In October 2015, Starbucks hired its first chief technology officer, Gerri Martin-Flickinger, to lead its technology team. Starbucks maintains control of production processes by communicating with farmers to secure beans, roasting its own beans, and managing distribution to all retail locations. Additionally, Starbucks's Coffee and Farmer Equity Practices require suppliers to inform Starbucks what portion of wholesale prices paid reaches farmers. On June 19, 2018, Starbucks announced the closing of 150 locations in 2019.

36. FedEx Corporation

FedEx Corporation, formerly Federal Express Corporation and later FDX Corporation, is an American multinational conglomerate holding company focused on transportation, e-commerce and services based in Memphis, Tennessee. The name "FedEx" is a syllabic abbreviation of the name of the company's original air division, Federal Express, which was used from 1973 until 2000. FedEx today is best known for its air delivery service, FedEx Express, which was one of the first major shipping companies to offer overnight delivery as a flagship service. Since then, FedEx also started FedEx Ground, FedEx Office (originally known as Kinko's), FedEx Supply Chain, FedEx Freight, and various other services across multiple subsidiaries, often meant to respond to its main competitor, UPS. FedEx is also one of the top contractors of the US government and assists in the transport of some United States Postal Service packages through their Air Cargo Network contract. The company was founded in Little Rock, Arkansas in 1971 as Federal Express Corporation by Frederick W. Smith, a graduate of Yale University. He drew up the company's concept in a term paper at Yale, in which he called for a system specifically designed for urgent deliveries. While his professor didn't think much of the idea, Smith pressed on. He began formal operations in 1973, when he moved operations to Memphis. Smith cited his reasons for choosing Memphis International Airport included its location near the mean population center of the country and its lack of frequent inclement weather. The firm was named by Fortune magazine as one of the top 100 companies to work for in 2013, citing the company's choice to downsize with voluntary buyouts rather than involuntary layoffs. FedEx ranked No. 50 in the 2018 Fortune 500 list of the largest United States corporations by total revenue.

The company grew rapidly, and by 1983 had a billion dollars in revenues, a rarity for a startup company that had never taken part in mergers or acquisitions in its first decade. It expanded to Europe and Asia in 1984. In 1988, it acquired one of its major competitors, Flying Tiger Line, creating the largest full-service cargo airline in the world. In 1994, Federal Express shortened its name to "FedEx" for marketing purposes, officially adopting a nickname that had been used for years. On October 2, 1997, FedEx reorganized as a holding company, FDX Corporation, a Delaware corporation. The new holding company began operations in January 1998, with the acquisition of Caliber System Inc. by Federal Express. With the purchase of Caliber, FedEx started offering other services besides express shipping. In January 2000, FDX Corporation changed its name to FedEx Corporation and re-branded all of its subsidiaries. In April 2015, FedEx acquired their rival firm TNT Express for €4.4 billion ($4.8 billion; £3.2 billion) as it looked to expand their operations in Europe. In February 2016, FedEx announced the launch of FedEx Cares, a global giving platform, and committed to invest $200 million to strengthen more than 200 communities by 2020. In March 2018, FedEx announced the acquisition of P2P Mailing Limited, a last-mile delivery service, for £92 million to expand their portfolio. In June 2019, FedEx announced they would not be renewing their $850 million contract with Amazon for the company's U.S. domestic express delivery business. Amazon accounted for 1.3 percent of 2018 revenues. In August 2019, FedEx announced the termination of ground deliveries for Amazon as well. In December 2020, FedEx acquired ShopRunner, an e-commerce platform. On March 29, 2022, founder Frederick W. Smith announced he would be retiring as CEO and become executive chairman effective June 1st, 2022. The company named Raj Subramaniam, FedEx's current president and COO, as Smith's successor.

37. Kohl's Corporation

Kohl's is an American department store retail chain, operated by Kohl's Corporation. As of December 2021 it is the largest department store chain in the United States, with 1,162 locations, operating stores in every U.S. state except Hawaii. The company was founded by Polish immigrant Maxwell Kohl, who opened a corner grocery store in Milwaukee, Wisconsin in 1927. It went on to become a successful chain in the local area, and in 1962 the company branched out by opening its first department store. British American Tobacco Company took a controlling interest in the company in 1972 while still managed by the Kohl Family, and in 1979, the corporation was sold to BATUS Inc. A group of investors purchased the company in 1986 from British American Tobacco and took it public in 1992. Kohl's private brands generate nearly half of the firm's $19 billion in annual sales. These include in-house clothing brands such as American Beauty, Apt. 9, Croft & Barrow, Jumping Beans, So, Tek Gear, and Urban Pipeline. Kohl's uses a "racetrack" layout with a single aisle that circles the entire store, a layout borrowed from discount stores.

Kohl's is headquartered in the Milwaukee suburb of Menomonee Falls, Wisconsin. It became the largest department store chain in the United States in May 2012, surpassing its biggest competitor J. C. Penney. The company is listed on both the S&P 400 and the Fortune 500. In terms of revenue, the chain was the 23rd-largest retailer in the United States in 2019. As of 2013, Kohl's was the second-largest U.S. department store company by retail sales. In early January 2017, Kohl's shares fell 19% in value, in what The Wall Street Journal said was "the stock's worst day on record," and noted that it was a noticeable exception to the overall declining volatility of the market. The company ranked 157th on the 2018 Fortune 500, the annual list of the largest United States corporations, having earned revenues of $19.095 billion in 2017. In that year, Kohl's entered into a partnership with Amazon, which included a program where select stores would accept Amazon returns; in 2019 it was expanded nationwide. In 2018, Kohl's announced a pilot program to lease space to grocer Aldi and, the following year, to fitness center Planet Fitness, alongside up to 10 stores each.

38. General Motors

General Motors Company (GM) is an American multinational automotive manufacturing corporation headquartered in Detroit, Michigan, United States. The company is the largest automobile manufacturer based in the United States and one of the largest worldwide. It was the largest automaker worldwide for 77 consecutive years, from 1931 when it overtook Ford Motor Company, until 2008, when it was overtaken by Toyota. William C. Durant's Durant-Dort Carriage Company, of Flint, Michigan, had become the largest manufacturer of horse-drawn vehicles in the United States by 1900. Durant was averse to automobiles, but fellow Flint businessman James H. Whiting, owner of Flint Wagon Works, sold him the Buick Motor Company in 1904. Durant formed General Motors Company in 1908 as a holding company, with partner Charles Stewart Mott, borrowing a naming convention from General Electric. GM's first acquisition was Buick, which Durant already owned, then Oldsmobile on November 12, 1908. In 1909, Durant's GM acquired Cadillac, Elmore, Welch, Cartercar, Oakland (predecessor of Pontiac), the Reliance Motor Truck Company of Owosso, Michigan, and the Rapid Motor Vehicle Company of Pontiac, Michigan (predecessors of GMC). Durant, with the board's approval, tried acquiring Ford Motor Company in 1909 but needed an additional $2 million. Durant over-leveraged GM in making these acquisitions, and was removed by the board of directors in 1910 at the behest of the bankers who backed the loans to keep GM in business. The action of the bankers was partially influenced by the Panic of 1910–1911 that followed the earlier enforcement of the Sherman Antitrust Act of 1890. In 1911 Charles F. Kettering, with Henry M. Leland, of Dayton Engineering Laboratories Company (DELCO) invented and patented the first electric starter in America. In November 1911, Durant co-founded Chevrolet with Swiss race car driver Louis Chevrolet, who left the company bearing his name in 1915 after a disagreement with Durant.

General Motors is ranked 22nd on the Fortune 500 rankings of the largest United States corporations by total revenue. The company has manufacturing plants in 8 countries. Its four core automobile brands are Chevrolet, Buick, GMC, and Cadillac. It also holds interests in Chinese brands Wuling Motors and Baojun as well as DMAX via joint ventures. BrightDrop is the company's delivery-focused service. GM Defense produces military vehicles for the U.S. Department of Defense and the Department of State. OnStar provides vehicle safety, security and information services. ACDelco is the company's auto parts division. The company provides financing via GM Financial. The company is developing self-driving cars through its majority ownership in Cruise LLC. In March 2009, after the company had received $17.4 billion in bailouts but was not effective in a turnaround, President Barack Obama forced the resignation of CEO Rick Wagoner. General Motors filed for a government-backed Chapter 11 reorganization on June 8, 2009. On July 10, 2009, the original General Motors sold assets and some subsidiaries to an entirely new company, including the trademark "General Motors". Liabilities were left with the original GM, renamed Motors Liquidation Company, freeing the companies of many liabilities and resulting in a new GM. Through the Troubled Asset Relief Program, the United States Department of the Treasury invested $49.5 billion in General Motors and recovered $39 billion when it sold its shares on December 9, 2013, resulting in a loss of $10.3 billion. The Treasury invested an additional $17.2 billion into GM's former financing company, GMAC (now Ally Financial). The shares in Ally were sold on December 18, 2014, for $19.6 billion netting the government $2.4 billion in profit, including dividends. A study by the Center for Automotive Research found that the GM bailout saved 1.2 million jobs and preserved $34.9 billion in tax revenue. On January 8, 2021, GM introduced a new logo alongside a tagline "EVerybody in", with the capitalized "EV" as a nod to the company's commitment to electric vehicles. GM's new logo used negative space to create the idea of an electric plug in the "M" of the logo.

39. Dell

Dell is an American technology company that develops, sells, repairs, and supports computers and related products and services, and is owned by its parent company of Dell Technologies. Founded in 1984 by Michael Dell, the company is one of the largest technology corporations in the world, employing more than 165,000 people around the world. Dell sells personal computers (PCs), servers, data storage devices, network switches, software, computer peripherals, HDTVs, cameras, printers, and electronics built by other manufacturers. The company is well known for its innovations in supply chain management and electronic commerce, particularly its direct-sales model and its "build-to-order" or "configure to order" approach to manufacturing—delivering individual PCs configured to customer specifications. Dell was a pure hardware vendor for much of its existence, but with the acquisition in 2009 of Perot Systems, Dell entered the market for IT services. The company has since made additional acquisitions in storage and networking systems, with the aim of expanding their portfolio from offering computers only to delivering complete solutions for enterprise customers.

Dell was listed at number 51 in the Fortune 500 list until 2014. Its most recent rank on the Fortune 500 is 34th. It is the world's 3rd largest personal computer vendor by unit sales as of January 2021, following Lenovo and HP Inc. Dell is the largest shipper of PC monitors worldwide. Dell is the sixth-largest company in Texas by total revenue, according to Fortune magazine. It is the second-largest non-oil company in Texas (behind AT&T) and the largest company in the Greater Austin area. After going private in 2013, the confidential nature of its financial information prevented the company from being ranked by Fortune. It was a publicly traded company (Nasdaq: DELL), as well as a component of the NASDAQ-100 and S&P 500, until it was taken private in a leveraged buyout which closed in October 2013. In 2015, Dell acquired the enterprise technology firm EMC Corporation; following the completion of the purchase, Dell and EMC became divisions of Dell Technologies. Dell EMC as a part of Dell Technologies focus on data storage, information security, virtualization, analytics, cloud computing and other related products and services. The company aims to reduce its external environmental impact through an energy-efficient evolution of products, and also reduce its direct operational impact through energy-efficiency programs

40. Google LLC

Google LLC is an American multinational technology company that focuses on artificial intelligence, search engine, online advertising, cloud computing, computer software, quantum computing, e-commerce, and consumer electronics. It has been referred to as the "most powerful company in the world" and one of the world's most valuable brands due to its market dominance, data collection, and technological advantages in the area of artificial intelligence. It is considered one of the Big Five American information technology companies, alongside Amazon, Apple, Meta, and Microsoft. Google was founded on September 4, 1998, by Larry Page and Sergey Brin while they were PhD students at Stanford University in California. Together they own about 14% of its publicly listed shares and control 56% of the stockholder voting power through super-voting stock. The company went public via an initial public offering (IPO) in 2004. In 2015, Google was reorganized as a wholly owned subsidiary of Alphabet Inc. Google is Alphabet's largest subsidiary and is a holding company for Alphabet's Internet properties and interests. Sundar Pichai was appointed CEO of Google on October 24, 2015, replacing Larry Page, who became the CEO of Alphabet. The company has since rapidly grown to offer a multitude of products and services beyond Google Search, many of which hold dominant market positions. These products address a wide area including email (Gmail), navigation (Maps), cloud computing (Cloud), web browsing (Chrome), video sharing (YouTube), productivity (Workspace), operating systems (Android), cloud storage (Drive), language translation (Translate), photo storage (Photo), video calling (Meet), smart home (Nest), smartphones (Pixel), wearable technology (Fitbit), gaming (Stadia), music streaming (YouTube Music), video on demand (TV), artificial intelligence (Assistant), machine learning APIs (TensorFlow), AI chips (TPU), and more.

Google is well-known for its highly ambitious technological innovations aimed at solving humanity's biggest problems. Some of these innovations include quantum computing (Sycamore), self-driving cars (Waymo, formerly the Google self-driving project), smart cities (Sidewalk Labs), and transformer models (Google Brain). Google and YouTube are the two most visited websites worldwide followed by Facebook and Twitter. Google is also the largest search engine, mapping and navigation application, email provider, office suite, video sharing platform, photo and cloud storage provider, mobile operating system, web browser, ML framework, and AI virtual assistant provider in the world as measured by market share. On the list of most valuable brands, Google is ranked second by Forbes and fourth by Interbrand. It has received significant criticism involving issues such as privacy concerns, tax avoidance, censorship, search neutrality, antitrust and abuse of its monopoly position. In the third quarter of 2005, Google reported a 700% increase in profit, largely due to large companies shifting their advertising strategies from newspapers, magazines, and television to the Internet. For the 2006 fiscal year, the company reported $10.492 billion in total advertising revenues and only $112 million in licensing and other revenues. In 2011, 96% of Google's revenue was derived from its advertising programs. Google generated $50 billion in annual revenue for the first time in 2012, generating $38 billion the previous year. In January 2013, then-CEO Larry Page commented, "We ended 2012 with a strong quarter ... Revenues were up 36% year-on-year, and 8% quarter-on-quarter. And we hit $50 billion in revenues for the first time last year – not a bad achievement in just a decade and a half." Google's consolidated revenue for the third quarter of 2013 was reported in mid-October 2013 as $14.89 billion, a 12 percent increase compared to the previous quarter.

CHAPTER 1

ORGANIZATIONS ARE EXTENSIONS OF INDIVIDUALS

It has already been established that an organization is an extension of an individual. When an individual identifies his or her area(s) of expertise, based on his or her natural talents, and conceives an idea or makes a discovery that he or she cannot fully actualize by himself or herself, he or she often reaches out to other people for help. By reaching out to involve other people, an organization is formed. It is, therefore, important to understand the individual as the basis to understanding the organization he or she creates.

Every individual is born with talents and every individual has a destiny to attain. This may sound too religious but the fact is that every human being is created with certain measure of natural skills, natural gifts, natural abilities and strengths known as talents, with which to make certain amount of contribution to the good of humanity. This is known as 'destiny.' Destiny is simply described as the totality of the contribution of an individual to human development and progress. It is your divine assignment on earth - the ultimate reason why God brought you here. Ralph Waldo Emerson said this about talents:

> "Nature arms each person with some faculty which enables them to do easily some feat impossible to any other."[6]

Let me talk a little more about talents for proper understanding. Everybody possesses some talents. Those talents constitute physical abilities, mental capabilities, and social skills. They involve the special ways we use our six senses - sense of sight, sense of smell, sense of touch, sense of taste, sense of hearing, and sense of reasoning. They constitute the ways we use our voice in speaking, reading or singing, our hands in spinning, designing or writing, our legs in walking, dancing or sporting, our bodies in acting, swimming, or modeling, and our brains in discovering, inventing, or innovating. These are abilities we are born with in certain degrees. Above all, it is the ability to learn what we see others do. This is the culmination of all human abilities - the ability to learn and add to what we already know as a way of boosting our capacity to create solutions that add value to mankind in our interaction with the environment. By possession of talents, the human being is, therefore, creative in nature. But the extent of one's creativity depends largely on how one develops and utilizes these talents in proffering solution to the needs of mankind.

Figure 1.1 The Flowchart of Life

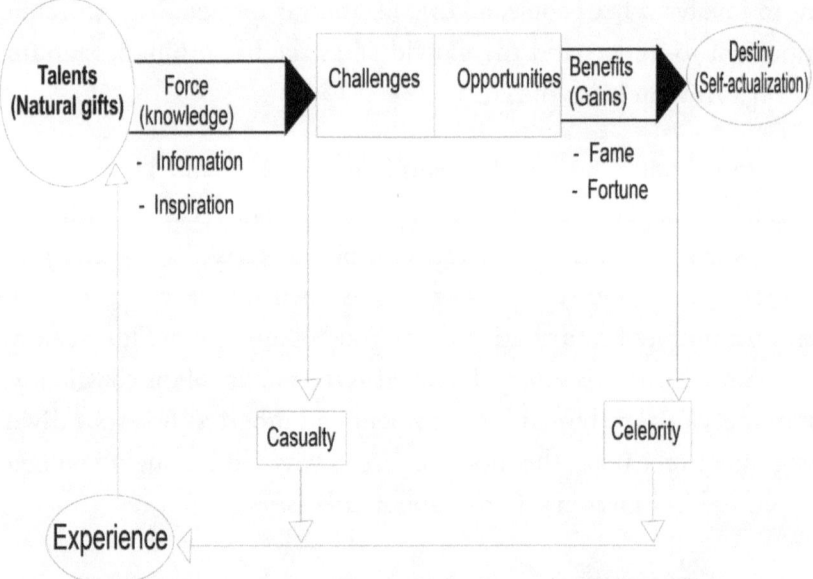

Above is a schematic representation of what I describe as the 'flowchart of life.' Our understanding of this diagram helps us in understanding our lives and how they function as well as how they are meant to function.

Talents

As I discussed in my book, Manifesting for Global Impact, published in 2013[7], there are 12 stages in our journey in life; the first stage being the birth or introductory stage while the last is the global recognition stage. Below is the complete list:

  Stage 12: Global Impact/Recognition stage
  Stage 11: Continental Impact/Recognition stage
  Stage 10: National Impact/Recognition stage
  Stage 9: State or Regional Impact/Recognition stage
  Stage 8: County or Local Impact/Recognition stage
  Stage 7: Community or Locality Impact/Recognition stage
  Stage 6: Family Impact/Recognition stage
  Stage 5: Matching Ability with Opportunity stage; The career stage
  Stage 4: Personal Advancement stage; The learning stage
  Stage 3: Destiny Discovery stage; Discovering your life purpose stage
  Stage 2: Talent identification/development stage
  Stage 1: Birth or Introductory stage

From the list above, stage 2 has to do with talent identification and development. In the earlier part of this chapter, I gave a detailed explanation about talents. Every individual has a couple of talents. The differences in the individual results of members of a particular career, profession, discipline or skill set is based on the extent of personal development. This is applicable to musicians, actors/actresses, sports stars, writers, news casters, doctors, teachers, scientists, lawyers, bankers, stock traders, pilots, engineers, etc. Talents must be developed or sharpened by constant exercise through practice, information update through research, and competition through real contests. A talent that is not being developed will soon become dormant. Remember, your talents are your basic tools for reaching your destiny. Those who engage in sports must develop their muscles, those who sing must develop their voices, those who model must develop their shapes and skin, those who carve and paint must develop their artistry, while those who write, design, discover, invent and innovate must develop their thought process. Everybody has some degree of natural talents. However, some environments encourage the development and utilization of those talents while other environments discourage their discovery and use. Talent development is a continuum and the more you develop your talents the more useful they become and the more resourceful you get at providing solution to common challenges. Your talent is, therefore, your natural resource for attaining destiny.

Destiny

Destiny has been defined as a predetermined course of events. So, an individual's destiny is predetermined even before he or she discovers it. Destiny has also been described as one's purpose in life, that is, the reason why you were created or the purpose for your existence. Destiny can also be your divine assignment; the responsibility God created you to undertake in this world. Breaking it down a little bit, we can say that your destiny is the solution you are meant to provide to humanity's common challenges to make the world a better place. It is also worthy to note that every destiny is potentially global. What this means is that every individual has the capacity to provide solution to global challenges. Destiny is neither local nor personal but global and divine.

From the list of the twelve stages in life, the last stage in our destiny actualization is the 12th stage, which is the global impact /recognition stage. Everybody has the potential to use his or her talents to provide solution at the global level. The fact remains that only a very few people get to this stage. Little wonder we have only 1% of the global population that control and enjoy 85% of the global wealth. There are needs everywhere beckoning for solution. From local to global levels, people are looking for solution to their personal, corporate, and general challenges. A local community may have its own challenge as the lack of clean water, a corporate organization may have its own challenge as the lack of customers for its products, while the global community's challenge might be the issue of global warming. HIV/AIDS, cancer, ebola disease, zika virus, COVID-19 pandemic, monkey pox and other forms of deadly diseases continue to pose health challenges to the global community. Then you have natural disasters such as earthquakes, tsunamis, volcanoes, and tornadoes that continue to destroy lives and properties. Plane crashes, auto crashes, and train crashes are some of the challenges that are begging for solution.

Can all the problems of the world be solved at any time? Never! Any day all the problems of the world are completely solved will mark the end of the world because people will no longer have jobs to do, passions to pursue, solutions to provide or challenges to overcome. Destiny will become irrelevant any day all the problems of the world are completely solved. If every individual fulfills his destiny in full, will there still be problems in the world? Yes! Every new generation of human beings has its peculiar challenges. Some of the problems we face in the world today were not there 50 years ago and some of the problems that the world will face 50 years from now are not here yet. It has often been said that the most successful human being on earth probably did not attain more than 25 percent of his or her destiny or utilize 25% of his or her potentials. This means that all the discoveries, inventions, and innovations we enjoy in the world today constitute less than a quarter of what we could have enjoyed if every human being used his or her talents to fulfill his or her destiny to the fullest. So, there is a huge gap between what we are doing and what we can do. The human being has some great potentials that he does not often realize in his lifetime. Hear what the legendary American journalist and author, Norman Cousins, had to say about this:

> *"The greatest tragedy in life is not death; it's what dies within us while we're still alive."*[8]

This quote has continued to change my life as it continues to challenge my potentials. The average human being is so loaded with great potentials. In fact, creativity is part of the natural endowment of every human being. You can only know what you are capable of doing when you are faced with challenges. No wonder challenge is a major part of our daily lives as shown in 'the flowchart of life.'

Challenges and Opportunities

Life is full of challenges as well as opportunities. Between talents and destiny are challenges and opportunities. They are all within the environment. If there were no challenges, people will not strive for anything in life. Absence of challenges means there will be no discoveries, no inventions, and no innovations. In fact, challenges were put in place to prepare us to look inwards and discover the enormity of the abilities we have within and to figure out how we can convert those abilities into solutions. You must have heard the saying that 'necessity is the mother of invention,' meaning that there would be no invention if there were no necessities. Challenges are opportunities for creative solution to those who understand what life is all about. It is those who take up the challenges, seek for solution, and offer hope to the society, that eventually end up as celebrities. A good example is Facebook. There was a need for a cheap means of communication across the globe. The telephone and the fax machine already provided a solution but at a cost that is beyond the reach of the common people. Now, through Facebook, hundreds of millions of people across the globe can give and receive information anytime and any day in writing, in voice, in pictures, and in videos at a little or no cost. Simply known as part of the social media platforms, this discovery has led to a huge revolution in the global information and communication industry and has greatly altered, if not obliterated, the traditional media industry. This is an incredible discovery! Do you know what the co-founder and CEO of Facebook, Mark Zuckerberg, enjoys these days? Fame and fortune! Let me shock you a little bit. Anybody else could have done what Zuckerberg and his colleagues did. It could have been you or me! There are still so many things that have not yet been discovered. As I write this book, there are still so many problems seeking for solution. There are so many diseases seeking for cure just as there are so many products yet to be developed. The environment has several opportunities which sometimes present themselves in the form of challenges.

Force

Depending on individual experiences and perspectives, where some people see challenges others see opportunities. Such is life! This does not mean that there are no real challenges. Even those who see all life's offerings as opportunities also face challenges all the time; a good dose of it. For example, if you interview two of the richest men on earth, Jeff Bezos and Elon Musk, the founders and CEOs of Amazon and Tesla respectively, they will tell you that it was not an easy task at the beginning and has never been. They faced numerous rejections, humiliations, limitations, intimidation, stagnation, and frustrations along the way. Does that sound familiar? it is the same with everybody. Entrepreneurship is not an easy task. So, what is the difference between those who persevere to the end and those who give up along the way? This is where 'force' comes in. Challenge is a barrier that requires a force to break through. Until force is applied, fame and fortune are denied. Until you are ready to fight your way through, you may never experience a breakthrough.

Knowledge

The greatest force in life is knowledge. This is why someone once stated that 'knowledge is power.' Knowledge provides the force for the pursuit of destiny. Those who do not acquire and apply this force end up as casualties while those who do end up as celebrities. There are two forms or sources of knowledge: 1) informational knowledge and 2) inspirational knowledge.

Informational knowledge accounts for about 30% of the force you need to break through life's challenges, explore available opportunities, create desired opportunities, and attain destiny in a grand style. We get information (or knowledge) through our school teachers, clergymen, television, radio, bill boards, books, newspapers, magazines, music, friends, parents, bosses, co- workers, etc. By listening, observing, and reading, we acquire informational knowledge. So, all our years in school account for a smaller percentage of the knowledge we need to become solution providers as well as celebrities. This is why the most educated people on earth are not necessarily the most successful! They are still struggling with the 30%; and 30% is not a pass mark in any examination! So, one can still be a failure with all the education acquired over scores of years. This does not in any way undermine or demean the importance of formal education in our success in life. In fact, I encourage everyone to get as much education as he or she possibly can because it is going to boost your capacity in the use of the rest 70%. Come to think of it, what do we actually learn in school? Other people's ideas, discoveries, inventions, innovations, experiences, and solutions! The school system gives us information about what is already in existence and how we can take advantage of it. The school system also exposes us to the existing challenges that are begging for solution but hardly helps us find the solution. The reason is simple. Finding solution to an existing challenge is entirely personal. Name those who made outstanding discoveries and you will realize that most of those discoveries happened outside the walls of the school. For example, Thomas Edison, Henry Ford, Wright brothers, Alexander Graham Bell, James Watt, Galileo Galilei, Leonardo da Vinci, Elon Musk, Jeff Bezos, Sam Walton, John D. Rockefeller, Walt Disney, Oprah Winfrey, Tyler Perry, Mary Kay Ash, Milton Hershey, Maxwell Kohl, Michael Dell, etc. Even people like Bill Gates and Mark Zuckerberg who made their discoveries at school, had to drop out of school to fully develop and commercialize those discoveries. The school may give you an idea but does not give you the solution. I must admit that our teachers and professors are doing a great job in the area of educating us to discover and develop our unique strengths as to convert them into instruments of solution. But you do not need to hold a doctoral degree before you can discover a solution to the challenges of your immediate locality or that of the global community. We have a long list of people who dropped out of school once they discovered certain solution. If you know what you want in life, you will know it when you find it!

The second form or source of knowledge is inspiration. Inspirational knowledge constitutes about 70% of the force you need to break through life's challenges, explore and exploit available opportunities, create desired opportunities, and attain destiny in a grand style. What is inspiration? Inspiration is the act of receiving sound and superior intellectual ability through supernatural influence. Some refer to it as instinct, concept, perception, imagination, fantasy, etc. It is a form of receiving divine ideas for human solution. Most, if not all, of the discoveries, inventions, and innovations came as inspired ideas and when those who receive them work to perfect them over time, they become solutions. Inspirations can come through imaginations, revelations, dreams, visions, meditations, research, adventures, stories, teachings, observations, interactions, etc. They can be sparked off by an idea in a book, news media, religious sermon, words of music, advertisement, movie, etc. An inspiration can emanate from where and when you least expect it. The air is filled with divine ideas which continue to be released for the solution of each generation's challenges. Those who pick these ideas end up as celebrities while those who do not end up as casualties.

Inspiration is not the same as creativity but it sure enhances creativity. Inspiration is a divine force of knowledge. Inspiration is the source of supernatural instinct for creating unique solutions. Creativity is natural to every human being and not just random to a few people. Everyone has some measure of creativity. Anybody can receive inspiration and anyone can be creative. Whatever idea that is received by inspiration must be developed into reality. That takes a lot of personal effort. An inspired idea that is not developed amounts to nothing! Inspiration is the birthplace of new ideas for new or better solutions. Inspiration is the realm of possibilities. Through inspiration, there is no human situation that does not have a solution. All things are possible, literally. For example, the law of gravity, a scientific theory, had concluded that heavy objects cannot fly since anything that goes up must surely be forced down by gravitational force. But then two brothers received an inspiration that defied this scientific law. Orville and Wilbur Wright went ahead to design, develop, and fly the first airplane. Before Thomas Edison finally invented the electric bulb, history has it that he made about 999 attempts that failed. Why did he go on with the 1000th attempt which eventually worked? Inspiration! Inspiration acts as an internal force that continues to push you until you have achieved your objective. Inspirational knowledge gives us the idea that translates our talents into solutions. Informational knowledge mostly gives us the idea that validates and consolidates our talents. Those who acquire much of informational knowledge and less of inspirational knowledge end up as job seekers while those who receive much of inspirational knowledge, even if they acquire less of informational knowledge, end up as job creators. Through their ideas, they establish the various organizations that create jobs and wealth, which enables them to join the 1% that controls 85% of their national wealth. Inspirational knowledge is the key to outstanding success in the pursuit of destiny. Go for it!

Receiving inspiration is one thing, taking action is another. Those who fail to take necessary action required to realize the ideas they received through inspiration are not any better than those who do not receive inspiration at all. Also note that inspired ideas are transient. If one misses it, another picks it. If you pick it but delay to take action needed to convert it into an instrument of solution, another person will pick it. Whatever idea that is released by God cannot be taken back. Sometimes, more than one person can pick up an idea at the same time. This is the reason why certain inventions or innovations can be taking place in different parts of the world simultaneously. This is quite incredible!

Let me talk more about the word ACTION. Knowledge, both informational and inspirational, does not amount to a force unless we take the necessary action. I can boldly conclude the following: Talent + Knowledge + Action = Force required to overcome challenges and create solutions. By expanding the equation, we have Talent + Information + Inspiration + Action = Force required to pull down the wall of opposition, explore the world of opportunities, and attain outstanding success in life. Though talent is naturally given, knowledge must be personally acquired, and force individually applied. Unfortunately, there is no easy way out!

Action

In one of my books[7], I defined ACTION as: **A**ggressively and **C**onscientiously **T**ake-up **I**dentifiable **O**pportunities **N**ow. It takes people who are aggressive to apply the force needed to have their desired breakthrough. If you think success is for the easy-going gentle fellows, you may have to think again. Success does not come on a platter of gold. Success does not come to those who sit down somewhere and wish that they were successful. Success comes to those who work and walk towards it. Successful people are not those who possess two heads, three hands, or four legs. Successful people are ordinary people who achieved extraordinary results by combining their natural talents and acquired knowledge with necessary action. They overcame daunting challenges along the way, explored and exploited opportunities, and provided ideas and solutions that made the world a better place. Imagine what the world would look like without airplanes, automobiles, telephones, computers, ships, trains, radios, televisions, houses, roads, railways, airports, seaports, bridges, clothes, shoes, books, stoves, petroleum products, music, movies, air conditioners, electricity, Internet, social media, prescription drugs, arms and ammunition, calendar, telescope, satellite, transmitters and decoders, submarines, furniture, refrigerator, microwave warmers, ovens, fans, photocopiers, printers, scanners, pens, cameras, phones, microphones, microscopes, thermometers, DVD players, clocks, wrist watches, remote controls, etc. The list is endless! Without all these discoveries, inventions and innovations, the world would be chaotic, to say the least. Yet, those who brought all these into existence were men and women like you and I who set out to work on an idea received by a spark of inspiration. It took some of them months while it took others years to realize their goal of providing a solution to the challenges of mankind in their time. What if they failed to take action when they saw the opportunity? What if they had ignored their instinct? What if they had procrastinated? What if they had folded their arms and expected some kind of miracle? Maybe the world would still be in utter darkness by now.

Be a solution provider

It is the solution you provide that takes you through the stages of life and lands you at the peak (i.e. stage 12). if you provide solution at the community level, you receive community recognition. If you provide solution at the regional or state level, you equally receive regional or state recognition. In the same vein, if you provide solution at the global level, you will receive global recognition. There are a couple of men and women the world cannot forget in a hurry based on the solution they provided in the areas of health and medicine, politics, education, sports, science and technology, religion, fashion, entertainment, media, agriculture, arts and crafts, and commerce and industry. I referred to these as the twelve of pillars of the earth and they represent the 12 systems of the world; reflecting all the careers, professions, jobs, institutions, and faculties of human endeavor; where needs occur and where solutions can be provided. I will discuss more of these later in this chapter.

Every destiny has the potential to be global. This means that there is no local destiny. However, the level you attain in life in the pursuit of destiny is directly proportional to the scope of the solutions you provide. You cannot be providing solution at the community level and be expecting to gain recognition at the global level. It is only those who profer solution to global challenges that receive global recognition. So, the level you reach in life mostly depends on the efforts you are willing to make. We have often been told that our destiny is in our hands. The stage is set and the race is on. The level you reach in life depends on how you combine your natural talents with the knowledge at your disposal to form a force that would smash the environmental challenges, explore the opportunities, and attain destiny by providing solution and adding value at various stages of life. Each time you try and seem to fail, refuse to settle as a casualty. Learn to turn your failures into an experience and make it part of the force you now have with which to attack the challenges more aggressively, explore the opportunities more intelligently, and attain destiny in a grand style. This is exactly what highly successful people do on a daily basis.

The realities of life

In one of my books, I defined LIFE as:

>**L**earning daily (i.e. acquiring right knowledge)
>**I**mproving daily (i.e. developing the knowledge into strength)
>**F**ocusing daily (i.e. setting specific targets), and
>**E**ngaging daily (i.e. taking necessary actions).

What are you 'learning' today? What constitutes your knowledge base? What kind of knowledge are you spending your time and money acquiring? Remember, you cannot operate beyond your level of knowledge. As stated earlier, there are informational and inspirational forms of knowledge. All the information you acquire amount to nothing if not backed by inspiration. 'Improving' what you learn is a way of converting your knowledge into strength for solution. Until what you know becomes a solution that the world needs, you cannot go far in life. We must, therefore, continue to improve daily. This is the reason why inventors spend so much time testing and assessing their inventions as a way of improving their capacity to provide needed solution. Innovations also come from continuous improvements of existing processes and procedures. On a daily basis, we must continue to 'focus' on the needs in the society so that we can set our targets right and provide the needed solution to the real needs of the society. Necessity, they say, is the mother of invention. Until a need is met, success cannot be achieved. We must focus our energy on the areas where we have an advantage to provide solution. You cannot be everything at the same time. You must have a target in life. Jack of all trade, they say, is master of none. You must maintain your own lane. Those who keep jumping from one lane to another often meet disaster along the way. There is a particular solution or set of solutions you are meant to provide to your generation. You need to concentrate on that. Never leave your own area to jump into someone else's space. This is called destiny crisis and so many people are already caught up in this web. For example, there are so many people who have no business being medical doctors, yet they go ahead to study medicine just because they hear, or someone else convinced them, that there is so much money to be made in the medical profession. We ought to remember that in the pursuit of destiny, money is secondary. Money comes naturally based on the solution you provide. Fame and fortune are the natural benefits of successfully fulfilling destiny. 'Engaging daily' entails taking the necessary action required to provide solution. A force that is not being applied soon becomes a farce, a joke. Inaction, or procrastination, is the basis of most failures today. If everybody is taking the right action at the right time, the world would have less and less failures.

We have hundreds of millions of human beings who fail to take the necessary action but rather sit somewhere and complain that things are not working. The fact is, until force is applied, motion is denied. This is the same as the law of inertia in physics. It will amount to a waste of resources if we acquire all the knowledge combined with our natural talent and then fail to put them into productive use. The graveyard continues to be the greatest place of waste in the world because there lies the remains of musicians that never sang, poets that never composed, authors that never wrote, actors that never performed, athletes that never competed, leaders that never led, professors that never taught, inventors that never discovered, soldiers that never fought, pilots that never flew, pastors that never preached, doctors that never treated, orators that never spoke, architects that never designed, entrepreneurs that never started any business, and world changers that never initiated any form of change, etc. This colossal waste continues to occur because someone failed to take the right action at the right time. For us to attain the level of success we desire, we must be ready to **l**earn daily, **i**mprove daily, **f**ocus daily, and **e**ngage daily. This is the LIFE we ought to live, there is no other way!

There is no limit to learning in life. We learn every time and everywhere. Those who cannot learn often discover that they cannot live, not to talk of lead. Learning is not only through reading. If you cannot read, listen. If you cannot hear, observe. If you cannot see, just ask questions. By all means keep learning for it is your knowledge base that determines your self-confidence and it is your self-confidence that determines how far you go in life. Continuous learning boosts our knowledge base on a continuous basis and positions us for greatness in life. Life is a give-and-take game. If you know nothing, you have nothing; if you have nothing, you give nothing; and if you give nothing, you gain nothing. Life can also be seen as a marketplace where everybody is both a seller and a buyer. Some are selling products while others are selling ideas; some are selling services while others are selling information; others are selling skills while others are selling experience. If you have nothing to sell in the marketplace of life, you will definitely find life very difficult. Have you discovered what you can give in exchange for what you need? There is something unique about you. There is something that differentiates you from every other person. There is something you have that the world needs. There is a solution you are meant to provide to this world, but the world is not going to wait forever. If you fail to deliver, another will take over. Such is the reality of life!

The twelve pillars of the earth

I had the privilege of being the first to discover and write about the twelve pillars of the earth in my 2013 book titled 'Manifesting for global impact.' In that book, I made a stunning discovery about the

12 different systems and how they continue to shape and reshape the world from generation to generation. In fact, I realized that the main duty of human beings is to add value to the earth by participating in one, some, or all of the twelve pillars of the earth. And when they do, they are simply helping to shape the earth.

It will interest you to know that I made this discovery directly from the Bible. In Genesis chapter one, verses one and two, the Bible States and I quote:

> *"In the beginning, God created the heavens and the earth. And the earth was without form, and void; and darkness was upon the face of the deep. And the spirit of God moved upon the face of the waters." (Old King James Version of the Holy Bible).*[9]

From the above scenario, we see creation and then devastation. This means that there was a problem after the initial creation, which led the earth to be submerged in water. How long it took to happen, I do not know! At this point, the world became shapeless (without form), empty (void), and dark (darkness). Three problems were visibly present on earth at this time: shapelessness, emptiness, and darkness, causing the need for restoration, which God began in Genesis chapter one verse 3:

> *"And God said, let there be light: and there was light."*[10]

Notice that God skipped the first challenge of 'shapelessness' as well as the second challenge of 'emptiness' to take care of the third challenge of 'darkness.' The reason is that darkness is the greatest enemy of progress. No matter the amount of progress you make in the dark, it remains irrelevant because nobody is going to notice it. Darkness undermines visibility, beauty, love, hope, peace, progress, productivity, and every good intention. Based on this concept, the discovery of electricity (i.e. light) has given boost to the productive capacity of the world through industrialization which has changed everything. We can't even begin to imagine what would happen if electricity suddenly goes off from the world for a period of 24 hours. In fact, electricity supply seems to be the main reason for the difference between the developed world and the 'developing' parts of the world. With light, a 24-hour-per-day work is possible. This boosts your production level and enhances your capacity to make supplies necessary to meet the needs around the world on different time zones. Lack of light (that is, electricity) limits the productive capacity of a nation and makes it an underdeveloped nation. 'Let there be light!'

After taking care of the looming darkness by providing light, God proceeded to solve the problem of emptiness by restoring and filling up the earth with things that were lost as a result of the devastation. This includes separation of the waters in the sky from the waters below; separation of the land from the waters; making of grasses, herbs, trees; calling up the sun, moon and stars; making the fishes, fowls, birds, animals, insects, etc. We see this in Genesis 1 verses 6 to 25. Here, the earth was fully restored. Firstly, the land was full of vegetation and animals of all species: the grasses were green, the herbs were edible, the trees had fruits and the fruits had seeds in them for further production; and rhinos, dinosaurs, dragons, lions, tigers, leopards, antelopes, giraffes, deers, elephants, cattles, goats, sheep, etc., were everywhere for human consumption. Secondly, the waters were full of different species of fishes and other sea animals such as whales, sharks, dolphins, hypos, etc., for human consumption. And lastly, the air was full of different species of birds and other flying animals such as eagles, hawks, vultures, doves, pigeons, etc., meant for human consumption. Everything was in abundance when God solved the problems of darkness and emptiness. The big question now is, when did God solve the remaining problem of 'shapelessness?' Did he ever solve it? If he did not, why? These are mysteries that require divine inspiration to unravel.

It is evident that God did not solve the problem of 'shapelessness' instead he created man to solve it. After the initial creation and devastation of the earth, the creation of man became the perfection of the restoration process of the earth. Watch this, each time God restored things, he said everything was good but when he created man, he declared that 'everything was very good;' Indicating that man is the completion of creation as man will continue to perfect, or complete, the restoration process by adding shape to the world through being fruitful, multiplying, replenishing the earth, subduing it, and having dominion over it. See Genesis 1: 26 – 31 below:

> *"And God said, let us make man in our image, after our likeness: and let them have dominion over the fish of the sea, and over the fowl of the air, and over the cattle, and over all the earth, and over every creeping thing that creepeth upon the earth. So, God created man in his own image, in the image of God created he him; male and female created he them. And God blessed them, and God said unto them, Be fruitful, and multiply, and replenish the earth, and subdue it: and have dominion over the fish of the sea, and over the fowl of the air, and over every living thing that moveth upon the earth. And God said, behold, I have given you every herb bearing seed, which is upon the face of all the earth, and every tree, in the which is the fruit of a tree yielding seed; to you it shall be for meat. And to every beast of the earth, and to every fowl of the air, and to everything that creepeth upon the earth, where in there is life, I have given every green herb for meat: and it was so. And God saw everything that he had made, and behold it was very good. And the evening and the morning were the sixth day."*[11]

So, man, being an extension of God, is meant to solve the last challenge of the earth, which is that of 'shapelessness,' by working to keep the earth in proper shape. To shape actually means to make something fit for a particular purpose, that is, to adapt, adjust, and regulate something for a greater or higher purpose. This is exactly what the five-fold mandate of man in Genesis 1:28 indicates. Therefore, to shape the earth is man's duty and responsibility – the ultimate reason for the creation of the human being. If this is so, how then does man actualize this mandate?

The earth is made up of the air, the land, and the sea and the human being is supposed to operate in these three areas. According to scientific research findings, while planets are hostile to life, the earth is the only planet that has the necessary conditions to sustain every living thing: its temperature, the humidity, the force of gravity, the atmospheric air, the soil texture, the rivers and the shores, the landscape with hills and valleys, and so forth. At creation, God literally handed over the earth to man to operate. God gave us natural talents as critical tools with which to effectively conduct our operations here on the earth. Let me explain the five-fold mandate for proper understanding.

a) To be fruitful

By this mandate, God expects human beings to be fruitful in the earth. To be fruitful means to produce useful and good results. It also means to bear fruit and be productive (in terms of productivity) and to add value to the earth. This is not in terms of producing more human beings but in terms of working diligently to add value to whatever results we are producing. God created the earth, and he wants us to make good use of all that he has created and to achieve great results in all our endeavors in order to make the earth a better place. Man has been given the ability to redesign what God has created to suit his special purpose. For example, when we gather various flowers from the seashore and plant them in beautiful arrays around our homes, and it adds aesthetic beauty to the premises, we are being fruitful. If we channel water from the stream to dry ground in order to water our crops, we are being fruitful. If we use wood from trees to design furniture and fittings, we are being fruitful. So, whatever products we produce, whatever services we provide, and whatever ideas we present, we are being fruitful.

Fruitfulness actually means producing good results and adding value to what is already in existence. Natural habitats are different the world over. Some regions are temperate while others are tropical. In whatever location one finds himself, one has what it takes to develop that place for one's good. This is why those who live around rivers are purely fishermen, those who live on arable land are predominantly farmers, while those who live around forests are basically hunters. In whatever natural environment God places us, he has made enough provision for our sustenance on one hand, and on the other he has given us something distinct which the rest of the world may be lacking, and can actually benefit from, if we properly develop it for economic exchange. The first man to develop an engine-powered boat must have lived around the coastal areas. By this singular invention, he exercised the mandate of fruitfulness by using his natural talent in this area and today an improved version of his invention (cargo ships, trawlers, submarines, war ships, etc.) are being used for the benefit of many all over the world.

When one collects and bottles up oxygen for use in the hospitals and in space shuttles, that person is being fruitful. That is, he or she is developing and making better use of the gifts of nature by enhancing their forms, shapes, sizes, and so forth. That person is adding value by being productive. Those who crossbreed various species of animals in order to get an improved species are simply being fruitful and productive; adding value to what God has created for the greater benefit of human beings. Those who bud various orange species on one orange stem so that one orange tree produces different oranges on different branches are simply fulfilling the mandate of being fruitful. What fruitfulness does is that it adds value to nature and gives man a greater level of benefit. This is the first assignment that God gave to man on earth and every human being has the capacity to be fruitful. The major challenge is to develop that capacity and to put it into use. God has given man the potential to be fruitful and so many people are using this great potential already.

b) To multiply

By this mandate, God expects human beings to multiply in the earth. To multiply means to increase in number or to add a quantity to oneself a specified number of times. It is to reproduce or bear other human beings that will take over from you when you must have gone. God does not desire that the earth be left empty, so he put into man and other creatures the ability to procreate their kind within a particular length of time. God believes in continuity and does not want to leave a vacuum in the earth. If man should be extinct in the earth, then God's desire for man to be in charge here would have been dashed. To forestall this, God gave human beings the ability to be reproductive. God had finished the work of creation so there would never be a time that the earth would lack human beings, except, of course, if God himself decides to destroy men and women. But if there is no multiplication or reproduction among human beings and other species, the earth will go extinct someday.

c) To replenish

By this mandate, God expects human beings to replenish the earth. This is the third and very important mandate that God gave to human beings. To replenish means to refill or renew a supply or stock. This means to be creative and bring in those things which are in short supply in the earth. This is the most sensitive aspect of the mandate, the aspect that actually positions men to be like God; creating those things which the earth lacks but needs for survival. The only difference between God and human beings is that God created out of nothing, but human beings create from the materials already in existence. Man's creative tendency is for inventions, innovations, and discoveries. This is the mandate that has brought a whole lot of improvement in the world. The airplanes, the trains, the automobiles, the ships or ocean liners, the rockets, the telephones, televisions, computers, power plants, and manufacturing machines, to mention but a few, are products of creativity. God did not create airplanes, ocean liners but metal alloys from which relevant raw materials are derived. God did not create electricity but water, sun, wind, oil and gas which are major sources of electric power. God did not create cement but limestone that is the main raw material for its production. God did not create buildings, roads or bridges but solid and liquid materials which are used for their construction. Human beings invented these things based on the creative ideas which they were born with. By this creative ability, the human being is able to develop natural materials for higher use and greater benefit. Every human being has what it takes to be creative, but unfortunately only a few develop and utilize it. Creativity is what brings solution to the many challenges of humanity. There is absolutely no limit to the creative ability of human beings. Ask any inventor and he will tell you that whatever your mind can conceive, your hand can achieve. What you believe is what you receive!

d) To subdue

By this mandate, God expects human beings to subdue the earth. To subdue means to bring under control or make quieter and less intense. There are certain things that God created on the earth which may not be to the best interest of human beings. So, God gave us the free hand to bring such things under control. For example, we can sand-fill a valley or a waterlogged space, or level a hilly area in order to build houses or construct a freeway for our convenience. By this action, we are subduing the earth. We can uproot trees within certain areas of a forest in order to build or construct roads. We can build concrete barricades along the riverbanks to prevent the river from overflowing into our neighborhoods, and we can also build bridges across rivers and valleys and walk across without any problem. All these are parts of the activities of subduing the earth. Bringing the earth under subjection means to carry out certain actions that will reduce the negative impact of nature on humanity as well as the society. The ability to subdue the earth has been released to man. This is why people device so many ways through which to reduce the adverse effect of nature on humanity. God made the sun to give light in the day and the moon to give light in the night. Scientists have proved that the moon derives its light from the sun by reflection and is able to give brightness at night, but you will agree with me that the moon does not appear every night. So, how do we see at night when the moon is not up there? To resolve this, God gifted human beings with the ability to invent light giving devices such as lanterns and electric bulbs. This singular creative activity has helped turn darkness into light and night into day; making it possible for activities to be carried out around the clock without the restrictions of natural darkness. This is an act of subduing the earth and every individual has the ability to do so.

Furthermore, subduing the earth can be seen in the area of medical discoveries. Couples are now taught what to do in order to determine the gender of the baby they are expecting. Children born with sickle cell anemia can now be transformed by the outright removal of the infected blood and the transfusion of new blood that is free from the disease. Research work has also been concluded in the area of delaying or curing aging in human beings. Kidneys can now be transplanted, and human hearts can also be transplanted. Virtually every organ or part of the body can be transplanted all in a bid to sustain life and make it worth living. By subduing the earth, we are amending nature to suit our purpose. The natural law of gravity states that whatever goes up must surely come down. By implication of this law, it may seem impossible to make anything that flies in the air like the birds, without falling down due to atmospheric pressure. But the invention of the airplane has proved this law to be totally wrong. Heavy equipment can now be carried in cargo planes from one country to another through the air without the airplane being forced down by the force of gravity, which is a natural phenomenon. The invention of the airplane has subdued the natural law of gravity. The first person to invent the airplane received an idea or inspiration to create something that can fly. Through various trials and errors, the airplane eventually came on board, defying the law of gravity. Today, we can travel from France to Frankfurt, Lagos to Libya, Indiana to India, Ghana to Canada, and Shanghai to South

Africa all by air. The aircraft is an incredible creation of the human brain!

e) To have dominion

By this mandate, God expects human beings to have dominion over the earth. Dominion is the authority to rule or govern and is from the root word 'dominate'. To dominate means to have a commanding influence over something or to be the most influential or conspicuous person or thing. God designed the earth for human beings and placed them in a position of authority here. The authority to administer this world (air, land and sea) was given to human beings by God. To have dominion over the earth is to exercise leadership and political authority in the earth. Every authority to control events on earth was given to human beings and nothing can take it away.

Actualizing the five-fold mandate and completing the assignment of shaping the earth

To actualize the mandate, man must work. By working, man keeps the earth in proper shape. What does man work with and what does he work on in a bid to shape the earth? To answer the first part of the question and balance the first part of the equation, man must work with his talents. I have already discussed extensively about talents; what they mean, what they represent and how they can be used. Now, the second part of the question is about what to work on. This is very critical because we cannot work in a vacuum and then expect value to be created; only God can. Human beings must work on something. We must engage our talents in working on or in the various systems of the world in a bid to add value and fulfill destiny. I have earlier referred to these systems as the twelve pillars of the earth. These are the systems that control all the faculties of human learning, careers of human endeavor, and professions of human engagement. All the various works of life revolve around these twelve systems and they work together to provide 'frames' that 'shape' the earth. We must emphasize on these two words, FRAMES and SHAPE, because they are very significant in our further discussion. The Bible actually talks about 'frames' in Hebrews chapter 11 verse 3 when it said and I quote:

> *"Through faith we understand that the worlds were FRAMED by the word of God, so that things which are seen were not made of things which do appear."*[12]

Below is a comprehensive list of the 12 systems of the world (which are 'pillars of the earth'):

1. Science & Technology
2. Health & Medicine
3. Agriculture
4. Politics
5. Education
6. Commerce & Industry
7. Fashion
8. Religion
9. Arts & Crafts
10. Media
11. Entertainment
12. Sports

Figure 1.2
Relationship among the 12 pillars of the earth

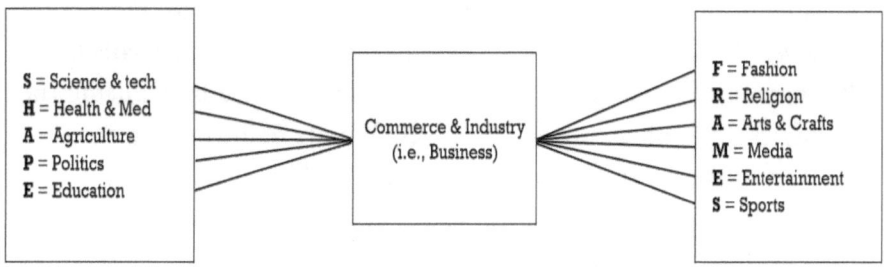

From figure 1.2, eleven out of the twelve pillars of the earth signify that these pillars are actually the 'frames' that 'shape' the earth. They determine what is being done, how it is being done, where it is being done, who is doing it, and why it is being done. I have already established earlier that God created man in his image and likeness and handed over to him the responsibility of solving the problem of 'shapelessness' in the earth. God did not build the bridges; the human being did. God did not build the houses, construct the roads, manufacture air crafts, computers, radios, televisions, telephones, or create the Internet, to mention but a few. Human beings like you and I did. All these discoveries, inventions or innovations have helped to make the earth more palatable for human habitation. You can now communicate between Ghana and China, commute between Austria and Australia, transact between New Jersey and New Delhi, watch in real time at Belgium the events that are taking place in Brazil. Through advancements in science and technology, for example, the entire world has become a community of over seven billion human beings relating with one another in ways that would never have been thought possible a few decades ago.

Through advancements in health and medicine, for example, disease found in some parts of the world can now be treated with drugs discovered in other parts of the world. There is a greater level of exchange in ideas and information leading to more and more solutions provided to those that have serious medical condition or severe health challenge. Medical exploits made in India can now be accessed and applied by medical experts in Indiana while a medical research conducted in a University in Kentucky can lead to medical breakthrough for a disease ravaging lives in faraway Kampala or Kuala Lumpur. With more cures discovered, more lives are been saved around the world on a daily basis. By these efforts, human beings are shaping the earth by reducing the negatives and enhancing the positives. We are adjusting the earth to suit our purpose for a better environment and living conditions. Man literally has the ability to control what nature has provided by adjusting it in such a way that would reduce its negative effects, increase its positive impact, and make the world a better place for all humanity.

Commerce & Industry

The pillar of Commerce and Industry plays a major role in the world. This is the system that facilitates production, distribution, exchange, and consumption. It is the linchpin and the link between other pillars. It is where the money is made to sustain and advance all other pillars of the earth. It is the pillar that tends to control most events in the world because 'money answereth all things.'[13] Any discovery that provides solution also makes money. Any discovery in health and medicine that has no commercial value is no discovery at all. Any invention or innovation in science and technology that cannot be exchanged for cash is of no use. Any pillar that does not make money through the provision of solutions cannot be sustained. Let us consider the entertainment industry, for example. Any movie that cannot recover the cost of its production plus a reasonable return on investment will not attract a producer to invest in it. Also, a musician whose music album does not move in the market cannot attract sponsorship from the business community. Unless your talent develops a solution that is marketable, you may never record an outstanding success. From experience, the entertainment industry happens to be the pillar where money is made real fast. So much money can be made in a limited time. This is because entertainment is very transient; it depends largely on the mood of the persons being entertained and mood, we know, changes with time. This is why music producers strategize to make all their money within days of the release of a new musical album into the market. Once that initial euphoria about the music dies down, not much money can be made. This is also true with movies. So, if you are a musician, a movie actor or a comedian, you must add aggressive marketing to your natural talents in order to succeed big time. No matter how you sing, act or talk, if you do not have a strong marketing support, your talent may soon become latent.

The Pillar of Commerce and Industry cannot be overemphasized. The amount of influence this system has on other systems is quite enormous. Take for example the Pillar of Politics. People that are successful in commerce and industry tend to influence political decisions by throwing money around during political campaigns, party events, and during political celebrations. They also engage lobbyists and pay their bills for the main purpose of influencing political decisions in favor of their business interests. This is the reason why the government delays in taking certain drastic measures against the corporate community like banning the manufacture and sale of substances that are known to be harmful to humans but very profitable to corporations such as cigarettes, alcohol, toxic food preservatives, and some prescription drugs, etc. Some individual investors make billions of dollars from the distribution of the products of these businesses every year and, so, cannot afford to let the government shut down one of their major sources of income. Subsequent chapters of this book will highlight how commercial and industrial organizations run, as well as ruin, the world one action at a time. But the fact remains that all the money made around the world each day comes as commercial transactions or industrial operations. Those who operate in the pillar of sports, for example, must convert their spotting prowess into entertainment, engage managers and marketers, who in turn liaise with the world of commerce and industry to convert sports entertainment into a money machine by making spectators pay to watch it. Those who operate in the pillar of fashion, for example, have to make designs that appeal to the market. The clothes, shoes, handbags, hats, ties, scarfs, etc., not only provide covering but must also attract funds that cover the cost of their production plus a reasonable return on investment. Those who are into the pillar of arts and crafts must also design, decorate, and deliver materials that provide both indoor and outdoor aesthetics to our environment. They, however, do organize exhibitions and shows where they raise millions of dollars every year in support and appreciation of their wonderful contributions in making the world a more beautiful place. Those who operate in the pillar of media, for example, do provide the platform for information dissemination but those who benefit from the information being disseminated, such us commercial and other advertisers, must pay the full cost of such services.

To show how the 12 pillars reflect the various subjects, faculties, careers, and professions, see the table below:

Table 1.1 The connection

S/N	Pillar	Related academic subjects	Life careers, professions and jobs
1	Science & Technology	Mathematics, Chemistry, Physics, Biology, Geography	Information & Computer tech, geology, engineering, General construction, lab works, etc.
2	Health & Medicine	Biology, Chemistry, Physics, Health Science, Agric Science	Medicine, pharmacy, nursing, public health tech, nutrition, environmental protection, etc.
3	Agriculture	Agric Science, Biology, Chemistry, Geography, Food and animal science	Farming, animal husbandry, horticulture, zoology, culinary tech, forestry, poultry, fishery, etc.
4	Politics	Government, Economics, history, civics, Sociology, Philosophy, law, taxation	Politics, law, International relations, Public relations, public admin, law enforcement, military
5	Education	All basic subjects, local and foreign languages, arts, psychology, sociology, etc	General teaching, education admin, curriculum development, mentoring, counseling, etc.
6	Commerce & Industry	Economics, commerce, mathematics, accounting, taxation, insurance	Entrepreneurship, Business mgt, finance, accounting, taxation, insurance, public admin, HR, etc.
7	Fashion	Economics, history, sociology, textile tech, designing and color tech	Fabric designs, tailoring, interior decoration, hair styling, textile production, shoe making, modeling, etc.
8	Religion	Religious studies, history, sociology, psychology, law	Theology, Religious affairs admin, counseling, family therapy, etc
9	Arts & Crafts	Economics, history, sociology, computer tech, designing and color tech	Painting, designing, carving, sculpturing, molding, computer graphics, photography, printing
10	Media	Languages, literature, voicing tech, history, government, law, socio-logy	Public speaking, journalism, tv/radio broadcasting, show hosting, events moderation, etc.
11	Entertainment	Music, literature, theater arts, history, sociology, dancing, singing, acting, etc	Musician, music director, actor, movie director, comedy, events management, tourism management, scripting, etc.
12	Sports	Physical education and exercise, swimming, jumping, running, gymnastics	Basketball, football, running, jumping, baseball, soccer, racing, swimming, biking, kayaking, sports coaching, etc

Every faculty, career, or profession belongs to one or two of the 12 pillars. Some of the careers are overlapping and seem to belong to more than one pillar. Also notice that developments in one pillar can advance operations in another pillar. For example, the discovery and development of computers under the pillar of science and technology has led to remarkable improvements in health and medicine, commerce and industry, education, media, etc. Also note that the products from the pillar of agriculture serve as raw materials in the pillar of commerce and industry. Satellites and transmitters are scientific discoveries, but they play major roles in the media industry. Also note that all of the discoveries in all other pillars serve as items of exchange in the pillar of commerce and industry. They are either exchanged as ideas or information, paraded as invention or innovation, or traded as products or services. Some are tangible goods while others are intangible services.

There are a host of other faculties, careers, professions, disciplines, trades, and human endeavors or pursuits that are not mentioned in table 1.1 above but no matter what it is, it definitely has a place among the 12 pillars. Thoughts and events can now be grouped in line with the 12 pillars. Communities and corporations can now operate much better based on the proper delineation of these twelve systems. Organizations and nations can be better managed based on these 12 systems while government departments and agencies can now be better structured based on these twelve major systems that determine everything we do around the world. It should be noted that no pillar is more important than the other. However, the importance of each pillar depends largely on the needs of a particular people at a particular time. It is also important to note that any nation which is leading the advancements in most of the pillars will absolutely lead the world as a superpower. In table 1.2 below, an attempt has been made to show the leading countries of the world in terms of their global operations and strategic positions in each of the twelve pillars.

Table 1.2

Pillar	The two leading countries in the world
Science & Technology	U.S.A. and Israel/Japan
Health & Medicine	U.S.A. and India
Agriculture	U.S.A. and China
Politics	U.S.A. and China
Education	U.S.A. and U.K.
Commerce & Industry	U.S.A. and China
Fashion	France and Italy
Religion	Vatican City and Saudi Arabia
Arts & Crafts	India and China
Media	U.S.A. and U.K.
Entertainment	U.S.A. and India/Nigeria
Sports	U.S.A. and China

The human factor of an organization

Having discussed the natural talents and many potentials of a human being, let us see how all these relate to the main subject of this book – organizations. An organization is a group of people who pull their resources (ideas, experiences, skills, strengths, and funds) together with the aim of attaining a certain objective or set of objectives. There are three groups of individuals that make up an organization:

a) The owner(s) or initiator(s) of the organization,
b) The managers of the organization, and
c) The workers at the organization.

The owners

The owners or initiators of an organization are those individuals who conceived the idea or nursed the ambition of creating a possible solution to a need in the society through the production of goods or provision of services. One individual can actually be an initiator of an organization.

History is replete with examples of individuals who initiated today's mega organizations. Apart from conceiving the idea to establish the organization, the owners or initiators also provide the initial capital requirement of the organization. This is the reason why they are often referred to as 'capitalists.' In the course of expanding the organization, the original owners or initiators do call on members of the public to contribute to the capital of the organization and become equity owners and shareholders through what is referred to as initial public offer (IPO) of its shares or units of stock at the Stock Exchange market. Those who purchase the organization's stock become part of the owners and are often called 'investors.' The main aim of an owner of an organization (initiator and investor) is to make profit or increase the value of his or her investment. People become part of the ownership of organizations for two major reasons: one, to make money by way of annual dividend, which is part of the profit of the organization that is shared among the shareholders, and two, to trade or convert their stock into cash when the value of a unit of stock must have appreciated to a reasonable level, say from $5 to $50. This constitutes the daily transactions that take place at the Stock Exchange markets across the globe.

Often, the original intention of the initiators of an organization, which is the production of goods or provision of services, is dwarfed by the profit orientation of the new investors. This reality places an immense pressure on the management of an organization, which must work to produce quality goods, provide needed services and at the same time make reasonable profit as to improve the firm's stock value. This pressure been mounted by the new capitalists, especially here in the United States, is beginning to create a paradigm shift in the way organizations are managed.

The managers

The managers of the organization are those employed by the Board of Directors of an organization (those elected by the shareholders to oversee the activities of their organization) to run the day-to-day affairs of the organization by planning what needs to be done, organizing the resources needed to do it, directing the personnel and procedures involved in doing it, and controlling the operations and processes to ensure that it is done with the least amount of resources possible so as to maximize the organization's profits and enhance shareholder benefits.

The managers form 'the management' of an organization, which is headed by the CEO or President. Due to the intensity of the pressure mounted on the management by investors or shareholders (represented by the board of directors), the managers of today's organizations now devise various means to do whatever is necessary to survive and succeed in the marketplace. A CEO who knows that he or she has a 5-year tenure would develop strategies and engage managers to explore and exploit every opportunity that would enhance his or her success record and, by extension, benefits within the time he or she spends in the organization, even if this situation will negatively impact on the organization's future operations. The board of directors sets a target for the CEO and promises him or her all kinds of benefits and perks (in the form of fat allowances, stock ownership, fully paid family vacations to any location in the world, etc.) if he or she meets or exceeds the set target. In a bid to meet the target and earn the juicy package offered by the board, today's CEOs are ready to do anything ranging from 'lobbying' government officials and 'bribing' regulatory institutions to compromise policies in favor of their organizations to manipulating the stock market to increase the value of their company's stock, intimidating the workers into accepting reduced compensation under often horrible working conditions, exploiting customers through high prices and shady deals, crushing competition by acquiring smaller organizations within its industry of operations so as to become a mega or monopolistic organization, bulldozing their way into foreign markets where they are likely to influence foreign governments and create monopolies in their area of operation, and 'paying-off' the media to continue to report nice, and often over-exaggerated, things about them. The list goes on and on!

The mega organizations created by the activities of today's CEOs are often too big to be efficiently managed. The rising cost of operations as a result of payments that need to be made on a continuous basis to maintain the 'faulty' foundation on which these organizations are built, often lead to sudden collapse and the loss of the 'poor' investors' fund - usually their life savings or retirement benefits. These greedy CEOs often convince the government to provide a bailout fund to avoid the dire consequences such collapse can have on the national economy. They mismanage their organization's resources and walk away with billions of dollars in compensation while the helpless taxpayers are forced to pay for the bail out of these ill-fated and grossly mismanaged organizations. This is the new reality in the corporate world of the United States and around the world. The CEOs of mega organizations have become too powerful to be controlled by the government because in a free market economy, like ours, business operators should be given 'a free hand' to explore and exploit available opportunities and overcome existing threats for the sole benefit of the capitalist. The evolving 'brutal' capitalism is responsible for positioning corporations ahead of politicians in the helm of affairs of our dear nation. While the entire society is being shortchanged as a result of the excesses of today's big CEOs, the ordinary worker is struggling to survive.

The workers

The workers at the organization are those who are employed to handle the various positions and carry out the numerous functions required for an organization to produce goods and provide services. These include the line operators and line workers, the machine operators and office assistants, the warehouse staff and the maintenance crew, the accounts clerks and the office secretaries, the human resources staff and the security personnel, the forklift drivers and the crane operators, as well as the truck drivers and the receptionists. These are the guys that work their asses off on a daily basis to obey laid down corporate policies, follow official procedures, release needed materials at the right time, utilize right personnel to carry out daily operations, write routine reports, pay salaries, receive supplies, settle suppliers, deliver finished products to customers, receive payments, maintain vehicles, repair machines, preserve materials, secure the facility, deliver mail, answer phones, pay bills, provide electricity and water, keep the toilets clean, dispose waste, clear the floor of clutters, guarantee industrial safety, and to produce quality products that ensure continuous patronage. The list of what ordinary workers do in organizations is endless.

It, therefore, beats my imagination to see the CEO get all the millions of dollars in compensation in the same organization that pays its workers peanuts. Do the Boards of Directors of today's organizations believe that the CEOs are single-handedly achieving the great results in their organizations? Does it not amount to exploitation for a CEO to go home annually with more than 500 times what the average worker is paid in that same organization? Today, we have organizations where the CEO takes home at least $25 million a year while majority of the workers are struggling to make $25,000 in the same period. The ratio here is 1000:1! This is unacceptable! The Board of Directors must do a better job. The CEO is not the only member of the organization who does all the jobs to keep the organization afloat. Every other member of the organization plays a significant role and, therefore, deserves a reasonable compensation.

In a bid to control the voice and reduce the force of today's workers to negotiate better work conditions, most CEOs have ensured that unions are crushed. The American middle class, which is the working class, is fast losing oxygen in its lungs. The union is what sustains the working class and maintains the middle class. At least, there should be checks and balances within the organization. It takes workers' union to checkmate the excesses of the CEO and the entire Management of an organization. Unions are not only beneficial to the worker but also healthy for the organization. Mega unions can become political, no doubt, but to conclude that unions are the reason why the cost of manufacturing in the United States is higher than that of other nations is simply not true. Over the years in America, workers unions have grown to become a huge problem both to corporations and the workers themselves. The major reason is that unions have been hijacked by officials who are outside the corporations where work actually takes place. Another reason is that powerful union officials seem to be using the union platform to advance their political interests rather than the interest of the workers they claim to represent. Sometimes union officials take positions that hurt the corporation where their members work and when these corporations shut down or relocate over seas, the workers are the ones that will suffer the full consequences. The solution is that unions should be company-based and not industry-based. The workers within the organization should form and manage their union themselves. Instead of having one central union for auto workers, let employees of Ford Motors, General Motors, Stellantis, etc., have their separate unions. Instead of having retail workers union, let employees of Walmart, Target, Giant Eagle, Amazon, Kroger, Costco, Home Depot, etc., have their separate unions. This will enable unions to work realistically with management to improve the fortunes of their corporation for the benefit of all stakeholders.

Every member of the organization deserves to be treated with respect. Both the general manager and the gate man are equally important. Each has a unique role to play which the other cannot play effectively. An organization that can afford to pay millions to the general manager should at least pay a living wage do the gate man. Remember the saying: 'what is good for the goose, is also good for the gander.' If all the workers contributed to the success of the organization, I see no reason why some of them should go home as failures. In an environment where the cost of living is increasing on a continuous basis, it is only reasonable that every worker be duly compensated. The CEOs can have the millions but not at the expense of the average worker who also has rent to pay, bills to settle, mouths to feed, clothing to purchase, car to buy, fees to pay, and other needs to fulfill.

Every organization does have owners, managers, and workers. However, in a few sole proprietorship, an individual usually operates as the owner, the manager, and the worker. As the business grows, the owner/manager hires a helping hand or two. In partnerships, the owners are equally the managers and workers but usually have one or more staff to assist. In big corporations, there is usually a huge distinction between the owners, managers, and workers. While the owners of an organization are ably represented by the board, and the managers well represented by the CEO, no one seems to be representing the interest of the workers in the absence of the union. Workers in non-unionized organizations are often left at the mercy of their immediate supervisors or departmental managers. This situation has often resulted in various forms of abuse. No society prospers amid continuous exploitation of the masses by a few. These are the same features of aristocracy that Americans fought against. Without a strong middle class, American democracy is in serious jeopardy.

The growing trend in today's corporate America is that the same individual often holds the position of CEO as well as Chairman of the Board of Directors. This may be as a result of the amount of shares the person holds in the corporation. However, this is not a very healthy situation. As a management professional, I will advise that the two positions be separated. Let two people handle the two positions. Typically, the CEO is an employee of the corporation hired by the Board to oversee the general operations of the corporation. The CEO reports to the Board which determines his or her remuneration and reviews his or her performance periodically to ascertain if he or she is still fit for the job. Where the CEO is also the Chairman of the Board, he becomes the lord of the corporation. He or she personally determines his remuneration, reviews his or her performance, determines the direction of the corporation, hires and fires managers and other employees at will, etc. For publicly quoted corporations, the CEO cannot be the Chairman of the Board at the same time. The CEO must be answerable to a higher authority for the purposes of checks and balances. This also makes it easier to replace the CEO when he or she is no longer performing. If the CEO is the Chairman of the Board at the same time, you can imagine what will happen if he or she gets involved in an auto crash and is in the ICU.

Why 85% of all 21st century workers hate their jobs

A 2017 survey[14] reveals that 85% of all workers, including Americans, hate their jobs. This report should not be taken lightly. As a management expert, I can categorically state that this report shows that an estimated 85% of the workers in any given organization dislike their jobs and are barely hanging in because they need the money to pay their bills. When your job is no longer about an opportunity to contribute to the value chain of the organization but an occasion to make money to pay your bills, the organization is at a great loss. It has been long established that dissatisfied workers are less productive because they would come to work late as many times as are allowed and call off with flimsy excuses at the slightest opportunity. Such attitude negatively impacts on other workers who start by complaining about it and then later joining in repeating such unhealthy attitude if nothing is done to address it. The dissatisfied worker soon begins to use the organization's resources to search for job openings in other places.

If 85% of your workforce is dissatisfied with their job, this shows that productivity is only 15% effective. This means more machine breakdowns, more down times, more rework, more repair cost, more overtime pay to meet production targets and customer orders, more substandard products and services, more customer complaints, loss of loyal customers to competing firms, loss of income, and ultimately loss of profits. This is not the right place to be for any organization. Seeing how dangerous it is for an organization to have 85% of dissatisfied workers, what can be done to avert this nightmare?

Some of the basic reasons for employee dissatisfaction include:
    a) Zero opportunity for career advancement,
    b) Lack of employee participation in policy formulation,

c) Emphasis on performance alone at the expense of employee welfare, comfort and well-being,
d) Bad supervision due to untrained management, and
e) Toxic work environment.

Lack of opportunity for career advancement is the major reason for employee dissatisfaction in an organization. When there are no openings for promotion to higher positions, workers generally begin to look for places where their skills or experience will be put to better use for a higher pay. When a store officer knows that he will never grow into a store supervisor or store manager position someday, even when he has the capability to occupy those higher positions, he will have no other choice than to look elsewhere. There are organizations which prefer to hire people from outside to fill existing higher positions instead of giving opportunity to the workers inside. This is generally a bad practice except where there are no competent candidates within the organization. As much as possible, qualified, and experienced candidates within the organization should be considered first for supervisory and managerial positions before reaching out to the people outside. There is nothing wrong in training and mentoring a junior worker for a higher position if he or she shows signs of leadership. This practice ultimately helps to lower the rate of labor turnover.

Lack of employee participation in policy formulation is another basic reason for worker disaffection and dissatisfaction. As stated earlier, every worker is coming in with a set of skills and experience and desires to contribute reasonably to the organization's value chain. When workers are denied the opportunity to contribute ideas to the policy formulation process of the organization, and only required to carry them out without asking any questions whatsoever, they soon begin to feel unwanted. Nobody wants to stay in an environment where he or she is not wanted. Even at the family setting, whenever the parents take all the decisions and issue all the instructions without any contribution from other members of the family, the kids soon become withdrawn and rebellious. And as soon as they become eighteen, they leave home and never want to come back. Workers are not robots. Most times, the idea that will save a situation might not come from the most respected manager but from the most neglected janitor. Some of the solutions for which we bring in consultants and contractors and pay them so much to provide, might be provided by the least employee who was never given the chance. Organizations must give opportunity to each of its personnel to contribute ideas towards the formulation of policies, procedures, systems, structures, strategies, layout, and workflows. All workers should be allowed to contribute ideas for the improvement of their workstations. Failure to do this can lead to high employee turnover.

Emphasis on performance alone at the expense of employee welfare, comfort, and well-being is another critical factor that often results in employee dissatisfaction. There are some managers who care less about the people who are producing the results. All they know is work, work, and more work without considering the welfare, comfort, and general well-being of the worker. If the production target is 1000 units per hour, they would increase the speed of the machine to make the workers produce 1200 units instead. If there is a 45-minute lunch break, they would reduce it to 30 minutes. If the shift shuts down at 4:00 pm, they extend it to 5:00 pm without caring about how all these would impact upon the personal and family life of the employees. They do not believe that the employees have a life outside of the organization. They literally use the employees like slaves. Employees are often asked to quit if they do not like the job. This is disheartening! People usually appear on their first day on the job with mixed feelings of happiness and apprehension. It is the duty of management to make them feel at home, adapt to the new environment and make their best contribution to overall organization's success. Every organization must learn to balance employee productivity with employee satisfaction. You cannot pay your workers peanuts and expect them to roll out gemstones. If you do not care about the welfare and well-being of your workers, you will soon have a bunch of disgruntled, unhealthy, depressed, and unproductive workers running a dilapidated, unwholesome, hazardous, and unprofitable organization.

Bad supervision due to untrained management is yet another major reason why we have dissatisfied workers in any organization. A supervisor occupies the lowest echelon in the management strata of an organization and is the direct link between the workers and the management. Supervisors ensure that workers have all the materials they need to carry out their job in the most comfortable environment. Supervisors communicate management policies and procedures to the workers, provide adequate training, see to it that relevant work materials are available, and monitor to ensure that workers perform their jobs effectively. Apart from these, the supervisors also have the responsibility to send feedback to the management on challenges faced by workers in the course of their jobs, and ideas generated from workers on how to improve their duties. Supervisors also ensure that there is a harmonious working relationship among the employees under their units by creating an atmosphere of teamwork which enables workers to form an informal bond that helps them to perform their formal jobs. This results in the willingness of members of the team to pick up each other's lapses to achieve a desirable group result. Experience has shown that workers achieve so much more working as a team than they do working as individuals. But where the supervisor creates an atmosphere of division by forming a clique with his favorites instead of forming a team with every worker under him or her, those outside the clique often get dissatisfied, leading to negative trend in employee performance and productivity. Every member of the management team, from the strategic to the supervisory levels, should be thoroughly trained on the general principles and practices of management. They should also have hours of management development training every year to update their knowledge on new information as it concerns organizational management. Human beings are the most complex but most important resource in an organization. So, those who supervise them must be well equipped with the right tools to directly communicate, correctly train, and effectively lead the workers on a daily basis as they work to achieve individual performance targets, group production quotas, and overall customer satisfaction. A bad supervisor can ruin a good job. If half of the supervisors in organizations across America should receive basic training on management principles and practices, there would be at least a 50% improvement in employee morale as well as corporate performance.

Lastly, toxic work environment is another critical factor that results in dissatisfaction among workers within an organization. By toxic work environment I mean when the work environment is generally unsafe for human adaptation. There are some workplaces you walk into and you immediately notice thick dark smoke everywhere as well as excessive machine noise, leading to high incidence of injury among workers. No one wants to lose their health, limb or life working for an organization. I have worked in certain industrial environments where there was so much dust in the air because of mixing and packaging of flour used in the baking industry. The organization actually had protective nets but did not insist that workers put them on before commencing operations. We have seen incidents where workers develop certain diseases or lose their senses of smelling, seeing, or hearing after spending years in an organization. New workers who notice these anomalies might become dissatisfied and quit their jobs as soon as possible. There are some work environments that qualify as prison cells. Here, there is no regard whatsoever for the health and safety of the workers. The level of heat and noise emanating from the machines that are hardly up to five feet away from the workers is enough to fry their brain cells, blow their ear drums, and send them to their early graves. I seriously recommend unscheduled factory inspections by public health officials as to prevent numerous health hazards experienced by American workers on a daily basis. I do not think it is right for a worker to put in between 25 and 30 years of his or her life adding value to an organization only to retire with a heart, lung, liver or kidney disease resulting from his or her exposure to toxic chemicals, excessive heat, deafening noise, dangerous smoke, and unhealthy work environment. Prevention is always better than cure. Have you ever seen a CEO whose office is smoky, noisy, dusty, or hot? The average American worker should never be a deplorable, expendable, dispensable, and disposable element but an invaluable asset in the organization. He or she, therefore, deserves a fair share of a decent work environment devoid of excessive smoke, excessive dust, excessive noise, excessive heat, and anything that can hamper a healthy livelihood. No one should be signing his or her death warrant the day he or she signs up to work for an organization.

CHAPTER 2

ORGANIZATIONS HAVE FOUNDATIONS

The foundation of any building determines its strength and longevity. It is so with organizations. It has already been established that an organization involves at least two people coming together for the purpose of solving a problem or providing a solution that is practically impossible or extremely difficult for an individual to provide. Successful organizations must, therefore, begin with solid foundations. Foundation is the base upon which something stands. Foundations are basic principles, proven ideologies, and tested theories upon which something is built. If an organization is the extension of an individual, there must be a very strong relationship between the foundation for personal success, depicted in the flow chart of life, and that of the organization, depicted in the flow chart of an organization.

The objectives and resources of an organization

Every organization must have a specific objective or group of objectives just as every individual has a destiny. The objective of an organization is the reason for its existence just as the destiny of an individual is the essence for his or her existence. People do not establish organizations without a reason. In fact, people establish organizations as part of their destiny; their desire to provide solution to a greater number of people in a wider location with the help of other individuals. An organization is, therefore, a pool of human talents, ideas, and experiences with the intention of realizing a set objective or group of objectives.

Figure 2.1 below is the Flow Chart of an organization and it outlines the basic features of an organization. The overriding objective of every organization is to achieve sustainable growth by providing valuable solutions. These solutions come in the form of products and services, ideas and information, and inventions and innovations. Some organizations are established for the purpose of medical research while others are established for industrial operations. Some organizations are established to provide for legal needs while others are established for logistic services. Other organizations are created to provide financial services while others are established to provide insurance services. There are tens of millions of organizations around the world engaged in one activity or another: shipping, warehousing, wholesaling, retailing, security, electricity, telecommunications, media, entertainment, education, sports, religion, politics, fashion, arts & crafts, etc. However, the one thing which is common among them is that they are established for a particular purpose; to achieve a particular objective or set of objectives.

Figure 2.1 The Flowchart of an organization

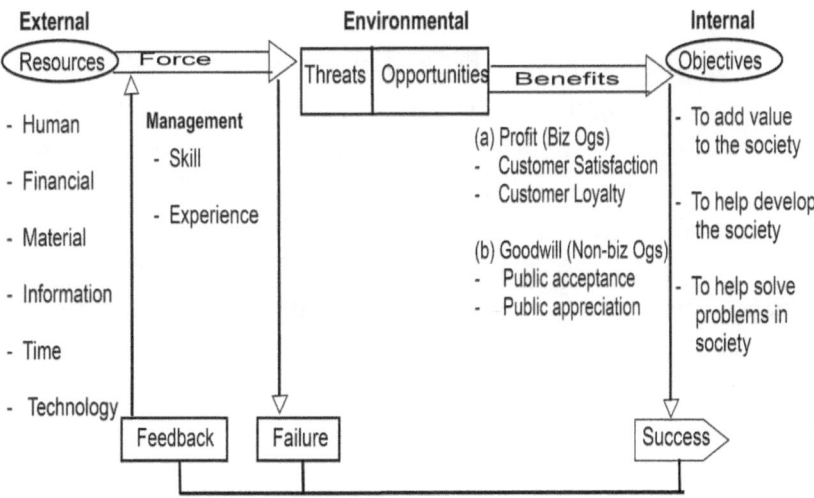

Apart from an objective, every organization must have a set of resources with which to actualize the objectives just as individuals have a set of talents with which to realize their destinies. These resources include humans, materials, finances, information, time and technology. No organization operates without some sort of resources. The human resources are the skills, experiences, talents, and knowledge possessed by all the people that make up the organization: the workers, the managers, or the owners. All these people bring their abilities and competences together under the umbrella of the organization in a bid to create a form of solution to certain problems within the society. This is the most valuable resource available to an organization. The success and failure of any organization depends to a large extent on how it handles its human resources. It has already been established that an organization is a group of two or more persons coming together to meet a need that is impossible for an individual. It is amazing to see what the average human being is capable of doing. Therefore, to bring many of such human beings together under the same roof to proffer solution to the challenges of mankind can lead to an unbelievable result. If the 21st century organization believes that the human being is becoming less and less important, then let us watch and see where this idea leads. Organizational energy is often released through human synergy. So, you must believe in the people, trust them, invest in them, and have an expectation of them if you want to get the best out of them. People are the basis for organizational success.

Material resources include the machines, raw materials (from the air, land and sea), computers, furniture, telephone, factory buildings, office complex, office supplies, tools, vehicles, etc., that an organization uses on a day-to-day basis to achieve its objectives. The nature of an organization determines the kind of materials it uses.

Financial resources form another important aspect of the resources available to an organization. This includes the initial capital required to purchase the materials as well as the cash needed to run operations and pay bills on a day to day basis often referred to as working capital or operating capital. Insufficient working capital has been the cause of many business failures, especially in the first 24 months of commencing operations. You are not in business just to make money; you are equally in business to spend money, sometimes a whole lot of it, before the expected income starts trickling in. It is better to not start an organization at all than to start with insufficient funds. Starting with insufficient funds is a road map to disaster!

The often-neglected parts of the resources available to an organization are information, time, and technology. The 21st century organization now realizes the importance of information to its survival: timely information about its customers, its competitors, it's labor market, it's immediate community, it's socio-political environment, etc. Sometimes the nature of information available to an organization can give it a competitive advantage over rival organizations. We now see most organizations spending millions of dollars to establish interactive websites to provide timely information and be in constant contact with the markets they serve. The online shopping activity based on e-Commerce is one example where information technology has enhanced customer relationship by making it easier for people to buy what they want at the time and place they want it and at the price they are willing to pay. People can now compare market prices from the comfort of their homes, pay with their smartphones, and take delivery at their doorsteps in a few hours.

Time, on the other hand, is a basic resource available to human beings even though we do not always consider it so. Time is both limited in supply and valuable in operations. This is the reason there is a price tag on time. Time is the basic resource in life. The way you manage time determines the way you will manage every other resource at your disposal - talents, skills, information, money, human beings, etc. Everyone has only 24 hours in a day and nothing more. Sometimes, time can be the difference between success and failure. The way we manage time determines our overall success in life. If you cannot manage time effectively, you may have difficulty managing other resources because nearly everything is based on time. I have defined time as follows:

Treating **I**mportant **M**atters **E**xpeditiously. (If something is important to you, you make time for it!)

Every opportunity available to an organization has a time tag on it. Opportunities do not wait forever. Organizations that treat time seriously are often the ones that succeed more than others. The ability of an organization to see opportunities before others and to take necessary action required to convert those opportunities into customer satisfaction is key to its survival and triumph. Most organizations spend a lot of money training their staff on time management because they now consider time as a valuable resource. Doing the right thing at the right time is what leads to success in life. This is also true for organizations. Since an organization is an extension of an individual, it cannot afford not to treat time with the seriousness it deserves. In the same vein, any nation that does not value time as a resource will continue to lag in global affairs. If you do not plant at the right time, your harvest will be lean. If you do not educate at the right time, your future generation will languish. If you do not treat a disease at the right time, life may be lost.

Technology is also one of the resources available to an organization. Technology is simply the method, way, and manner of producing products, providing services, or creating ideas. There are manual, mechanical, and electronic forms of technology. The form of technology available to an organization can be the source of its competitive advantage in the marketplace. Better technology most times results in improved products and services, reduced unit cost of production, more efficient utilization of materials, and better use of time. Technology as a resource can make all the difference between success and failure in an organization.

The force of an organization

From the flow chart of an organization, it is very clear that the environment poses threats and provides opportunities for the organization. Threats are challenges that tend to impede an organization's effort towards reaching its objectives. Threats make it difficult for an organization to actualize its set objectives. They are those things that stand in the way and tend to lead to failure. They often present themselves as insufficient resources, actions of competitors, activities of regulators, decisions of government, change in the lifestyle of the people, demands by host communities, agitations by civil society groups, etc. Opportunities, on the other hand, are those conditions that tend to facilitate the actualization of an organization's objective. The basic opportunity is the availability of a need to be met, a problem to be solved, and a solution to be provided. Once this is not there, the very existence of the organization becomes questionable. Every organization is set up for a purpose. That purpose is to meet an existing need, and the existence of a need to be met is an opportunity. The environment has a range of opportunities that only smart people can recognize. Those who see what others can't, usually get what others can't. Once an opportunity is identified, the need to overcome threats and exploit the opportunity becomes imperative. Every opportunity has challenges. Without challenges life would be boring. Challenges come to test the human ability to solve problems. The improvements we experience in the society are results of overcoming existing challenges.

Due to the presence of threats to an organization, there is, therefore, the need to have a force. A force that would break through the challenges, explore the opportunities, and actualize the organization's objective. This organizational force is the knowledge possessed by the people we refer to as 'the management.' The management of an organization is a group of people saddled with the responsibility of providing direction for the organization. Management combines its skill and experience with organizational resources to form a formidable force required to smash through the threats, exploit the opportunities, and attain organization's objective. A weak management is a weak organization, and a strong management is strong organization. The failure of an organization is often attributed to management's ineffectiveness. Management is the knowledge base of an organization. The quality of the people that make up the management team will determine the effectiveness of the organization in reaching its objective.

Organizational system and structure

Management is responsible for the overall direction of an organization. Management sets out the plan about what the objectives are, what the resources will be, what the processes will be, what the procedure will be, what the tasks will be, and what each member of the organization will need to contribute towards its overall success. To run an organization effectively and achieve its objective, management must develop a comprehensive system and establish a distinctive structure. Organizations thrive on well-defined systems and well-designed structures. This system includes the processes, procedures, and mode of operation necessary to achieve set objectives. It is the transformation process of the organization. It is the flow chart detailing the stages between the inputs and outputs of an organization. It answers the question 'how does the organization operate in a bid to convert its inputs to desired outputs?' Systems must be continuously monitored (M), corrected (C), and improved (I). The structure, on the other hand, is the proper arrangement of positions and functions necessary to ensure the continuous realization of the organization's objectives in a predictable manner. It spells out the formal interaction existing among members of an organization, the relationship of their functions, as well as the importance of each functional position to the overall success of the organization. It highlights the hierarchy of authority and outlines the flow of responsibility and accountability within the organization. It shows who reports to who and who is responsible for what. It is an overview of the communication channel among members of an organization.

A system and a structure are very essential to the success of an organization. You cannot develop the teamwork necessary to run an organization effectively if there is no deliberate system and detailed structure. The system is what must be transferred from one generation to another to keep the organization going. It is the secret recipe or the internal strength of an organization. It is often the distinguishing factor between one organization and another even though they are both operating in the same industry. The system defines and differentiates the organization while the structure runs the system. The structure must create a conducive environment for the continuous attraction and retention of the right quality and quantity of people required to effectively run the operations of an organization in such a way that same results are realized each time and every time. Since the organizational structure shows the job positions and functions, it also makes it easier to determine the minimum qualification and experience necessary to perform each job function. If you walk into an organization that has no system and structure or that does not follow its established system and structure, things can be chaotic. Questionable mistakes, material wastes, unnecessary delays, shifting of blames, and financial losses are some of the end results. Things work better in an organized set up and the two main ingredients that help to ensure 'a sense of organization' within your organization are system and structure. If you bring a team of experts into an unorganized environment, their expertise will turn into an escapade. Organizations must be effectively organized if they are to meet the objectives for which they were set up. If management does its job very well, an organization will not experience any form of failure. Successful organizations are the ones that have the kind of management that combines its skill and experience with the resources at its disposal to take advantage of environmental opportunities, overcome the threats, and actualize the organization's objectives.

Examples of systems and structures

Knowing the critical nature of systems and structures to the success of organizations, I will attempt to give some practical examples for a better understanding. It has already been established that a system represents the processes involved in the conversion of organizational inputs into organizational outputs (in the form of products, services, and ideas). It reflects the way and manner things are to be done in an organization that desires to actualize its objective. It is often put in place by those who established the organization (that is those who had the original dream about the purpose of the organization) or those who have been recruited to manage it. For example, a restaurant has a recipe for every meal. This may include the quantity of each item if a particular size of the menu is being prepared. If you increase the amount of each item in the recipe, without altering the size of the menu, the result will be different. Apart from determining the quantity of each item in the menu, the process will also include which item comes first, second, third, and last during preparation. It also includes how long it will take to add the second item, the third, and the last. It also establishes which two items should be mixed before adding the mixture to the other items. It should be noted that any of the procedures that is not followed will result to a different menu entirely. This is the reason why two people can use similar ingredients to prepare a similar meal but end up producing meals with different taste and quality. The different recipe (the procedure or the process) accounts for this difference. The method of operation or the step by step manner of getting things done is referred to as system. Every organization must have an established way of getting things done different from the way it is done in similar organizations. Any organization that does not have a unique system of providing solutions cannot survive in today's highly competitive marketplace.

The structure, on the other hand, is the established network of relationships to ensure that the system continues to operate as required. It determines who does what, who reports to who, and who gives instructions to who. It shows the formal line of communication existing within an organization and defines the extent of authority attributed to every job position. Above all, it delineates responsibilities and assigns functions to every member of the organization to ensure that consistent results are achieved each time and every time. Based on the restaurant example, the organization structure shows who is responsible for purchasing and storing the items in the menu, who gets the items ready before the preparation like washing, cutting, grinding, drying, etc. It also establishes who does the mixing, frying, baking, cooking, etc. It also states who welcomes the customers, who serves the meals, who clears the tables and who washes the dishes, etc. It should be noted that anybody who does not have a place in the structure cannot be a part of the organization. Also, if you find it difficult to draw the 'organogram' of an organization, you will always find it difficult to operate the organization, let alone achieve its objectives. It shows you are operating in chaos and confusion and nothing good can come out of such set of conditions. Below is a diagrammatic representation of an organization structure, also known as organogram (i.e. organizational diagram):

Figure 2.2

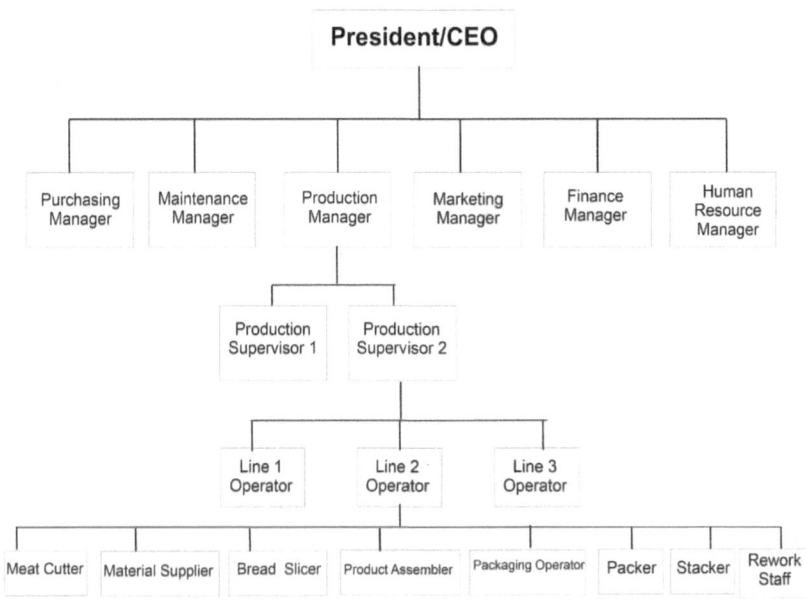

N/B: There are various forms of organizational structures ranging from functional to divisional, hybrid, and matrix. Each has specific characteristics and spells out the best set of conditions under which it can be applied.

Benefits of an organization

We must differentiate between the benefits of an organization and its objectives. We have explained earlier that the objectives of an organization include the solution it provides to the needs of the society. Benefits on the other hand are about what the organization gets in return for meeting the society's needs. For business organizations, profit is generally accepted as its benefit while non-business organizations receive what is referred to as goodwill. The profit made by business organizations is based purely on customer satisfaction and customer loyalty. These two concepts are very vital to the survival of an organization. Customer satisfaction comes when customer needs are met by the provision of the right product, service, or idea at the right time, at the right price, and in the right place. Everything must be right to achieve customer satisfaction. Customer loyalty, on the other hand, comes because of long-term customer satisfaction. Loyal customers are those customers that have decided to pitch their tent with a particular brand or organization. It is worthy of note that the number of loyal customers a business organization has determines its position in its industry of operation. Every industry has what we call a market leader, a market challenger, market follower(s), and market nicher(s). Here, an industry will be described as a group of firms or enterprises engaged in the same line of products or services and serving the same customers so that if a customer patronizes one, he cannot patronize another at the same time. An example will help to explain this concept. The US telecommunications industry has organizations such as AT&T, Verizon, Comcast, Charter, T-Mobile, Sprint, US cellular, and a host of other organizations that provide a wide range of telecom solutions (products and services). As at the time this book was written, one of them (AT&T) is the market leader based on its largest customer base while another one (Verizon) is the market challenger; that is, the one that has the next largest number of customers and is fighting to become the next market leader. All other organizations within the telecom industry are either market followers (companies that simply follow whatever the market leader does by adopting its successful strategies) or market nichers (companies whose products serve segments too small to be of interest to firms with larger shares of the market). Every business organization must identify its position in the industry of its operation as to figure out how to reposition itself for the next level. Your market position is also referred to as the value of your market share. These are terms that must be understood by business operators if they want to do well within the industry they operate. Details on business organizations will be discussed in subsequent chapters.

Non-business organizations do not receive profits as their benefits rather they enjoy what we call goodwill. Goodwill comes through public acceptance and public appreciation of the solutions a non-business organization provides. For example, the US Food and Drug agency (FDA) does not make profits but enjoys goodwill based on the public's acceptance and appreciation of its regulatory achievements in the food and drug industry by working to ensure that Americans receive safe drugs and consume healthy foods. If this agency of government fails to carry out its job effectively, more Americans might get sick for consuming bad food or die from using substandard drugs. So, the benefit the US government gets for spending tens of millions of dollars annually on the FDA is in the public acceptance and appreciation of the role of the FDA in working so hard to reduce the consumption of contaminated food products and the ingestion of adulterated pharmaceutical products. If FDA fails in its major function of regulating the production, distribution and consumption of foods and drugs, then the tax-payers money spent on it annually would be unjustifiable. Another example of non-business organization is a non-governmental organization that funds and conducts research aimed at finding lasting cure for breast cancer. This organization raises money from corporate bodies as well as individuals in a bid to advance research in discovering a cure for breast cancer. Its objective is usually to provide solution for the eradication, reduction, or treatment of breast cancer and its benefits are public acceptance and public appreciation. However, such a research institute can commercialize its findings by licensing it to a pharmaceutical company and then receiving royalty from the proceeds for use in funding future research efforts.

Foundations also form part of non-business organizations. A foundation raises funds to pursue a particular course of action that is beneficial to the society. An example is an environmental protection foundation. The job of such a foundation would include gathering and disseminating of relevant information about the effects of environmental pollution or degradation and ensuring that relevant stakeholders are well versed on the dangers inherent in their actions and in-actions with regards to the environment. Such a foundation also engages in lobbying the Congress to pass relevant laws to protect the environment as well as monitor the implementation of those environmental laws by relevant government agencies.

Organizational Environment

Every organization operates within the environment. There is a continuous interaction between the organization and its environment for the supply of resources or inputs and the use of outputs. The organization depends on the environment for human, material, financial, information and other resources required to carry out its operations and actualize its objective. Where the environment does not provide adequate resources, the operations of the organization will be scuttled and its objective jeopardized. This is the reason behind the establishment of certain organizations in certain locations. It is either an organization is located close to its source of raw materials or it is close to the market or customers it serves. This choice is, however, based on the cost-benefit analysis of obtaining the organization's resources vis-a-viz that of reaching its target market.

Apart from being the source of inputs and the outlet for its outputs, the environment also provides opportunities and poses threats to the organization. Here, the environment is described as those conditions that are external and either facilitate or devastate the operations of an organization. Those conditions that 'facilitate' or make it possible for the organization to attain its objectives are, therefore, referred to as opportunities whereas those that devastate or make it difficult for the organization to actualize its objectives are, therefore, referred to as threats. Environmental factors are categorized as economic, social, political, legal, technological, physical, industrial, and global. Changes in the conditions within these environments can influence actions as well as outcomes for the organization. Table 2.1 gives details of how environmental conditions affect and influence organization's performance and survival.

Table 2.1

Environmental factors	Effects on the organization
Economic	A set of economic factors do affect the operations of an organization. These include economic stage of the nation (boom or recession), inflation rate, unemployment rate, access to funds for investment or expansion, availability of needed resources, etc. Favorable economic conditions boost organizational performance while the reverse is the case for unfavorable economic conditions. E.g. The period of high inflation generally has negative effect on the performance of organizations because operational cost increases while customer demand shrinks.
Social	A set of social factors do affect the operations and performance of organizations. Some of them are changes in taste, fashion, demography, education, and religion as well as activities of labor unions and civil society groups. For example, the activities of the green movement - a coalition of civil society groups for the protection of the environment - can adversely affect the survival of an organization whose major source of raw materials allegedly leads to environmental degradation like fossil fuel, wood, paper, rubber, coal, etc.
Political	The activities of the government in power can limit or expand the operations of an organization. Public policies, rules and regulations continue to be changed in line with public pressure, demand by interest groups, and activities of opposition parties, criminal gangs, and terrorist groups. When these changes occur, certain organizations are negatively affected while others are positively affected. For example, the decision by the Trump Administration to build a wall along the US/Mexico border will negatively affect some organizations that are located along the Mexican side of the border while positively affecting local producers of those products that are normally imported through that border line.

Legal	A set of legal factors do affect the operations of an organization. Changes in the laws of the land can adversely affect the survival of an organization. For example, if a new law is passed that prohibits the production and distribution of tobacco products, tobacco manufacturing organizations will be forced into extinction. New laws can raise corporate taxes, reduce profits, and discourage investment in certain sectors of the economy. Also, the absence of a sound legal system that protects private investments as well as private property ownership will discourage the establishment of certain organizations in designated locations.
Technological	A set of technological factors do affect the operations of an organization. Technology is a general term used to describe the forms, tools, techniques, and activities used in transforming the inputs of an organization into desired outputs. The basic element that causes transformation in the society is advancement in technology. Once technology changes, organizations must either adopt it, adapt to it, or face extinction due to excessive competition from the organizations that do. The rate of change in technology in the 21st century is so alarming that a new item can become obsolete in a matter of weeks.
Physical	A set of physical factors do affect the operations of an organization. Physical factors have to do with the conditions of the physical environment where the organization is located. You cannot locate an organization in an environment that is prone to natural disasters such as earthquakes, tornadoes, hurricanes, flooding, thunderstorms, etc. If you do, you might wake up one day to realize that the organization is gone with the storm. The physical features of the organization should also give easy access to anyone who wants to relate with the organization such as customers and suppliers. If you locate your organization in an unfriendly neighborhood as well as a dangerous terrain, you scare away major stakeholders.

Industrial	A set of industrial factors do affect the operations of an organization. An industry has been described as a combination of organizations engaged in similar operations and targeting the same customers. Every organization belongs to a certain industry and is affected by the conditions prevailing within that industrial market. The industry size and stage, the position of the firm in the industry, and the activities of the market leader, have a great deal of influence on the operations of any organization. New entrants must have an in-depth knowledge of the industry they plan to be a part of. How bright is the future of the industry? What other alternatives do customers have in relation to the products and services of that industry? For example, those who wish to start an airline transportation business should not only consider how many airlines there are at present but also how effective other means of transportation is such as bus services, train services, and boat services. The reason is that the more people use buses, trains, and boats as effective means of transportation, the less they will have need for airplanes. An unmet need is what gives birth to a new business. Remember, a business without customers is a disaster waiting to happen!

Global	A set of global factors do affect the operations of an organization. The world is said to be a global community these days meaning that whatever happens in one part of the world can have a serious impact on what happens in other parts of the world. Distance is no longer a barrier in the international community. An organization in Austin, Texas is now in competition with another organization in faraway Australia. A firm operating in Ghana is now afraid of another firm operating in Canada. Whatever products they are producing or services they are providing, organizations now know that they are in competition with other organizations engaged in similar operations in other parts of the world. I once quoted that 'competition is real, and when we try to localize it, we applaud ourselves as champions; but when we globalize it, we often realize that we are so far behind. To remain a local champion in a global community is not only self-deceiving but self-defeating.' Organizations that used to be market leaders in their national domain now realize that they are in competition with organizations outside their national boundaries who have better alternative products at a cheaper price. This scenario has led to new trends such as outsourcing of products or parts of a product, and/or relocation of an entire production facility to a foreign country. For example, an auto company that is manufacturing cars in the United States may have all the various parts of that car produced and shipped from other parts of the world. The only operation taking place in the United States might just be 'assembling of the parts.' As a result, it is becoming difficult to say that those cars were manufactured in the United States. It will be even more correct to say that today's cars are global cars. Organizations now relocate their entire production operations to another country, produce there and then ship to other parts of the world for sale. The global environment is redefining the way and manner organizations are undertaking their operations.

Having discussed the important role the external environment plays in the daily operations and long term survival of an organization, the best thing the leadership of an organization can do is to scan the environment on a continuous basis in a bid to identify challenges and take care of them before they become threats, as well as identify opportunities and exploit them before a rival organization does. Environmental changes and challenges are inevitable and the way and manner an organization responds to them is critical to its survival and success. Successful organizations are those that have developed speed, skill, and strategy in responding to the threats and opportunities within the environment they operate.

Speed: This connotes how fast you respond to environmental changes and challenges. Speed is time-based and most opportunities do not wait for a long time. Time is an organizational resource and the first organization to identify and exploit an opportunity is usually the first to lock into the benefits at the expense of late comers. Also, organizations that are fast enough to spot potential threats and find ways to confront, avoid, or adapt to them usually last longer than others.

Skill: This connotes the knowledge base of an organization usually made up of the training and experience of members of that organization. Speed without skill leads to loss of resources while pursuing an opportunity or fighting a threat. Market leaders often have an advantage of skills over other players in the industry because of the ability to attract the best skilled workers within the industry. This provides the right talent set necessary to take advantage of current and future opportunities as well as fight against both existential and potential threats.

Strategy: This connotes a specific action plan designed to overcome a certain environmental threat and take advantage of an existing opportunity. Strategy involves the use of skill and speed and tends to target a specific opportunity or threat at a specific time and location. For example, an organization might decide to set up an ad hoc team of experts to tackle a particular environmental threat or explore an environmental opportunity while other organizations might use the existing traditional structure to take care of the situation while still running normal operations. Some organizations have a Research and Development unit for the purposes of identifying and offering new products or approaches in a bid to meet changing market demands and varying customer needs. Members of the marketing department of organizations do not only engage in activities that promote their organizations' products and services but also constantly conduct a market research on the competitor's products and services for the purpose of countering the negative effect on their organization's market share.

Organizational Management

While discussing the force of an organization, the term 'management' was mentioned briefly. There, management was described as the force necessary to pool all resources together and then direct them towards the attainment of organization's objective. Management is, therefore, the engine of an organization. Just as an engine is the driving force of an automobile, so is management the driving force of an organization. The strength of the management is the strength of the organization and the weakness of the management is the weakness of the organization. Knowing how important management is, this section shall be devoted towards shedding more light on the authority and responsibility of the management of an organization.

Management happens to be the most misunderstood and, therefore, the most misapplied aspect of an organization. The reason is that everyone believes he or she can occupy a management position and 'manage' an organization. It is, however, pertinent to note that 'management' is not just a group of people saddled with the responsibility of issuing orders in the organization. Management is the process of effectively achieving the objectives of an organization by efficiently utilizing the organization's resources. Management is the overall process of determining an organization's objective, attracting the organization's resources, establishing a system and structure for the operations of the organization, and ensuring that the entire arrangement is properly monitored and controlled as to actualize the set objective at the right time and with the right amount of resources. All these are achieved by applying the management functions of planning, organizing, directing, and controlling.

Functions of management

Planning is the primary function of management and it involves determining ahead of time what needs to be done (that is, setting the objective), determining and attracting the needed materials for the operations (that is, acquiring the resources), deciding how to do it (establishing the system), and deciding on how to arrange the people needed to do it (determining the structure). These four aspects of the planning function of management are very critical to the growth and survival of an organization. Setting the objectives of an organization depends on a lot of variables and once there is a mistake as to the objectives, every other part of the organization's life will be flawed. It would look like building a house on a faulty foundation. No matter how beautiful the house is, it is bound to cave in some day. It is just a matter of time. Acquiring the resources needed to carry out the operations of an organization and actualize its objective is part of the planning function of management. The material, financial, human, and other resources must be planned for and acquired by management ahead of commencing operations. If you are not sure of the objective, you cannot be certain about the resources you need to attain them. Establishing a system for an organization is designing the process of getting things done. The planning function of management helps to establish the plant layout or a flowchart of what needs to be done first and how, followed by the second and third until the end. It determines the quantity and quality of materials needed for each operation, how to use and store them, and how to ensure that everybody understands and operates them for consistent results. Determining the structure is deciding each job function, determining the skill and experience needed to carry out the job function, deciding the person who gives the instruction, the person who prepares the report, and the person who checks to see that those jobs are carried out as specified. If one of these four aspects of the planning function is faulty, the entire organization will be on the verge of a breakdown long before attempting to meet its set goal.

As part of the planning function, the management of an organization sets out its mission and vision amid the broad objective. It is very important to distinguish between these two critical aspects of the organization. When I walk into the reception room of an organization, the first thing I look out for is the mission and vision statement. Most of the time what I see is statement full of confusion, ambiguity, and misrepresentation. Some of the organizations actually think that the two terms mean the same thing while others exchange the meaning of one for another. These two terms mean and represent two different things though they stem from the same root called 'objective.' An organization's **mission** is a statement of its fundamental purpose. It sets out the basic objective of the organization and outlines the resources at its disposal with which to reach that objective. For example, the mission statement of a food processing organization may read like this:

> "ABC Foods offers the best food products to its esteemed customers in the meat processing sub-sector of the United States food industry from a plant operated in a purely automated and extremely hygienic environment by a team of highly skilled and motivated team. At ABC Foods, we ensure that we put a smile on the face of every customer each and every day."

The above example summarizes what ABC does, how it does it, and the resources it has with which to do it. It focuses on the customer's need for a healthy product as well as the organization's capability to provide such a product with highly skilled and experienced staff in a highly automated environment. Note that excellence is the watchword here.

An organization's **vision**, on the other hand, is a statement of its long-term goal. The vision statement sets out the position the organization intends to attain within the industry in a future time frame. It is always handled by the senior management of an organization and concentrates on the overall future direction of the organization. It is usually represented with the sign of an 'eye' showing that it helps the organization see beyond its current position into a future position it wishes to attain over time. Sometimes, it can include the resources or strengths at the disposal of the organization with which to reach that goal. For example, the vision statement of the food processing organization may read like this:

> *"ABC food intends to be the leader in the meat processing sub-sector of the United States food industry and beyond by continuously expanding its research and development efforts towards offering the best meat products to its highly esteemed customers with the best technology and most qualified and motivated workforce."*

Organizing is another function of management apart from planning. Organizing is the assigning of tasks and allocating of materials required to achieve the goals of an organization. Organizing rests on the foundation of the system and structure established in the planning stage. Since the planning stage decides the job functions, sets the minimum skill and the experience required to carry them out, and outlines the official relationship and formal line of communication among members of the organization, the organizing stage simply positions people on the job functions for which they are most qualified, and allocates the materials required to get the job done. Based on this scenario, planning and organizing share the function of 'staffing' which some authors include as a distinct function of management. The management function of organizing helps to eliminate confusion by ensuring that the right person occupies the right position to get the right job done at the right time and with the right materials.

Directing is another function of management. Directing is the management function of providing leadership and offering the motivation required by the employees in their day-to-day activities towards contributing do the achievement of organization's objectives. It is usually handled by the lowest level of management called the operational management. That you have the right worker with the right materials does not often guarantee the attainment of set objective. Human beings are the most complex of all the resources of an organization and must be treated with utmost respect and dignity to get the best out of them in terms of performance and productivity. The right leadership must be provided, and the right motivation offered. Leadership is the influence you exact on people to make them unleash their full potentials while motivation is the inward conviction a person gets based on the words and actions of a superior officer that makes him do things in unique ways than he would have done otherwise. Certain job tasks are difficult but not impossible. Management must, therefore, provide the leadership necessary for each person to release his or her full strength as well as offer the motivation needed for each person to believe that he or she can do anything. With these scenarios in place, there is no limit to what the human being can achieve. There must be constant flow of healthy communication between the management and employees if desired results are to be achieved. Information is like blood to an organization. Just as insufficient blood or bad blood is injurious to the human life so is insufficient information or bad information to an organization. Communication is a vital ingredient of the directing function of management.

Controlling is another function of management. It is the process of continuously reviewing and constantly correcting the processes and procedures of the organization as well as the activities of employees as they work daily towards the attainment of organization's objectives. Processes and procedures undergo changes as operations expand or shrink. People are also bound to make mistakes and machines are bound to malfunction from time to time. Things seldom go as planned. The ability of management to intervene on time to remedy the situation is very critical to the organization's success as it helps to reduce wastes, restore order, boost confidence, as well as channel available resources and human efforts towards the achievement of the organization's objectives. The management function of controlling ensures that current performance is measured against established standards and compared with previous performances, deviations promptly identified, causes established, and corrective actions undertaken to forestall further occurrence of the anomaly. Controlling helps to match performance with expectation as to ensure that set objectives are actualized as planned (with the right resources and at the right time) or adjusted as needed, based on the realities on the ground.

Levels of management

Here, we look at management as a group of people saddled with the responsibility of performing management functions in an organization. People become members of management by virtue of their job positions and functions. Anyone who participates in planning, organizing, directing, and controlling the operations of an organization is a member of management. There are some organizations with a handful of managers while a host of others boast of having an array of managers based on their size and stretch. Some organizations have operational branches around the world and so have hundreds, if not thousands, of managers carrying out the functions of planning, organizing, directing, and controlling. Levels of management is, therefore, the categorization of members of management based on how much or how little they participate in each of the core management functions. We have three distinct levels of management: top level management, middle level management, and lower level management.

Top level management: These are executive members operating at the highest echelon of the organization's hierarchy. This involves the president or chief executive officer of the organization, the vice presidents as well as members of the Board of Directors that oversee the activities of the executive officers. These people set the overall direction of the organization through planning. They decide the overall objective of the organization including the mission and vision, the markets to operate in, the product lines to produce, the services to provide, the sources of finance, future expansions, etc. They generally take decisions on how the organization's resources should be allocated in taking advantage of opportunities in the chosen market. This level is often referred to as the Strategic Management due to its focus on the future direction of the organization rather than the day-to-day or week-to-week operations. Some of the activities they engage in include expansion of the facility, location or relocation of the plant, sourcing of funds, merger and acquisition activities, international operations, and relationship with government as well as the host community.

Middle level management: These are managers operating at the middle section of the organization's hierarchy. The middle management involves departmental managers, divisional managers, plant managers, facility managers, area managers, etc. They break down the strategic plans into tactical plans and set monthly and weekly targets towards the achievement of the overall objective. As a result, this level is often referred to as tactical management. It is the link between the top level and the lower levels of management. They engage (that is, hire and place) people in various job functions and ensure that they know what they are expected to do. They perform more of the organizing function and are often specialists in their field of operation.

Lower level management: These are managers operating at the lower level of the organization's hierarchy. Lower management involves supervisors, foremen, and all those who oversee the daily operations and monitor the activities of the rank and file of the organization. They are often referred to as the operational management or frontline management. They perform more of the directing and sometimes the controlling functions of management because they provide leadership and motivation, communicate the organization's expectations, and work to ensure that operations run in line with set standards. Those who occupy this level of management often possess the technical knowledge of the units or sections of the organization they are meant to supervise. Surprisingly, most supervisors do not have a deep understanding of their jobs. A supervisor is the link between the management and the rest of the workers. As a link, the supervisor has dual responsibilities; one, to the management he or she represents and, the other, to the workers he or she supervises. As supervisors bring information, instruction, and ideas down to workers, they should also take reports, requests, and recommendations up to the management. It cannot be a one-sided game. This feedback segment is what leads to improvements in the organization.

Observation has shown that most of our 'untrained managers' focus more attention on exercising authority than in providing direction to the people they are working with. They think management is all about dishing out orders and expecting compliance. First, it is a big mistake for a manager to say that his or her subordinates are 'working for him.' The fact is both the manager and the subordinates are working together for the organization. The organization is usually a separate legal entity. Every other person is either part of the ownership, the management, or other employees. With this understanding, managers ought to be team leaders to their team members rather than superiors to subordinates. Any manager that assumes the position of a boss all the time often goes out of touch with other people, creates an atmosphere of disharmony, and weakens the organization's capacity to actualize its objectives. Members of today's organization must work as a team to effectively realize the goals of the organization.

CHAPTER 3

ORGANIZATIONS COME IN DIFFERENT FORMS

As shown in earlier discussions, organizations come in different forms. In this chapter, attempt shall be made at identifying the various forms of organizations as well as their similarities and differences. We should note that the major differences among the different forms of organizations are in their objectives and how they go about fulfilling them. It is also significant to observe that various organizations are actually extensions of the twelve pillars of the earth.

S/N	PILLAR	CORRESPONDING ORGANIZATIONS
1	Science & Technology	Scientific research institutions and foundations, Technological organizations, Engineering and construction operations, energy and power plants, space and weather centers, telecommunications, etc.
2	Health & Medicine	Health institutions, hospitals, medical laboratories, pharmaceutical firms, medical research institutions, etc.
3	Agriculture	Agricultural research institutions, farms, poultry, fisheries, animal husbandry, horticultural firms, food centers, food regulators, etc.
4	Politics	Political organizations, national, state, and municipal governments, departments and agencies of government, the civil service, military formations, law enforcement agencies, regulatory organizations, global institutions such as the United Nations, etc.

5	Education	Educational institutions: universities, colleges, high schools, middle schools, elementary schools, skill acquisition centers, talent development institutions, training centers, capacity builders, etc.
6	Commerce & Industry	Business organizations: industrial firms, commercial enterprises, service firms, transportation companies, aviation firms, courier services, banking, insurance, taxation, real estate, import, export, stock market, Forex trading, wholesale, retail, etc.
7	Fashion	Fashion and modeling firms, cotton processing, textile, and fabric production, designing and sewing, beauty and hair products, shoe and bag designers and manufacturers, etc.
8	Religion	Religious organizations: Churches, Synagogues, Mosques, Temples, religious centers and agencies, etc.
9	Arts & Crafts	Arts and craft organizations, painters, sculptors, decorators, interior and exterior designers, photography, graphic designers, metal designers and welders, etc.
10	Media	Media organizations: Television, Radio, print and publishing, advert and marketing agencies, internet, communication agencies, etc.
11	Entertainment	Entertainment organizations: Music, Movie, Comedy, theaters, amusement parks, zoos, dance and drama groups, etc.
12	Sports	Sports organizations: Sports teams such as football, basketball, baseball, rugby, hockey, racing and swimming, National, State and Local Sports institutions, International sports agencies such as FIFA, IOC, etc.

It is very clear that the twelve pillars of the earth, also known as the 12 systems of the world, have become the authentic basis for the categorization of organizations into various forms. So, the discussion on the different forms of organization will be done in line with the order of the twelve pillars as outlined above.

1. Organizations under the Pillar of Science and Technology

Technology development is an outcome of scientific research efforts undertaken by individuals or group of individuals. Technology includes the tools, machines, techniques, methods, and actions taken in the production process to convert inputs into outputs. The basic needs of every human being have been identified as food, clothing, and shelter. The natural environment may have provided us with food, clothing, and shelter but not always in the form and shape we need them. For example, nature provided streams, fruits, nuts, vegetables, fishes, birds, animals, etc., as food for mankind but some of them cannot be consumed in their raw state. Technology helps us to process and transform the raw food materials into desired forms that give us the best satisfaction and nutrition that our body needs for strength, growth, immunity, and survival. Research in Science and Technology has enabled man to discover various ways of making foods available in the form, time, and place that we need them. Stream water can now be purified and stored, fruits and vegetables can now be harvested and preserved, fishes can be caught and dried, and chicken can now be processed and frozen, etc.

Clothing is another fundamental need of mankind. Nature provided leaves and tree branches but we know that those are not enough to cover our nakedness from harsh environmental conditions. With better tools at his disposal, man has been able to use animal skins for covering. As technology improved, man has developed better ways to cloth himself in line with the varying climatic conditions in his place of abode. The same reason why those who experience temperate cold with winter snows, dress in winter coats whereas those who experience tropical heat mostly put on light summer cloths.

Shelter is another fundamental need of mankind. Nature provided the early man with caves and forest trees as shelter from harsh environmental conditions such as snow, rain, sun rays, etc. As people expanded and migrated away from caves and forests, the need for a better shelter arose. Over the centuries, improvements in science and technology have led to improvements in shelter. We can now cut down trees, split tree drunks into timber, and use the timber to build houses, construct furniture, and provide fittings. We also use concrete blocks, stones, glass, bricks, and cement to build houses and provide decent shelter. Improvements in technology based on scientific research, discoveries, inventions, innovations, and developments have helped humans to record monumental improvements in the way they interact with the environment in meeting their daily needs for food, clothing and shelter.

These improvements did not just happen. Individuals and groups of individuals made them happen. Once individuals come together, an organization is formed; whether it has a name or whether it is registered or not. There are numerous scientific, technological and research organizations around the world. The result from their diligence is leading to improvements in the various aspects of our everyday lives. NASA (National Aeronautics and Space Agency) is such an organization and IAEA (International Atomic Energy Agency) is another. Others are National Academy of Sciences, Center for Science and the Public Interest, Council for Chemical Research, Geoscience Research Institute, Hydrologic Research Center, Improvement Science Research Network, National Space Institute, Glenn Research Institute, Governor Gray Davis Institute for Science and Innovation, Institute for Creative Technologies, Broad Institute, American Institutes for Research (AIR), and a host of others. Research leads to discoveries and most discoveries result in inventions or innovations in technology (or methods of production of goods and services). Almost all colleges as well as tertiary education institutions are involved in research and development activities. When we succeed in bringing a team of researchers together under one roof, there is no limit to what can happen. There is no problem without solution!

2. Organizations under the Pillar of Health and Medicine

Organizations are formed to solve problems, meet needs, or proffer solutions to the myriad of challenges within the society. Organizations under the pillar of health and medicine are established with the objective of providing health care services to those suffering from sicknesses or diseases. Pharmaceutical companies are also health organizations. Some of the causes of sicknesses and diseases include protracted lack of sufficient rest after the day's job, lack of regular exercise for normal blood circulation, eating of junk food, exposure to extreme cold or heat, dehydration, loss of blood, challenging pregnancy, genetic disorder, untreated wounds, internal injuries, organ failures, etc. Prevention of any sickness is always better than its cure because it saves you money, time as well as discomfort. However, when sickness cannot be prevented, cure becomes necessary. Our hospitals are established and equipped to treat and, possibly, cure sicknesses and diseases based on discoveries from medical research. Surgeries can be conducted to replace or repair the affected body parts or organs while drugs can be prescribed to eliminate the symptoms or delay the spread of the disease. The universal challenge in the field of health and medicine is that we are yet to find cure for some of the diseases that are ravaging the world today. Our doctors, nurses, pharmacists, medical laboratory experts, medical consultants, and a host of other service providers work so hard to diagnose, treat and cure sicknesses and diseases. Sometimes they succeed and at other times they fail. Medical practitioners have severally confirmed that healing is mostly 'natural 'but you must place the body in a certain condition to initiate the healing process. This is exactly what our medical and health workers try to do.

Hospitals are health organizations and they operate in different forms. There are private hospitals, public hospitals, corporate hospitals, joint hospitals, and specialist hospitals. There are also primary hospitals, secondary hospitals, and tertiary hospitals. Private hospitals are health organizations that are owned and operated by a principal medical practitioner with the help of other partners or employees to deliver health care in locations where they are non-existent or for health conditions in which the medical practitioner is a specialist. For example, diagnostic laboratories, eye clinics, dental clinics, foot clinics, ear clinics, etc. This kind of hospitals are usually small in size with only one branch or two in an area where the principal medical practitioner can personally reach.

Public hospitals are health organizations owned by the government and operated by doctors and other medical and health workers employed by the government. For example, a state government can constitute a hospitals' management board to oversee the affairs of state-owned general hospitals located in major cities across the state. Such hospitals usually engage in general health care and tend to refer special cases to specialist hospitals. State general hospitals undertake prenatal training, child delivery and maternity services as well as post-natal care for moms and their new babies at a minimal cost. They also carry out general immunization services to members of the public as preventive measures against contagious sicknesses and diseases.

Corporate hospitals are health organizations owned by private investors but operated by their medical employees for the purpose of rendering health care services that are either general or special in nature to members of the public usually at a cost higher than that charged by public hospitals. Joint hospitals are health organizations which are jointly owned by the government and private investors. It is a blend of public/corporate hospitals for the purpose of improving service delivery to patients. In this case the government owns the facility while the private investor brings in the management, hires the staff, and operates the facility as a corporate hospital. Specialist hospitals, on the other hand, are health organizations that are either owned and operated by the government or the private sector but that tend to specialize in the treatment of specific sicknesses or diseases at the exclusion of others. For example, cancer treatment centers, children hospitals, orthopedic hospitals, neurological hospitals, spinal injury hospitals, etc.

Some nations categorize their health organizations into primary, secondary, and tertiary. Primary health care organizations or hospitals deal with preventative healthcare services such as immunization against the six child-killer diseases, prenatal training, postnatal care, and minor health issues such as cold, flu, cough, body pains, minor domestic injuries, etc. Secondary health care organizations or hospitals deal with major sicknesses and diseases that are general in nature such as digestive issues, circulatory issues, respiratory issues, etc. Here, the objective is not to prevent but to cure. Special cases are usually referred to tertiary health institutions. Tertiary healthcare organizations or hospitals are established and equipped to treat special sicknesses and disease with the services of specialist medical practitioners. Cases that are referred to this level of health care are categorized as critical and life threatening and, therefore, require the attention of medical consultants who are experts in the field. Examples are cancer, orthopedic, neurological and spinal cord cases, etc.

Health and medical organizations play a major role in safeguarding the health of the nation both for productivity and re-productivity. Any nation that has a poor health care system risks the loss of its future generation through high infant mortality, loss of pregnant women during child delivery, loss of part of the population over minor preventable diseases, as well as loss of those with special diseases for lack of local experts to treat them. The Center for Disease Control (CDC), the National Health Institute (NHI), and the Food and Drug Administration (FDA) are health organizations which work to prevent diseases or regulate the activities of health and related organizations.

3. Organizations under the Pillar of Agriculture

The need for food cannot be overemphasized. Every human being eats to live. We need food to maintain our body metabolism; providing us with the nutrient we need for daily activities and the immunity our body needs to fight against sicknesses and diseases. Agricultural organizations are, therefore, responsible for providing the natural food that we eat daily as well as the raw materials needed by the industrial sector to process and preserve food for future consumption. As at today, there are at least 7.8 billion human beings in the world. Can you even begin to imagine what it will take to provide food for this number of persons on a daily basis? it is simply amazing! The air, land and sea have been naturally blessed to produce things that sustain the human life. The air provides the oxygen human beings and animals need for breathing as well as the carbon dioxide plants need for their food processing activities. The land provides plants and from plants we have flowers, trees, grasses, seedlings, and food. Food comes in the form of fruits, vegetables, nuts, grains, suckers, tubers, fibers, etc. The land also sustains animals and birds from where we get the meat we need for food. The sea provides the fishes and a host of other sea foods which come as delicacies when served in our meals. Examples are shrimps, lobsters, periwinkle, crayfish, crab, snail, etc.

The early man started by gathering fruits and vegetables for food. As time went by, he discovered that seeds from the fruits he consumed gave 'birth' to other trees that produced the same fruits. So, farming was conceived. As he developed relevant tools, he started hunting for animals as part of his food. When the human population expanded and food was becoming scarce due to the distance between the location of shelter and the source of food, the need for planting and animal husbandry became obvious. It soon became clear that if you want a bumper harvest, you had to plant more. This is how farming advanced to its current commercial stage where, with the use of improved tools and techniques, a few men and women can now grow and process the food consumed by tens of millions of human beings around the world. Quite incredible!

Agricultural organizations are those organizations that engage in activities that lead to food production, processing, storage, and preservation. Agricultural production happens at corn farms, poultry farms, fish farms, vegetable farms, flower farms, seedling farms, rice farms, beans farms, yam farms, cassava farms, tomato farms, potato farms, peanut farms, sugar cane plantations, millet farms, onion farms, carrot farms, pepper farms, water melon farms, palm plantations, apple plantations, pineapple plantations, coconut plantations, orange plantations, mango plantations, strawberry plantations, pawpaw plantations, guava plantations, plantain plantations, banana plantations, pear plantations, cotton plantations, coffee plantations, cocoa plantations, grape farms, cattle farms, pig farms, goat farms, and sheep farms, etc. By having these farms around our homes, it is now much easier to produce more of different species of food in a limited land space. Chemicals that improve soil nutrient and farm yield have also been discovered and applied.

Results of scientific research have also helped to boost agricultural produce over the years and made food abundantly available for human consumption. The big question, however, is 'do we have enough food storage that would take care of our food needs for the next 12 months assuming there is a global poor agricultural yield this year?' Your guess is as good as mine!

The commercialization of agriculture has moved most agricultural organizations into commercial and industrial operations. In fact, agro-based business is the primary business that never lacks customers. Everybody must eat every day! Whether you have shelter, clothing or nothing, you must eat else you will join your ancestors sooner than later. No matter how bad the economy is, no matter how poorly paid a worker is, and no matter how sad we feel about the situation, we must eat. This makes agricultural organizations critically important in our society. All organized farms are agricultural organizations. Some of the agricultural organizations that support farmers include the following: Dairy Farmers of America, National Federation of Young Farmers, Northeast Organic Farming Association, American Farm Bureau Federation, National Farmers, and American Poultry Association, etc.

4. Organizations under the pillar of politics

The pillar of politics is all about governance and all the activities that directly support it. It has been mentioned that nations, regions, states, counties, municipalities, and communities are organizations. They are organizations because they involve a collection of people for the attainment of a certain objective or group of objectives. For example, a nation is a collection of states or regions which either share similar cultural heritage, accept similar social values, adopt similar property rights, or wish to abide by similar set of rules. They may not dress the same way, eat the same food, or speak the same dialect but their *agreement* to live together as one makes them a nation. As a result, the need to select or elect leaders to run the affairs, enforce common rules, ensure conformity to existing regulations, protect lives and property, and defend the territorial integrity of that nation, becomes imperative. All organizations that engage in any of these and related activities are political organizations. These include political parties, national governments, regional governments, state governments, municipal governments, city governments, military formations, the civil service, regulatory agencies, law enforcement agencies, etc.

Political parties are political organizations that participate in the governance process by educating the public on their manifesto, attracting members to the party, selecting and preparing candidates for election, participating in elections, and supporting their successful candidates all through their political career. If the political parties present wrong candidates, the electoral process will produce wrong winners and the nation will grapple with wrong leaders. It is a chain reaction! If we desire to have good leaders in a democratic setting, political parties must be re-positioned to present the right candidates. The management of political parties should be strengthened to organize the operations of their parties in such a way that the right candidates are always presented for election. A political party that fails to identify and present right candidates for elective positions has denied the society the good leaders it deserves.

National governments are organizations under the Pillar of Politics. The national government is a group of people selected or elected to manage the affairs of the nation in line with existing rules and regulations put together in the constitution and any other ordinances or codes that have been accepted as a guide to the actions and reactions of all the members or citizens of that nation. Most democratic nations have three arms and three tiers in their governance structure. The three arms are the executive, the legislature, and the judiciary while the three tiers are the federal, state, and local governments. The federal government oversees the affairs of the nation at large and the state government runs the affairs of the state while the local or county government directs the affairs of the local area or county. The three arms of government are present in the three tiers of government. The executive arm of government undertakes the day-to-day management of either the nation, the state or county by ensuring that existing policies are followed, laws obeyed, necessary programs implemented, needed projects executed, personal and property rights protected, lives preserved, human health sustained, healthy environment maintained, right information disseminated, available resources judiciously applied to tasks, crime rate reduced, emergencies responded to, jobs provided, and civic duties performed by all citizens and other residents. This is a huge task that requires seriousness on the part of those who desire the position, and the acceptance of those who are willing to make the necessary sacrifice to actualize such objectives. If those who desire political positions are not serious, and if those who are willing to make the necessary sacrifice do not accept to lead, the current state of the society will be hijacked and its future jeopardized.

The nation is an organization and the government is its management. Every nation has its threats and opportunities. If it's 'management' does not develop a formidable force to overcome the threats and take advantage of the opportunities, the nation cannot actualize its objectives which include internal unity, external peace, economic prosperity, protection against invasion, and general freedom and progress of its people wherever they may be. If nations are organizations, which, of course, they are, then their proper management becomes of paramount importance. A weak national management or government produces wrong policies, embarks on unwanted projects, executes irrelevant programs, makes unrealistic laws, engages in public exploitation, condones waste of resources, supports the weakening of educational and other institutions, promotes disunity among citizens, creates fear among the citizenry, establishes unsustainable healthcare system, encourages environmental degradation, shows lack of value for lives and properties and, therefore, presents a bad example for the citizens to follow. Incidentally, what happens at the federal level has a ripple effect at the state and county levels.

The legislature is the arm of government that is responsible for making laws that are relevant to the good governance of the society. The right laws must be made by the legislature for the executives to implement. If the laws are wrong, everything else will go wrong. The legislators must exhibit internal cohesion, focused attention, and people orientation if the right laws are to be enacted. The issue of congressional division based on party inclination or social affiliation is the greatest undoing of the American society. If legislators truly understand the enormity of their responsibility in the management of the nation, their posture and performance will absolutely change. Internal division weakens the system and makes it vulnerable to external destruction. Let us not forget that the legislature also carries out an oversight function of every aspect of government. This is a critical assignment which establishes and reinforces the principle of checks and balances in government. If human activities are left unchecked, abuse is often inevitable. However, legislators must be unbiased and nonpartisan to carry out their oversight functions most effectively.

The judiciary is the arm of government that ensures that the laws are rightly interpreted in times of conflict, and offenders or violators brought to justice. If the judiciary fails to carry out its activities in the most effective manner, laws will be misunderstood and broken with reckless abandon. Violators will often go unpunished, thereby enabling members of the society to operate with utmost impunity. The integrity of the judiciary as an unbiased umpire is the strength of the government as the people's representative. Therefore, members of the judiciary cannot afford to fall short of the society's expectation.

Other organizations under the pillar of politics include military formations, the civil/public service, regulatory agencies, law enforcement services, and all other institutions that support the operations of government. The military must be organized to defend the land from external invasion as well as internal aggression. Most of the time, the respect of a nation derives from the strength of its army. Security is what is needed to defend freedom. A nation that cannot defend itself is a prey to the enemy. The civil service is needed to run the bureaucratic institutions of government. These institutions carry out various functions in a bid to execute or implement the policies, programs, and projects of government. These institutions are the various departments, ministries and agencies of government that operate or supervise the transportation systems, the health care systems, water resources, electricity supply, energy supply, customs and immigration functions, communication systems, public parks and gardens, public libraries, educational programs, the court system, the prisons, environmental protection, national budget, taxation, insurance, etc. The civil service carries out the operational functions of government.

Regulatory agencies, on the other hand, are institutions of government which work to control private sector participation in the economic and other aspects of the society's life. Rules must be established and boundaries set if individuals are to perform within the expectations of the society. Food producers must be monitored so they do not end up poisoning members of the society in their greed. Drug producers must be monitored so they do not end up giving us medicines that do not cure our ailments but leave us worse off. Health care providers must be closely monitored so that people receive the health care they pay for and nothing less. Transporters should be monitored so that they do not end up becoming agents of death and devastation. Home builders must be monitored so that they provide homes that guarantee comfort and safety instead of disaster and trauma. Education providers must be monitored so they do not end up churning out educated illiterates who cannot contribute to societal development. Employers of labor must be monitored so they do not reduce their workers into mere slaves. The Stock Exchange must be monitored so that it is not used to fund projects that destroy rather than build up the society. Broadcasters and media platforms must be monitored so they do not end up misinforming and misleading the society. Sports women, men and institutions must be monitored to avoid cheating. Judges must be closely monitored so they do not sell justice to the highest bidder. Regulation is necessary to avoid public exploitation and economic sabotage while protecting public safety and health and restoring the people's confidence in the society where they belong. The free market system, also known as capitalism, does not connote the absence of regulation but the freedom of entry and exit by anyone who desires to participate in economic activities. Government has the responsibility to regulate all aspects of national life because the absence of regulation is the foundation for abuse. Regulation simply means setting the limits for operation to avoid exploitation by operators. The presence of any form of exploitation depicts the failure of government.

Law enforcement agencies ensure that all legal provisions are adhered to by members of the public. They also arrest, investigate, and prosecute erring members. Laws are mere statements on paper unless they are enforced. Laws are generally established standards to guide individual actions and behaviors and to control corporate activities within the society. The Police Department, as a law enforcement agency, ensures that these laws are strictly followed no matter who is involved. For example, there are traffic lights and speed limits on every road as established by law to ensure public safety by reducing auto crashes and saving lives. If these traffic laws are not enforced, members of the public will continue to violate them, over-speed their vehicles and cause avoidable auto crashes that claim innocent lives and destroy properties. A society where existing laws are not enforced will surely degenerate into a state of chaos and anarchy. However, our law enforcement agencies must be adequately trained and effectively managed to actualize their mandate without posing a new threat to the society they are established to protect and defend. The right people must be engaged as officers, right training extended, right gears provided, and right motivation put in place so that our law enforcement agents can perform their jobs without fear or favor, apprehend criminals without having to fear for their lives, and peacefully go back to their family and loved ones at the end of each day's activities. Law enforcement officers are not public enemies. They are ordinary men and women who have decided to devote their lives, skills, strengths, and experience in enforcing the law, fighting crime, and ensuring that everybody is safe. If all police departments should shut down for a week, we will know if they are important or not.

5. Organizations under the Pillar of Education

Education is the process of transferring knowledge from one generation to another. No society grows without some form of education. People need to learn their past and understand their present to discover their future. A people without a history is a people without a foundation and a people without a foundation is a people without a future. Education enables us to tap from the knowledge of our ancestors, avoid their mistakes, and chat a better course for a greater society. Education also helps us to access other people's discoveries, inventions, and innovations and learn how to apply them in solving today's problems and meeting tomorrow's challenges. Education can be formal or informal.

Informal education is the one we get from family and friends, neighbors and colleagues, partners and acquaintances, billboards and signboards, radio and television, music and movie, town halls and religious houses, etc. These are unstructured ways of passing knowledge from one person to another. For example, parents teach their kids how to eat, dress, talk, greet, shower, wash, clean, sweep, and how to treat other people with respect. The things we learn from our homes help us to exhibit positive attitude while relating with other people either within the home or outside of it. When you relate with someone who has a poor, or no, home training, the experience is usually corrosive and the result quite regrettable. If parents fail to teach their children these basic manners at home, they become half-baked and when they come into the larger society, they embarrass both themselves and their parents and every other person around them.

Formal education is a structured and institutionalized process of passing knowledge from one person (the teacher) to another person (the student). All the institutions that are involved in this process are referred to as educational organizations. Our schools are educational organizations and they must be organized in such a way as to make it easier for them to pass on knowledge. It is also important to note that the knowledge been passed on is based on the twelve pillars of the earth. Incidentally, one of the pillars is conspicuously missing in our education system; the Pillar of Religion. We now live in a society that considers religion, and the moral codes it teaches, as an anathema but still expect the society to operate at a high moral standard. For example, we removed bibles from our public schools where they are needed and placed them in jail cells where it is too late. We give our kids electronic devices that expose them to all forms of social vices and then expect them to possess high moral values. As a result of this moral gap caused by social negligence, our schools have become bullying clubs, racist centers, and sexual harassment rendezvous. Our kids are no longer safe at school. More parents are now forced to organize private coaching classes for their kids or place them on online educational programs just to shield them from the harassment and violence out there.

Our colleges have been turned into rape centers with most victims suffering in silence while perpetrators freely go about their business without any form of accountability. We now have so many colleges that ban religious activities but promote cults and fraternities. We know that the holy Bible contains the most comprehensive and indisputable account of creation yet we have college professors who teach our kids that God did not create anybody or anything. They insist that human beings evolved from ape through a series of developmental processes but fail to explain why today's apes are not developing into human beings or human beings developing into higher species of homo sapiens. Our kids are now being taught that one's gender is a matter of choice and not by implication of birth. They are taught that one can actually chose not to be either male or female. This is insane! The kind of knowledge we pass on to our kids these days is very confusing and counter-productive, yet we want them to act as though nothing is wrong. The level of moral decadence and criminal tendency we find among our youths is a result of what they are constantly learning from the society.

Educational organizations at all levels must be organized and managed in such a way as to pass on positive knowledge to our kids so that they are well positioned to contribute meaningfully to the development of an egalitarian society, where everyone is a major stakeholder. The owners, operators, managers, teachers as well as regulators of educational organizations must be tasked to do more towards ensuring that we are raising the next generation to be people of high moral character, free thinkers, focused enthusiasts, team players, hard workers, risk takers, as well as self-confident people, and not arrogant, lazy and self-seeking folks who are very much after what the nation can do for them rather than what they can do for the nation. Our schools must become a place where every child, regardless of his or her gender, race, color or religion has an equal opportunity to learn, develop, and contribute his or her strengths and skills to the overall good of the society without any fear of intimidation or victimization.

6. Organizations under the Pillar of Commerce and Industry

The Pillar of Commerce and Industry has been described as the connecting instrument of all the pillars of the earth. This is because that is where all the money is made. Anybody that understands the importance of money knows that there are so many things you cannot do without it. Other names for Commerce and Industry are trade and investment, and the business world. Every economy depends on the creation and exchange of value to survive. Value is, however, determined by the joint forces of demand and supply, which place price on each of the items of value. Every day, millions of billions of dollars change hands as people seek to meet their needs for food, clothing, shelter, safety, security, beauty, relaxation, entertainment, convenience, and luxury. As a result, new products and services are introduced daily, rendering obsolete what used to be the best products and services a couple of years ago. New businesses spring up almost at the same rate as they go down, leading to waste of billions of dollars that could have been channeled to somewhere else. Do people really understand the world of business?

Business is any commercial or industrial activity engaged in with the sole purpose of making profit. Profit is the incremental value of a business enterprise. It is the return on investment. However, there are five levels of profitability: businesses either lose profit, break even, make profit, increase profit, or maximize profit. Everyone in the economic value chain desires a greater value for whatever they are willing to part with. Be it the producers, the sellers and the buyers, everyone wants to out-negotiate the others in a bid to make higher returns on whatever value they are willing to give in exchange. If the value you receive is higher than the one you give, you make a gain and where it is lower, you make a loss. To make a profit, a business must make an income that is higher than its cost of operations. This means that a business must offer something of value so that what other people are willing to pay for it is bigger than what it costs to produce it. This shows that price is determined more by the value of an item than by the cost of its production. This is very critical if a business must succeed. If the value the end user of a product or service places on it is very high, you can charge any price for it and he would pay but if the value is very low, your negotiating power as a businessman or woman is gone. Our business schools teach us that we must first identify a business opportunity before going into any kind of business endeavor. By this they mean that we should identify the existence of a need within an environment and then find a way to meet that need profitably. Beyond that, we now know that the value the customer places on that need means a lot if you must offer solution at a profit. Not every market need has the potential to meet the profit need of a business enterprise. This is the basic reason why many businesses fail in their first two to five years. It is also the reason why old businesses fail, especially those that refuse to continuously analyze the value placed on their 'offerings' by their customers. The value a customer places on a product or service changes over time based on the importance of the item to his or her immediate need as well as the presence or absence of a better or cheaper alternative. Profit is the main motivation for going into business. It is the measure of business success and the driver of entrepreneurship. Profit attracts investors to an enterprise and sustains the value of its stock. The future of an organization depends largely on its profit potential. However, not all great businesses record substantial gains at the beginning of their operations. Some may even record losses for a few years before gains start flowing in. Profit comes in different forms and shapes.

Levels of profitability

I mentioned earlier that there are five levels of profitability available to a business:

a. To lose profit
b. To break even
c. To make profit
d. To increase profit, and
e. To maximize profit

To lose profit is to make an income, from an item of sales, that is lower than the cost of producing or providing that item. This is a general understanding of loss. But we must separate the cost of an item in a way as to identify its 'profitability,' that is, its potential to yield profit over time. Every cost of an item is divided into variable cost and fixed cost. Variable cost is that unit of the total cost that is directly related to the production of an item. For Example, the labor cost of the factory workers who are directly involved in its production, the machine time, wear and tear, the electricity used, the raw materials used, the transportation of materials used, etc. The fixed cost is that unit of the total cost that is not directly related to the production of an item. For example, the rent paid on the facility, the salary of administrative staff, the telephone bill, the heating bill, the water bill, the vehicle maintenance charge, the building maintenance cost, payments to security contractor, the cost of machines and equipment, advertisement, publicity and public relations charges, and other business charges, etc. This cost is said to be fixed because they do not depend directly on a particular item of production. Most of these costs will still be paid whether there is production or not. Most new business owners are in a hurry to cover both the variable cost as well as the fixed costs that they miss out on a business opportunity that has long term profit potential. They fix their initial prices with the aim of recovering the total cost and as a result price their products far beyond the value the customer is willing to place on them and the price he is able to pay for them. You can only conclude that you made a loss when the price of your product does not cover the variable costs of its production. Once the price covers the variable cost, the excess, which we call 'profit' becomes a contribution to the offsetting of the fixed cost. Over time, the fixed costs will be taking care of and the business enterprise will be more profitable.

By way of further explanation:

i. To lose profit means $R - C = -P$; where R = Revenue from sales
   C = Variable cost, and
   -P = Loss

ii. To break even means $R - C = 0$; where R = Revenue from sales
    C = Variable cost, and
    0 = Zero profit (no gain, no loss)

iii. To make profit means $R - C = P$; where R = Revenue from sales
     C = Variable cost, and
     P = >0 (Gain)

iv. To increase profit means $\uparrow R - C = +P$ or $R - \downarrow C = +P$;
    where $\uparrow R$ = More revenue from sales
    R = Revenue from sales
    C = Variable cost, and
    $\downarrow C$ = Less variable cost
    +P = More gain

Here, it is evident that there are two conditions that can lead to making more profit in a business venture: increasing the revenue from sales or reducing the variable cost. To increase your revenue from sales, you need to find ways to sell more of the products. This is where 'marketing' comes in. You must design a desirable marketing program to generate more sales. There are still people out there who have need for your product but have never heard about nor seen the product and the solution it provides. You must discover the best medium of communicating the product idea to the target market in a bid to generate more sales. You can't afford to let the electronic billboards and unending TV jingles of big competitors scare you from reaching the potential customers within your neighborhood. Why increasing sales is important to increasing profit is because if you multiply a unit of profit with millions of items sold, the profit builds up into millions of dollars as well. Where it is becoming difficult to increase revenue from sales, the entrepreneur must seek for ways to reduce the variable cost of operations. You must find cheaper sources of raw materials without compromising quality. You must also find ways to reduce internal waste and the cost of labor, transportation, storage, insurance, etc. If revenue from sales remains the same while the variable cost reduces, the business is going to experience an increase in profit as well.

v. To maximize profit: $\uparrow R - \downarrow C = ++P$; where $\uparrow R$ = More revenue from sales
$\downarrow C$ = Less variable cost
$++P$ = Maximized gain

Here, it is very clear that there is only one condition that can lead to the maximization of profit by a business enterprise. Now, what do we mean by profit maximization? To maximize profit is to increase profit to a maximum limit or to make the most profit that is possible within the industry or your level of operation. It is important to note that not many business organizations attain this level of profitability in their lifetime. Let me explain! I have already stated that to maximize profit depends on one condition only. That condition is 'working to increase revenue ($\uparrow R$) and reduce cost ($\downarrow C$) at the same time.' It sounds too simple in pronunciation but very complex in implementation. The reason is that it takes more cost to increase revenue. Fact is, to produce the extra items for sale will mean purchasing more materials, paying more in labor costs, spending more on transporting the items, engaging in more marketing programs that help to generate sales. All these add up to the total variable cost of every unit of production. So, how can we increase revenue and reduce cost at the same time? This is where 'management' comes in. I have, therefore, summarized the daily duties of every 'professional manager' into two categories: striving to increase the revenue of an organization, and struggling to reduce its cost. When managers perform these two assignments simultaneously, they are maximizing the profit and performance of their organization. Profit maximization equals utilizing the least cost in actualizing the best result. This is the whole essence of the management function. It simply means effective and efficient utilization of resources. So, if you are not maximizing profit, you are not managing properly. There is no difference between you and the so-called hundreds of millions of managers around the world. The task of management is not a child's play. No wonder many organizations fail annually for lack of good management. I can categorically say that big organizations are the worst when it comes to the challenge of profit maximization. The reason is not far-fetched. In a bid to maintain their market position, big organizations spend so much on sales promotion, public relations, events sponsorship, community development, publicity, advertising, etc. They, most times, forget that these activities cause a substantial increase in their cost of operation as well as reduce their gross profit. For example, imagine a situation where Coca Cola and Pepsi give out free giant-sized refrigerators to all grocery stores that sell their products. Also, imagine where Verizon and AT&T give out free cell phones to millions of their subscribers. Imagine also where a clothing store asks its numerous customers to buy two items and get one for free. These are items that must be paid for, which go a long way towards increasing the cost of operations. If these costs are not reflected in increased prices, which they hardly do due to intense competition, they do result in a substantial decrease in profitability.

Size-based classification of business organizations

There are various sizes of business organizations which have been so categorized for decades based on the amount of capital outlay and the number of employees. In this book, I am going to differ from this traditional classification of business into something that I have discovered in my years of research, consultancy, and practice in the Business Management profession. Here, I have classified business organizations based on the number of customers they serve and the spread of their operations. This classification establishes and maintains strong universality. As a result, we have:

i) Micro business organizations

Micro business organizations are usually very small and often operate within a local community and serving only those customers who live around. For example, an individual may decide to open a coffee shop, a wine bar, a repair shop, or a grocery/convenience store within their neighborhood. A family may also decide to operate a restaurant or pizza shop across the street to cater for the food needs of people living within the neighborhood. Nearly all sole proprietorship and most partnerships fall within the category of micro business organizations because they mostly have a single store, office or site to serve the people within that locality. A sole proprietorship is owned and managed by an individual but usually has friends, family, and a few employees who help out from time to time. Most partnerships exist in the form of two or more professionals, technicians or experts coming together to use their skills and experience to serve a local community. For example, CPAs, doctors, lawyers, auto repair and towing technicians, plumbing and painting technicians, building and construction technicians, lawn mowing and landscaping technicians, real estate professionals, staffing agents, metal bending and welding services, etc. With time and concerted effort, micro businesses do grow into medium business organizations.

ii) Medium business organizations

Medium business organizations are usually bigger than micro business organizations, have a few branches and operate within the boundaries of a county or state. For example, in the United States, some banks, savings and loans firms, and insurance companies operate within the space of a particular state. There are also telecommunications companies and Internet service providers that operate within the limits of a state. Some hospitals (private or public) also operate and serve customers within a particular state, obeying the laws of the state and contributing to its overall development. Most of the business organizations that fall within the scope of medium businesses are a few partnerships and a host of private limited liability companies that channel their strengths and focus their attention on serving the needs of customers or clients within a particular state. Due to the nature of their operations and the size of their resources, medium business organizations always resort to limiting their services within the boundaries of a state as expanding beyond that environment might pose a serious challenge on their resource availability and managerial capacity. With time and due diligence, medium businesses can grow into major business organizations.

iii) Major business organizations

Major business organizations are those businesses that have nationwide operations with numerous branches to cater for the need of their customers within a national boundary. Most public limited liability companies and a few private limited liability companies fall within this category. For example, insurance companies such as Allstate, Nationwide, State Farm, Farmers, Liberty Mutual, GEICO, Progressive, American Family, etc.; banks such as JPMorgan Chase, Huntington, Wells Fargo, Bank of America, Key Bank, Citigroup, Northwest bank, BBVA compass bank, etc.; airlines such as United, Delta, Spirit, America Airline, Southwest, Alaska, JetBlue, etc.; and telecommunications companies such as US cellular, Sprint Corporation, Verizon, AT&T, T-Mobile, Simple Mobile, etc. We also have mortgage institutions that operate nationally just as you have electricity corporations, transportation companies (air, road, rail and river), pharmaceutical companies, courier and logistic services, hotels, retail stores and restaurants (e.g. USPS, Walmart, K-mart, Giant

Eagle, Target, Sears, Kohl's, Burlington, KFC, Dominos, Burger King, McDonald's, Dunkin's Donut, Buy-Rite, etc.); publishing companies (e.g. Page publishing, Dorrance publishing, McGraw Hill, Pearson, Harper Collins, Gallup press, Bantam, Wiley, etc.); and television stations (such as FOX, CNN, ABC, CNBC, NBC, CBS, HSNBC, etc.) There are so many business organizations that render services that are national in scope and coverage. A host of these business organizations also produce products that are sold throughout the country. These are major businesses and some of them do extend their services beyond the shores of the nation to become mega businesses.

iv) Mega business organizations

Mega business organizations are those businesses that have global operations with branches in nations other than their parent countries. For example, auto mobile companies sell their products in almost all the nations of the world. Computer and other electronic companies also sell their products across the nations of the earth. Companies such as DHL, UPS, FEDEX, Coca Cola and Pepsi have operations in nearly all the nations of the world. Facebook and Microsoft corporation have a combined global customer base in billions. Citigroup, Walmart superstores, McDonald's, Starbucks and other American corporations now have numerous branches outside of the United States in places like Canada, China, Japan, Mexico, Brazil, U.K., France, Israel, India, Russia, Australia, Germany, and many more. The Boeing Corporation sells its air crafts in nearly all the nations of the earth. General Electric also has operations around the world. American companies that produce cell phones (such as Apple) have the entire world as their market. With an estimated 7.8 billion human beings, the world is a mega marketplace. Any business organization which products or services are in high demand across the globe will exert some level of global influence. Social media companies are doing just that. To achieve and maintain this global outreach, mega business organizations work so hard to improve their system, enhance their structure, and sustain the quality of their offerings in the midst of daunting challenges such as cultural barriers, currency differences and fluctuating exchange rates, logistic problems, political pressure, and usually difficult and varying regulatory environments. Sometimes a change in regime can ruin your business overseas. At other times, an acceptable advertisement in the United States can become an obituary announcement for your product or service in another country due to language differential and existing stereotypes and superstitious beliefs. These are some of the threats mega business organizations contend with daily as they seek to satisfy their heterogeneous market segments across the globe. Their size, scope of operation, access to funds, and use of improved technology are some of the advantages that can make a whole lot of difference in the ability of the management to withstand the storm and keep the mega business organization afloat in its effort to meet the needs of billions of human beings across the globe and also bring home billions of dollars as a return on investment.

Mega businesses are global businesses. Business organizations do not become mega overnight. In fact, no business starts out as a mega business organization. It is major business organizations that grow into mega business organizations. Effective management is the only tool that can help a major business grow into a mega one. No major business should launch into over-sea operations when it is not yet prepared to face and surmount the many challenges that plague global businesses. The challenges are huge and so are the benefits.

The stock exchange

The Stock Exchange market is a very important part of business and it operates within the boundaries of a country even though investors from other nations can trade within the market. Examples are The New York Stock Exchange, London Stock Exchange, Paris Stock Exchange, Shanghai Stock Exchange, Tokyo Stock Exchange, etc. As the name implies the Stock Exchange market is an arrangement in which investors buy and sell company stocks or shares for profits on a daily basis. It affords people the opportunity to purchase stock from any quoted company of their choice and to also sell their existing stock of any quoted company whenever they deem fit. Those who sell at a price higher than it cost them to acquire make a gain while those who sell at a lower price make a loss. Most times, the market operates on speculations. If there is a speculation that the profitability of a quoted company is expected to be on the rise due to a major breakthrough from its research and development efforts, people will likely rush to buy its stock in order to take advantage of the expected higher dividend to be distributed to the shareholders of the company. This raises the demand for the stock of that company, causing those existing stockholders who are willing to sell, to offer their stock at a higher price, make their own gains and get away. If the company declares more profits and distributes more dividends to its shareholders at the end of the day, those who bought the stocks would have made a good deal. If not, the reverse will be the case. However, there are some individuals and corporations that have studied the trend and can predict the ups (bulls) and downs (bears) in the stock exchange market. Some of these predictions have been found to be correct while a host of them did not pan out well, leading to losses and regrets. The final decision to buy or sell at any time must remain that of the individual investor.

Companies also raise funds at the Stock Exchange market. This happens in two ways: initial public offers (IPO), and subsequent public offers. The initial public offer occurs at the time a company becomes a new member of the Stock Exchange and offers a number of its stock for sale to the public (individuals and corporate investors) at a fair price. This price is usually a reflection of its current financial standing which depends on its profitability portfolio, the industry it belongs, the value of its products and services, and the nature of its management team. No investor wants to put his or her money where there is limited chance of success. The subsequent public offers occur when a quoted company needs a lot of money for a major expansion. The cost of acquiring a bank loan to fund such an expansion might be huge and might plunge the company into a debt position thereby reducing its profitability portfolio as well as its position in the Stock Exchange market. Selling additional stock to raise the money becomes the most viable option. Usually, the company will offer these stocks at a price a bit lower than the current market price of its stock in a bid to attract higher level of patronage both from existing shareholders as well as new investors. By purchasing and owning the stock of a company, an investor becomes a stockholder and part of the ownership of that company. If an individual investor or a corporate investor owns a substantial amount of stock in a particular company, that individual or organization is said to have controlling shares and, therefore, expected to participate more in its decision-making process, especially in the formation of its Board of Directors and the appointment of a CEO.

There is, however, a difference between the Stock Exchange market and the Stock Exchange Commission. The Stock Exchange Commission is a government agency which regulates the activities of the stock exchange market by establishing the rules, ensuring all parties play by those rules, and sanctioning erring members. Often, those who are appointed to head the Stock Exchange Commission are major investors themselves or those who have skill and experience on the general operations of the Stock Exchange market, the general nature of business organizations, the intricacies of the financial market, and the expectations of government from the business environment. The various tiers of government (federal, state, and local) can also raise funds from the Stock Exchange market by offering secure bonds: short term, mid-term, or long-term bonds.

7. Organizations under the Pillar of Fashion

Fashion can be described as the way and manner people of all times clothe themselves. One of the basic needs of man is clothing. Others are food and shelter. Fashion represents the popular style of cloths, jewelry, hats, shoes, bags, footwear, makeups, hairdressing, and costumes, etc., and the general dressing of a particular time, place, and people. Dressing has become a major distinguishing factor among people of diverse cultures. It should also be noted that people of different cultures often dress in line with the prevailing climatic conditions of their physical environment. Those who live in places where the temperature is cold most of the year will often dress in thick clothing, covering most parts of their body while those that dwell in areas with predominantly warm temperature will put on light clothing, not covering most parts of their body. Fashions also differ in terms of age, occupation and social status, and most times the people we refer to as celebrities tend to lead the way in new fashion styles and designs.

Fashion has gone beyond mere dressing to personal branding. Knowing fully well that people are often addressed the way they are dressed, fashion is fast becoming a matter of personal identity. Most celebrities are now much more interested in what they put on and the person that designed it than in what they do in their fields of endeavor. In modern fashion, it is those who are naturally gifted or who have been adequately trained in textile designs and decoration that determine the kind of materials or styles that people wear. The French and Italians have proven to be the best fashion stylists and designers around the world. What is trending in the global fashion industry is that clothing can be designed in one country, produced in another country, and sold in a different country. It is also pertinent to note that, with advancements in technology, clothing is becoming standardized so that the same designs and styles can be used by everybody everywhere; making it easier for companies to mass-produce in one location and ship to various locations at the same time. Although clothing designs are done mostly in France, Spain, Italy, the UK and the United States, most textile factories are located in India, China, Pakistan, Mexico, Indonesia, Taiwan, Bangladesh, and Vietnam, etc.

The fashion industry employs tens of millions of the global labor force as it has different layers of production activities ranging from fabric design to textile manufacturing, style creation, clothing production, tailoring or sewing, storage, shipping, marketing, retailing, etc. A greater portion of global economic output can be attributable to the fashion industry as well. Organizations that process cotton, fiber, textile, leather, fur and wool are within the fashion industry as well. Organizations that design, manufacture, distribute and sell clothing materials are part of the fashion industry. Organizations that promote, advertise and hold modeling and fashion shows are also part and parcel of the fashion industry. People who sew in their shops and firms that sell sewing materials are also operating in the fashion industry.

Just like the food or agricultural industry, the fashion industry makes a whole lot of money each year and, therefore, contributes immensely towards global economic growth by providing jobs to individuals and income to families, providing a platform for cultural exchange, providing revenue to government through corporate taxes, import and export duties as well as income taxes from employees, ensuring that one of the basic needs of man is met in the most trendy way, and making sure that clothing materials are distributed according to the needs of various parts of the world, from the point of production to the point of consumption. Notable among global clothing companies are Christian Dior, Nike and Inditex. In the United States of America, the top clothing companies include Nike, Adidas, Ralph Lauren, Old Navy, GAP, Levi Strauss & Co, Michael Kors, Coach, Tommy Hilfiger, American Eagle Outfitters, and Under Armour. These companies rake in billions of dollars annually from clothing to footwear, perfumes, ear rings, necklaces, bangles, bracelets, handbags, ties, socks, caps, hats, synthetic hair, hair care products, beauty accessories, scarfs, masks, under wears, winter coats, hand gloves, wedding gowns, religious outfits, academic gowns, costumes, military service uniforms, other professional uniforms, school uniforms, sports garments and accessories, etc. Fashion is redefining the global socio-cultural interaction and making the world one global community. For example, the Levi Strauss jeans is won by people of different ages, races, color, gender, regions, religions, political orientations, economic status, and professional affiliations. It has helped to equalize everyone everywhere. This is what fashion can do!

Organizations under the Pillar of Fashion are also business organizations and must be well organized and managed in a bid to actualize their objectives of ensuring that men, women, boys, girls, and children around the world get the clothing they need, at the time and place they need it, and at the price they can afford.

8. Organizations under the Pillar of Religion

Religious organizations, also known as faith-based organizations, are organizations that handle spiritual and supernatural aspects of the human society. They help to nurture people's beliefs, establish moral standards, and ensure that human beings maintain continuous interaction with the supernatural. Almost all religions believe in the existence of a Supreme being known as God, and that He is the force behind creation, procreation, invention, discovery, agricultural production, healing, miracles, signs, and wonders, etc. They also believe that life itself is a gift from God and emphasize on the need to guard it jealously. It is true that people have created more problems in the world under the guise of religion. It is also a fact that more lives have been destroyed in this world as a result of what people refer to as religious crises. Some people still hide under the aegis of religion to hate, insult, fight, injure, abduct, rape, torture, kill, enslave, imprison, and discriminate against other people. Some religions criticize and condemn other religions while others simply want to eliminate other religions and their adherents. Yet all religions preach love, peace, unity, and the sanctity of human life. So, religion is not what divides or destroys us; it is bad people that hide behind religion to destroy humanity. They achieve this evil by poisoning the hearts and minds of their listeners and followers, creating enmity between them and the rest of the world. The truth is whenever religion is used as a tool for political agenda, it becomes toxic.

The pillar of religion is not for destruction rather it is for emancipation. It helps people to gain insight into supernatural benefits which can manifest in the form of divine inspiration needed for incredible discoveries, witty inventions, and unlimited innovations. I have already stated earlier that knowledge is the force required to break through the challenges of life and take advantage of existing opportunities in a bid to get to our destiny in life. It was also established that knowledge comes in two forms - information and inspiration. I also presented the fact that inspiration carries more weight, as much as 70%, than information which carries the rest 30%. Inspiration is, therefore, needed most if one wants to make it great in life. Most discoveries, inventions and innovations come by way of divine inspiration and instruction. Inspiration gives you what information can't, keeps you going when information can't, and takes you where information can't. Information is a natural force; inspiration is a supernatural force.

When religious organizations exert the right influence on their people, empower them with the right knowledge, and reposition them as solution providers rather than attention seekers, the world will experience an unprecedented release of divine inspiration needed to meet the ever changing needs of the human race. The more we deny the need for spiritual renewal, the more we distance ourselves from the unique opportunity to meet the needs of the society. There is a greater power that keeps the entire universe in constant equilibrium; makes the sun to shine, makes the rain to fall, makes our crops and plants to grow and produce fruits and vegetables, makes the plants to produce enough oxygen required to sustain human life, causes the winds to blow, causes the moon and the stars to appear at night, and ensures that rivers neither dry up nor overflow the entire human race. There is a greater power that also ensures that the mountains do not collapse on us, ensures the earth does not fall out of space, and keeps the solar system in place, etc. That greater power is God. To deny the existence of God is to deny the existence of life.

There are numerous religions around the world ranging from Judaism to Christianity, Islam, Hinduism, Paganism, Confucianism, Buddhism, Shintoism, Sikhism, Taoism, Zoroastrianism, Jainism, and Baha'ism, etc. These religions form organizations such as synagogues, churches, mosques, temples, shrines, and other places of worship and have hundreds of millions of people in membership. Some of them also establish schools, banks, publishing houses, parks, hospitals, and other institutions to serve the needs of their members and the public.

Religious organizations must be well organized and properly managed to fulfill their objective of ministering to the spiritual needs of their adherents and making them productive members of the larger society. Religion cannot be used as an instrument of destruction to the very society it seeks to preserve. Everybody must not accept your religious ideas or views. This does not in any way mean that they hate you as an individual. It simply means that they have the right to choose what to believe and what not to believe and you must respect that right. All religions must preach and practice love, peace, unity, freedom, happiness, and high moral values. Our places of worship must be devoid of hate, disunity, and acrimony. Those in leadership positions in our religious organizations have a responsibility to make this happen.

9. Organizations under the Pillar of Arts & Crafts

Art is the use of skill and imagination in the production of things of beauty while craft is an occupation requiring special skill. This system involves all activities that need both artistic and practical skills such as pottery, weaving, jewelry making, sculpting (e.g. designing statues and tomb stones), drawing and painting, carving and molding, etc. It involves the use of wood, stone, metal, glass, plastic, paper, calabash, raffia, bamboos, and fabric in creating designs for decoration, beautification, demarcation, and commemoration. As pointed out earlier, it reflects in such areas as carving, painting, sculpturing, photography, digital graphics, and sign writing. Carving is the act of making an object or pattern by cutting away material from wood or stone. Painting is the act of using pens and paints of different colors to produce images on a paper, cloth, walls or other materials such as glass, metal, plastic, etc. Sculpturing is the act of making a solid object of artistic value by molding or shaping with paper, cement, clay, etc. Photography is the act of capturing images with still or video cameras. Digital graphics is the act of designing images, pictures, schematics, and projects with the aid of computer programs while sign-writing is the act of designing signposts, billboards, etc., with pen, paint or printer.

The work of arts and crafts are usually in display in public places such as parks, gardens, museums, banks, libraries, schools, airports, hotels, conference halls, government offices, bridges, bus stops, train stations, state boundaries, sports stadiums, golf clubs, radio/TV stations, community centers, places of worship, business showrooms, art theaters, hospitals, etc. The field of arts and crafts can simply be described as creativity exemplified. This is an area that shows the level of natural skills human beings possess. It shows man's ability to create something amazing from something of little or no value. An ordinary piece of wood can be converted to an object of aesthetic beauty by the work of arts and crafts. Things taken from a junk yard can be redesigned into artistic masterpieces by crafts men and women who are naturally gifted in designs. A human face can be carved on a stone or painted on a wall in such a way as not to keep you in doubt about the person whose image is being depicted. The work of arts and crafts are used to preserve and promote cultural histories, capture and cultivate current knowledge, as well as present and project future trends of the society.

There are numerous organizations operating within the pillar of arts and crafts. Examples of such organizations are American Craft Council, The Center for Art in Wood, United States Artists, World Crafts Council, The Society of Arts and Crafts of Boston, American Art Pottery Association, etc. The amount of money that exchanges hands at international art exhibitions points to the fact that this system of the world has a lot of potentials for those who are naturally endowed with designing abilities. We have heard of a single piece of artwork being traded for tens of millions of dollars. Works of art readily become items of business due to the high demand for original art creations by naturally gifted members of the society.

Apart from big organizations that prepare, protect and promote arts and crafts men and women, as well as organize art exhibitions, individual artists or a group of them can form art and craft enterprises to display and market their works to members of the public. Those who are into designing jewelries and crafting tombstones are good examples of arts and crafts organizations where people walk in to admire and patronize incredible works of art. Children's toys are also good examples of the work of arts and crafts. Art and craft organizations do rake in billions of dollars annually from around the world. People who are naturally gifted in these areas should rise up and begin to contribute to the beauty and overall development of society with their various works of arts and crafts. Just as any other form of organization, arts and crafts organizations must be well organized and effectively managed to provide the designs required to make the world a better place for all of us. We live in a world where everybody has something of value to contribute and when we exchange what we have with what we need, everyone becomes complete and the world becomes better. Employment opportunities are also created when individual skills are tapped to establish organizations while income is generated to meet other needs of the society. When those who are endowed with unique capabilities in the pillar of arts and crafts unleash their potentials, the world gains in many more ways.

10. Organizations under the Pillar of the Media

The media is one of the major institutions of the world. Also known as the mass media, it is the system for communicating information to a large number of persons at the same time. Radio and television broadcasting, newspaper and magazine publication, and billboards and the Internet are forms of mass information dissemination under the pillar of the media. The media assists in determining the direction of events in the society by shaping people's thoughts and influencing their actions either positively or negatively. It is through the media that important information concerning the policies, programs, and projects of both public as well as private organizations are communicated for proper understanding and timely response.

The media industry of the twenty-first century is unique in the sense that it combines high level technology with vast experience to offer world-class information to a global audience. For example, the events taking place in Syria in the Middle East can now be transmitted live to an audience in faraway Sydney in Australia in the form of real-time motion pictures via the Satellite. In a similar vein, a live TV show taking place in the City of Los Angeles, California can now be watched by a family in faraway Lagos, Nigeria through the cable network. In both a fascinating as well as challenging manner, the media has succeeded in 'globalizing' the world.

The social media is now challenging the traditional media by blazing the trail in real-time information dissemination. Individuals with smartphones can now audio-tape and video-record events as they occur, upload them on YouTube, Facebook, Instagram or Twitter and send to hundreds of millions of people across the globe through a network of friendly relationships. Right now, Facebook has at least two and half billion subscribers around the world and with a click of the button on a computer keyboard, information can be sent to this number of people at the same time. This is incredible! Debates have been generated on the social media concerning serious social and political issues and various groups with divergent views have often emerged from such debates. The social media has become the most active forum to sell your ideas, gather needed support, form a movement, and launch a protest on any social or political issue that interests you. It has become the new platform for socio-political change.

Media organizations appear in three different forms: media enterprises, media institutes, and media associations. Media institutes are educational institutions where people are trained in mass communication and journalism to be qualified to work in media organizations. Media associations are formed by workers and operators for their protection and promotion. However, media enterprises are business organizations formed for the dissemination of information to the public. They are involved in producing and presenting news, marketing programs, public relations activities, advertising programs, public affairs research, as well as political debates and are usually the link between the government and the governed. Through a series of merger and acquisition exercises, it is now very clear that only six media organizations control about 90% of America's media industry. The six media giants are Comcast, News Corp, Walt Disney, Viacom, Time Warner, and CBS. Major television channels, newspaper houses, satellite stations, public entertainment studios, and information centers are owned by these big six and they raise billions of dollars in revenue annually. Outside of the United States, the British Sky Broadcasting and the WPP are media giants in their own right; often covering media operations in the whole of Europe and beyond.

General information is also available online. The Internet has various search engines where almost unlimited information can be generated on any topic of concern ranging from science to geography, history, health, fashion, politics, economy, religion, sports, and entertainment, etc. Notable among these search engines are Google, Bing, Ask, AOL, Wikipedia, etc. As hundreds of millions of people around the world upload information of any kind daily, these search engines make them accessible to other people who might need them for research, information, education, and entertainment, etc.

Seeing how important the pillar of the media is to the shaping of public opinions, actions, and reactions, media organizations must be properly organized and effectively managed to be able to actualize their main objective of providing the right information to the right people at the right time and in the right location. It has already been established that knowledge is a force for pulling down challenges and exploring opportunities. It should also be recalled that information and inspiration are the two sources of knowledge. People usually take actions based on the information available to them. If we expect them to act in the best interests of the society, we must ensure that our media organizations disseminate the right information at all times.

11. Organizations under the Pillar of Entertainment

Entertainment is a unique system in the world but often erroneously grouped alongside the mass media. The pillar of entertainment involves that aspect of the society that provides entertainment through music, movies, dances, jokes/comedies, drama and so forth. Most times different forms of entertainment can be engaged to provide information and education to various segments of the society. Entertainment is the platform for amusement, excitement, and relaxation in a bid to calm the nerves and ease the tension arising from physical, intellectual, and emotional stress and strain. Life in the 21st century is loaded with numerous challenges that often result to physical exhaustion, intellectual exasperation, and emotional explosion as we struggle to make ends meet. This is the reason why vacation is so important in our lives. Vacation affords us the opportunity to break the chain of work routine, overcome professional fatigue, quench the heat in the human brain, calm the nerves in our muscles, slow down the excessive flow of blood in and out of our heart, and rejuvenate the entire body in readiness for the next set of activities. Vacation to nature reserves, zoos, museums, amusement parks, music concerts, movie theaters, and exquisite hotels and gardens offer us the opportunity for entertainment. To live life without any form of entertainment is to die slowly, daily.

The sources of entertainment have already been enumerated as music, movies, dances, jokes/comedies, and drama, etc. Music can be described as sounds arranged in a certain manner that is pleasant and exciting to the ears and conveys melody and meaning. It combines both vocal and instrumental sounds to provide rhythms, notes, melodies, and songs that relax our body, excite our soul, and uplift our spirit. Good music is like food to the soul. Music has a very strong appeal to people and is often played whenever people gather. Performing musicians are, therefore, very popular and tend to exert so much influence on their fans. Our late international pop stars like Michael Jackson, Whitney Houston, and Elvis Presley are good examples of the kind of influence musicians do have on the society. In fact, music has made more celebrities in the world than all other professions combined.

Music and dancing go hand in hand. Dancing entails the movement of parts of our body in response to music. It involves shaking, jumping, clapping, swinging, nodding, blinking, boxing, stomping, twisting, twerking, and every other physical movement you can think of. Our young people, the millennial, have taken dancing to a different level. A visit to some of the teen music and dancing competitions will confirm this. A musical video that lacks good dancing steps and moves may not sell as much as the ones that do have them. Certain musicians are often associated with certain dancing steps. When kids want to mimic Michael Jackson, they simply display his unique dancing steps. Even though dancing has now become much of a physical exercise, it is meant to entertain us by helping us to relax as we appreciate the unique skills certain individuals possess through their dancing steps. When we are eventually moved to join in the dancing, the excitement it provides can be long lasting. Trust me!

A movie, on the other hand, is a series of motion pictures recorded with sound to tell a specific story. A movie can be based on a true story or a fiction and can be shown in movie theaters, on television screens, or through the Internet. Movies serve as a platform for conveying valuable information through entertainment. Movies provide physical pictures that create a mental challenge which often results to new inspiration for providing needed solution. Good movies make lasting positive impact while bad movies make everlasting negative impact. Apart from music icons, movie stars are among the most popular human beings on earth. The amount of money made through music and movies runs into hundreds of billions of dollars every year and those who own and manage music and movie organizations are among the richest guys in the world. The United States of America still has one of the best rated movie and music industries in the world. Each year, scores of movies are produced in Hollywood, and watched around the world. Surprisingly, the second-best rated movie industry in the world in terms of the number, content and revenue generation potential is Nollywood, the Nigerian version of Hollywood. Bollywood of India is also among the best. Through movies, gifted actors and actresses perform specific roles to tell a story and to reveal the true message which the script writer seeks to convey to the society. Movies convey such messages that are either historical, cultural, spiritual, emotional, criminal, social, economic, ecological, or political in nature and help to not only entertain but also to inform, educate, motivate as well as incite and instigate.

Entertainment organizations include music studios, movie theaters, Actors Guild, music and movie production enterprises, and promoters, as well as movie or music institutes. Those who produce musical instruments are also in the entertainment industry. Those who write the scripts, act in the movies, record the movies, sponsor/produce the movies, provide the locations, prepare the costumes, select the actors, provide the audio and lighting, as well as those who provide one form of service or the other to the crew, are all operators in the entertainment industry. Entertainment organizations must be well organized and effectively managed to realize their ultimate objective of providing amusement, excitement, and relaxation that rejuvenate the soul and reinvigorate the body in readiness for another series of activities.

11. Organizations under the Pillar of Sports

Sports involves physical effort and skillful display by individuals either for pleasure or prize. These days sporting is used as a major instrument of competition between individuals, groups, institutions, communities, states, nations, and continents. It can also be used to assess physical superiority among nations, unfortunately. In each sporting activity, there is usually a set of standards that individuals must attain using their physical skill, natural stamina, and mental stability often built through years of physical training and muscle stretching. Sports competitions are held in specific locations, guided by special regulations, and moderated by unbiased experts. There are different kinds of sporting activities around the world ranging from games to races, cycling to motoring, swimming to skiing, jumping to gymnastics, boxing to wrestling, karate to kickboxing, tennis to taekwondo, golf to cricket, baseball to volleyball, football to basketball, and soccer to rugby, etc.

Apart from commerce, sporting is another strong instrument for peace and unity in the world. It has also become an instrument with which to measure the comparative strength of nations. Both the Federated International Football Associations (FIFA), and the International Olympic Committee (IOC) have become powerful institutions in the world due to the role they play in organizing annual, bi-annual, and quadrennial sporting competitions among nations of the world. The quadrennial Olympic competitions not only showcase the various sporting talents in different nations but have also become an opportunity for individual nations to discover, train, and equip them to stardom. International sports competitions have also enabled hosting nations to upgrade their local sporting facilities to meet international standards. Sports stars are among the celebrities around the world. If not for sports, the world would not have known such personalities as Michael Jordan, Mike Tyson, Mohammed Ali, Venus Williams, Serena Williams, Tiger Woods, Hulk Hogan, Tom Brady, Michael Phelps, Magic Johnson, Kolbe Bryant, Lebron James, Steve Curry, Maria Sharapova, David Beckham, Diego Maradona, Amando Pele, Roger Federer, Lionell Merci, Christiano Ronaldo, Roger Miller, and a host of others. Successful sportsmen and women suddenly become role models to upcoming sports stars as well as young enthusiasts as they are always held in high esteem.

In sports, physically talented people display their expertise to a cheering audience by combining natural skills with years of training to perform and attain extraordinary physical feats in the area of jumping, swimming, running, skating, skiing, boxing, wrestling, cycling, motoring, gymnastics, golfing, tennis, football, baseball, volleyball, and basketball, etc. Time after time we see old records broken and new ones created as ordinary men and women achieve extraordinary results through stretching their muscles, expanding their strengths, and increasing their stress limit to beat their opponents and win laurels that ultimately attract them fame and fortune.

There are various organizations or institutions that work collectively to groom our talented sports men and women to stardom. There are numerous sports academies, private coaching managers, sports councils, and sporting associations. Most communities have robust sporting facilities where young people with identifiable sports talents can visit and practice for self-development. Various organizations and communities do organize sports competitions where contestants are given the opportunity to showcase their talents and win trophies. Apart from being opportunities for competition, sporting events also double as sources of entertainment and oftentimes lumped together with the pillar of entertainment. But we now know that sporting is a distinct industry with its operators: participants, managers, regulators, sponsors, and other stakeholders. Other organizations also use sports celebrities to promote their products, services, programs, or ideas.

Looking at the amount of money spent in hosting sporting events either at the local level or global stage, as well as the huge salary paid to sports stars, there is no doubt that the pillar of sports has what it takes to contribute to overall societal development. Sports organizations must, therefore, be properly organized and effectively managed to discover sports talents, provide the right training and equipment, and prepare them to compete with others for gold as well as entertain the others for good. Our society will be incomplete without sports and everything that go with it.

Other organizations

There are other organizations that are worthy of mention. Some of them are what I refer to as social organizations. These are philanthropic, charity, or non-governmental organizations which identify certain challenges in the society, attract membership, and mobilize resources to take care of those challenges most effectively. There are millions of them around the world today. Some are operating at national levels while others are operating at international levels to ameliorate most of the numerous challenges facing our physical, political, social, and ecological environment. However, their activities still fall under one or more of the Pillars of the Earth. Examples are Habitat for Humanity, Clinton Global Initiative, Feeding America, United Way, Wounded Warriors Project, The Red Cross, Rockefeller Foundation, Bill & Melinda Gates Foundation, Ford Foundation, GAVI Alliance, International Rescue Committee, Save the Children, Christian Aid, Salvation Army, etc.

Another form of organization is the one I refer to as Regional or International Organizations. There are various organizations that connect a few nations or all the nations of the world for the purpose of solving certain common challenges which can be economical, political, religious, medical, or social in nature. Examples of regional organizations are the North America Free Trade Association (NAFTA), the North Atlantic Trade Organization (NATO), the European Economic Community (EEC), the European Union (EU), the African Union (AU), etc. International organizations, on the other hand, are organizations jointly formed by all the nations of the world to solve common problems that plague the entire universe. Prominent among such organizations is the United Nations Organization (UNO). There are numerous other organizations that act as extensions of the United Nations. Some of them are UNICEF, UNDP, FAO, WTO, UNESCO, WHO, IAEA, ISO, UNFPA, UNEP, UNOPS, ICC, ICJ, etc. We also have Amnesty International, Transparency International, and other global organizations that work so hard to ensure that nations as well as individual members of the global community are held accountable for their actions and in-actions towards promoting global peace, security, justice and progress.

Each of these organizations has specific objectives or a group of objectives and the only way these objectives can be actualized is when these organizations are properly organized and effectively managed.

The management or leadership of these organizations must have the capacity to articulate the real objectives, possess the ability to mobilize the right resources, and express the capability to utilize those resources in the attainment of set objectives in the most effective and efficient manner possible.

CHAPTER 4

ORGANIZATIONS ARE VERY IMPORTANT TO THE SOCIETY

In chapter 3, I presented a lot of facts to show how economic organizations directly or remotely impact other activities that take place around the world. Whatever happens in the rest of the pillars of the earth must be brought to the Pillar of Commerce and Industry for it to be appreciated, appraised, and patronized. Every sector of the society needs funds to thrive and the only place to raise this money is in the Pillar of Commerce and Industry. To achieve this need for funding, every result made in any pillar must be converted into a product, service, program, or idea to be exchanged for cash. This is the reason why music, movie and sports stars are as wealthy as captains of industries. Pharmaceutical companies, top medical specialists, fashion experts, media companies, entertainment producers, scientific inventors, commercial agriculturists, arts and crafts professionals, top religious leaders, creative educationists, as well as renowned political figures are also among the financially stable because they have a way of commercializing their expertise. Based on the foregoing, further discussions on organizations will revolve around economic organizations that operate under the Pillar of Commerce and Industry.

The importance of organizations to the society cannot be overemphasized. We need organizations just as we need each other. The importance of organizations to the society shall be discussed under the following headings:

a) organizations serve as the platform for expressing individual abilities, talents, dreams, and destinies.
b) organizations provide an opportunity for synergy.
c) organizations create employment opportunities for the people.
d) organizations produce the products and services needed by households to thrive and for institutions to operate.
e) organizations make global exchange possible.
f) organizations increase value to their owners and yield revenue to the government.
g) organizations encourage innovation by utilizing modern tools in production.
h) organizations contribute to the overall development of the society by meeting some of the infrastructural needs.
i) Organizations ensure the dreams of their founders continue to live long after they are gone.
j) organizations facilitate the transfer of knowledge from generation to generation.

Details will be presented below:

Organizations serve as the platform for expressing individual abilities, talents, dreams, and destinies.

In the first chapter of this book, I established the fact that organizations are extensions of individuals. Organizations don't just emanate from the vacuum. They are born as part of individual's abilities, talents, dreams and destinies and the need to reach more people and meet more needs in more locations. Every organization is someone's idea, and every idea is geared towards providing a solution to a preexisting need or perceived challenge in the neighborhood, community, or larger society. There is a limit to what an individual can achieve at a particular time. Through organizations, individuals can express their dreams, reveal their talents, exhibit their skills, showcase their abilities, and fulfill their destinies in better and higher ways than they would on individual basis.

For example, when a doctor establishes a hospital, his ultimate intention is to not only use his medical skill for the benefit of himself and his immediate family but also for the benefit of the entire community and beyond. The hospital as an organization, has provided the doctor with an opportunity to extend his abilities beyond his family. A doctor without a hospital is like a vehicle without a seat. The vehicle moves, no doubt, but does not solve the problem of transportation; the reason for its existence in the first place. Without organizations, individuals' abilities will be limited in scope as well as in benefits.

Organizations provide an opportunity for synergy.

An organization is usually the idea of an individual, but it involves the contribution of more than that individual. Organizations provide the opportunity to pull together people with different talents, skills, and experiences in a bid to meet the varying needs of the society. It has been established that the result of the combined effort of individuals is usually far greater than the summation of the result of their individual efforts. This is known as synergy! Working together as a team produces more results any time, any day. This means that without organizations, less and less results will be produced by the society.

When people come together in organizations, there is a new energy released for greater results; old ideas are challenged, new ideas flow, new methods emerge, more solutions are achieved, and greater results are recorded. Teamwork is one of the major benefits of organizations. Two good heads are usually better than one. No man is an island. No single individual has all the skills and expertise needed to solve problems. When people come together in organizations, they complement each other and make up for whatever area of weakness each of them might have. This creates the opportunity for improved results. Through organizations, diverse talents are brought under one roof for the greater good of the society.

An individual may have an idea but lack the funds necessary to turn it into a solution. Another individual may have the funds but lack the idea to put it into a productive use. Working independently, these individuals may end up as failures. But when they decide to pull their resources together to form an organization, amazing things can happen. Another example would help to buttress the synergy created through organizations. An individual that knows how to sing but cannot play musical instruments cannot make music and another individual that can play musical instruments but cannot sing cannot also make music. But when these two individuals come together, great music can be made. This is synergy! I can, therefore, conclude by stating that organizations are 'synergistic relationships.' Successful individuals never operate in isolation. They often tap from other people's resources such as ideas, time, money, energy, and, above all, talents.

Organizations create employment opportunities for the people

Whenever organizations are established, opportunities are created for job seekers. The person or group of persons that started an organization may be good in certain aspects of the organization's process and not in the other. To make up for this lapse, opportunities are created for other people to be employed to fill the gap. For example, when two engineers come together to start an engineering-based enterprise, they would need other people to take care of the accounting system, the customer/public relations aspect, the human resources functions, the marketing activities as well as the secretarial and administrative functions. This is the reason why entrepreneurs are the greatest job creators in the world. Any society that wants jobs created should simply initiate and implement policies and programs that encourage and sustain entrepreneurship. Some large organizations employ thousands of people who participate in producing products or providing services that meet the needs of their customers and that of the society at large.

Organizations provide employment opportunities for individuals who do not have the tools to go into entrepreneurship themselves. Not many people have the boldness to take the kind of risks involved in entrepreneurship. Some people rather have the skill and experience needed to add value to existing organizations. The unemployment rate of a nation reflects economic contraction or expansion as well as the ability and willingness of entrepreneurs to start up new enterprises, or for operators to expand existing ones. When new organizations are not being established and existing ones are not being expanded, jobs cannot be created. Worst still, when new organizations are not being established and existing ones are being downsized, jobs will be lost, and the unemployment rate would soar. Entrepreneurial skills are never in short supply in any society. What we lack is the right economic environment to inspire entrepreneurship. This includes availability of investment funds, low interest rates for loans, institutions that assist entrepreneurs with relevant information and guidance, and availability of the infrastructural requirements of the enterprise as well as ready market for its products and services. Unemployment is a huge challenge to any society and the only way to reduce it is to encourage the establishment of new organizations or the expansion of existing ones. This can be achieved through the establishment of deliberate policies and relevant programs which provide organizations with an enabling environment to thrive as well as support individuals with the resources they need to go into entrepreneurship. When small organizations expand, which is often the case, more employment opportunities are created. When employment opportunities are created, people are better positioned to utilize their talents in contributing to societal well-being. This is the whole essence of forming organizations.

Organizations provide needed products and services

If you look around, you will discover that most of the products we use today are produced by organizations and most of the services we enjoy are equally provided by organizations. There is a limit do what an individual can do. Let us assume that the manufacturing of automobiles is done by individuals, how many cars do you think will be produced in a year? Probably five by one of them multiplied by all of them, say 1000 producers. Cumulatively, we will have about 5000 vehicles, far below its annual demand in the State of California alone, here in the United States of America. The same way it is with other numerous products. When people come together in organizations, new ideas are generated that lead to product improvement, and mass production is achieved through automation. No one individual has the monopoly of knowledge and no single individual can operate all the machines in a factory all by himself. Other people must be brought in to assist. As new people are engaged in organizations, new and better ideas are generated leading to the introduction of new products and the improvement of existing processes and products. This scenario ultimately yields greater value to the final consumers. Mass production has been known to lower operational costs as well as unit prices.

The principle of 'two good heads are better than one' is leading professionals into partnering with their colleagues to form organizations. Skilled laborers and technical contractors are also collaborating to form organizations. People are becoming more comfortable dealing with corporate contractors than individual technicians. The presumption is that the combined effort of two people will ultimately yield greater results than that of one of them.

Just imagine how airplanes will be manufactured in a desired quantity if there were no organizations. What about rockets, ships, submarines, computers, televisions, air conditioners, washing machines, refrigerators, microwaves, smart phones, power plants, refineries, radios, and DVD players, etc.? The list goes on and on. The improvements we see in the products and services we consume daily have been made possible by organizations. Organizations play a major role in ensuring that products are in sufficient quantity and quality to meet the needs and demands of the society.

Organizations make global exchange possible

Just as individuals possess unique talents that are somewhat different from the one possessed by others, nations also possess unique resources that are lacking in other nations. These resources can be natural mineral, human, or agricultural in nature. This situation creates the need for exchange between nations; the basis for international trade or global commerce. Due to the intricacies of global trade, it takes organizations to move products from one nation to another.

Let us take a farmer for instance. A single farmer in Southern California can only produce enough to feed his family and then display any excess for sale at the front of his yard. This is what happens under subsistence farming where nearly every member of the community has a little piece of land to farm on and very little harvest resulting from it. With civilization and industrialization, many people left the farm to attend schools and later work in factories and warehouses. This diminished the number of farmers and the amount of land farmed; resulting in scarcity of agricultural produce which is in very high demand. This scenario necessitated the need for a group of organizations to be established for commercial farming and processing of agricultural produce for mass consumption. Now the agricultural produce grown in Southern California can be sold in faraway Manhattan, New York, where there may be no farmers at all. By this exchange, New Yorkers can enjoy the fruits and vegetables they cannot produce while Southern California receives the cash revenue it needs to purchase industrial processing machines from New York factories. This is exchange! It would have been very difficult for a single farmer to engage in such a complicated transaction but with organizations, the entire process is simplified.

When we extend this scenario beyond the United States, we see how scientific products manufactured in Ohio are used in laboratories in Ghana while the cassava pellets from Nigerian farms are used to feed livestock in Texas. Organizations make this exchange possible. The reason is simple. As one organization produces, another purchases, another ships, another clears, another transports, another stores in a warehouse and sells in bulk to wholesalers who resell to the retailers, who then sell to the final consumers. It is a chain of activities between the original producer and the final consumer, creating jobs along the way and generating income to stakeholders. This is what is called the economic value chain. With this scenario, the chocolate cookies produced in the United States can now be enjoyed in Cot d'Ivoire, West Africa where the cocoa paste was imported from in the first place. By this arrangement, American companies get what they need for chocolate production while kids in Cot d'Ivoire get the cookies they want for consumption; making everyone a winner. If organizations are not involved, it would be very difficult, if not impossible, for what is produced in one part of the world to be enjoyed in other parts where they are lacking.

Natural resources are unevenly distributed around the world. There are some natural resources that are in higher demand than others but are not found in abundant quantity in all the nations of the world. The only way such resources would be enjoyed by all is through exchange. One good example is petroleum and natural gas. Petroleum products are consumed by most of the global population daily in different ways. Many organizations are involved in the entire process of ensuring that these products reach every nook and cranny of the world as the scarcity of these essential products will not only devastate the industrial sector of nations but also destroy the entire process of their economic development. Just imagine a situation where Americans do not have access to enough gasoline for their automobile needs or a situation where their gas stoves suddenly run out of gas. This is better imagined than experienced! And if those organizations which are involved in ensuring that enough petroleum and natural gas products are moved from areas of production to areas of consumption fail to function effectively, the situation can be chaotic, to say the least. Organizations operate day and night to ensure that the economic chain, from production to consumption, does not break down. While most people are asleep, others are awake to ensure that the machines keep running and the vehicles keep moving to produce and distribute the goods and services that make their lives better on a daily basis.

Organizations increase value for their owners and yield revenue to government

As organizations provide goods and services to the society, they also raise revenue from it in exchange. This income is used to run the organization while the excess accrues to the owners or initiators of that organization as profit. For example, five people get together to form an organization to produce chocolate and milk beverage drink. They pull their financial resources together, take a bank loan to make up for the difference, rent a factory and purchase machinery, engage their skill and experience and hire others to make up for the needed manpower, purchase raw materials, set up the production layout, engage in aggressive marketing programs, and commence operations. After the items are produced, salesmen move into the market, customers place orders, deliveries are made, and income is generated.

From the income that comes in, bills are paid which include wages and salaries, heating and lighting, telephone and Internet, rent and logistics, and part of the bank loans and accrued interest. Raw materials are also purchased for the next batch of production while marketing programs are intensified to attract more customers and sustain existing ones. Whatever amount that remains at the end of the business cycle, usually a twelve-month period, or every quarter as the case may be, is what is referred to as the gross profit or net income of the business. From this amount, the organization pays corporate tax of between 25% and 40% and returns the rest as the net profit available for the owners of the business (shareholders) to share among themselves as the return on their investment (ROI).

As customers increase, more orders are placed leading to more production. More production means more expenditure on raw materials, wages, heating, lighting, logistics, etc., which tends to reduce the net profits in the short run but greatly increases it in the long run. To achieve this expansion in operations, the owners/investors may decide to plow back the entire profit from the last business cycle instead of accumulating more loan instruments from the bank. The resultant expansion from this low-cost capital ensures greater return on investment over time. This is the reason why successful business owners are among the richest people on earth. Business owners are also well respected by the society because the organizations they help establish end up creating needed jobs, providing or importing needed products and services, and raising all the tax incomes needed by government to execute infrastructural projects and fund other vital programs for the development and security of the nation.

Organizations encourage innovation by utilizing modern tools in production and operations

Innovations and inventions are useless on their own except if they are used to meet existing needs in the society. Manufacturing a super-fast computer with unlimited memory capacity will amount to an effort in futility if organizations do not use it to perform their operations more effectively. So, the only thing that drives innovation is that organizations need them in their efforts to produce better products or provide more excellent services for the society.

The auto industry, for example, has created opportunities for various inventions and innovations in science and technology such as the global positioning system (GPS) and the lane-and-crash control device under the concept of Artificial Intelligence (AI). If automobile organizations refuse to apply these new systems or devices, the inventors will be discouraged from creating more innovations. Also, if our airports fail to use drug detector machines as well as metal detector doors and scanners while checking in passengers and their luggage, the inventors of such technology will see no reason to continue in their research and development efforts. Organizations, therefore, help to sustain innovations by ensuring that the results of such innovations are put into effective use for the benefit of the larger society.

Most individuals can't afford to purchase and use bulldozers, tractors, forklifts, cranes, ships, industrial computers, commercial jets, cargo airplanes, submarines, rockets, and armored tanks, etc. Only big organizations do. If there were no organizations, these pieces of equipment probably would not be in existence today.

Organizations contribute to the overall development of the society

Organizations contribute to the overall growth and development of the society in so many ways. Through what is referred to as cooperate social responsibility, organizations participate actively in the development of their host communities and beyond. Organizations fund education scholarships, job training programs, school building projects, road constructions, environmental sanitation, modern medical equipment to community hospitals, water projects, electricity projects, etc. They also donate to charitable courses such as research efforts for the cure of terminal diseases (which include cancer, HIV/AIDS, diabetes, Hepatitis B, sickle cell anemia, blood clot, heart attack, stroke, spinal injuries, etc.), efforts at ending child hunger and children diseases, research for ending global warming, and research on improving child learning and development, etc.

There are so many ways organizations contribute towards improving our society and general well-being. Some organizations simply register as philanthropic organizations. Examples are the Rockefeller foundation, Ford foundation, The Red Cross, Bill and Melinda Gates Foundation, Clinton Global Initiative, Habitat for Humanity, etc. These organizations raise money and then channel it towards solving a particular problem in the society. Some provide shelter, food and medicine to refugees while others provide similar things to communities devastated by natural disasters such as flood, earth quake, hurricane, fire, tornado, etc. We can't even begin to imagine what would happen if these organizations were not there to assist in these times of utmost need. Death tolls will be on the rise and the suffering of survivors will only multiply. A number of organizations are really helping to solve our common problems and making the world a better place for us all.

Looking at it from another perspective, we can see that organizations create jobs, and jobs yield income to individuals with which they raise their families: feeding, clothing, housing, schooling, etc. Kids that are properly raised end up contributing immensely to the solution of society's myriad of problems. Organizations, therefore, provide endless opportunities for the growth and development of our society.

Organizations ensure the dreams of their founders continue to live long after they are gone

It has already been established that organizations are extensions of individuals. Organizations are established based on the talents and ideas of individuals and the need to reach a greater number of people with the solution coming from those ideas. It is, however, worthy of note that though organizations are products of human ideas, not all ideas lead to the formation of organizations. When highly talented individuals pass on, their talents often disappear with them. The only way to perpetuate those talents is to establish organizations around them. For example, Sir John D. Rockefeller died many decades ago but his legacy lives on through the Rockefeller Foundation which was built on his lifelong principle of philanthropy. Today's kids now know about John D. Rockefeller and tomorrow's kids will most likely know about the man who, without an iota of doubt, was the first billionaire in American history.

Another example is the Ford Motor Company founded by Sir Henry Ford over a century ago. This company has continued to perpetuate the ideas and legacy of the man who believed that automobiles should be within the reach of every member of the society and not just an exclusive reserve of a few wealthy people. Ford Motors has continued to thrive on those same principles long after Henry Ford had passed on. His name will never be forgotten in a hurry. So, if you want your ideas to live on, establish organizations around them. If you want your idea to continue to benefit humanity long after you are gone, establish an organization around it. The organization will not only preserve and promote your ideas but will also position and perpetuate your identity.

When organizations are effectively managed, they can last beyond our imagination. There are actually organizations that have lasted more than a thousand years. Japan seems to have a long list of business enterprises that have been in existence for so many centuries. For example, the Koman company of Japan, which is into hotel business, was established in 717 while Genda Shigyo of Japan as well, which deals on ceremonial paper goods, came into existence in 771. Germany, UK and France have a fair share of companies that have lasted for centuries. In the year 862, Staffelter Hof, a wine company, was established in Germany. Weltenburger, a brewing company, was established in Germany in 1050. In France, Monnaiede Paris was established in 864 to produce mint while Chateau de Goulaine was established in 1000 to produce wine. In the UK, The Royal Mint was established in 886 to produce mint while Otterton Mill was established in 1068. Here in the United States, some of the early organized set-ups were in the area of farming. Examples are Shirley Plantation (1613), Tuttles Red Barn (1632), Field View Farm (1639), Banker's Farm (1642), Emery Farm (1655), and Saunderskill (1680). Hotels and Restaurants were also established long ago which include Seaside Inn (1667), and White Horse Tavern (1673)[15]. Most of these organizations still exist today, some with new names and shapes.

Organizations facilitate the transfer of knowledge from generation to generation

Organizations engage in the training and retraining of their workers to ensure that every member understands and practices the processes and procedures involved in producing products and providing services in the organization. This training exercise helps to extend the original idea or an improved version of it to those who never met the founders of the organization. This is the reason why the concept of Ford cars remains while Ford employees come and go. Organizations develop unique cultures which every new member must adopt or adapt to in a bid to be a part of the team. This form of socialization by interaction helps to pass on the ideas, talents, skills, tasks, procedures, and strategies adopted in the production of the organization's products from one generation to another.

Knowledge is a force with which to overcome challenges, explore opportunities and reach destiny. When knowledge is lost, the society is shortchanged. Imagine a situation where Henry Ford did not establish the Ford Motor Company to teach other people how to manufacture automobiles, his death in 1947 would have been the end of Ford cars. Fortunately, he did! The people he thought, went ahead to teach other people and today we still have the Ford Motor company producing one of the best automobiles in the United States and around the world.

Coincidentally, all we learn in school are other people's ideas written down in books and taught within the environment of an academic organization. Educational institutions ensure that experts are brought together to pass on knowledge from one generation to another so that development is sustained, and the society perpetuated. Parents cannot teach their children all they need to know to be prepared to contribute meaningfully to the well-being of the society. Educational organizations must continue to be an effective platform for the transfer of knowledge from one generation to another generation. Improvements in the form of innovation cannot happen without new knowledge. New knowledge comes through new ideas from ordinary women and men like you and me. Let's get to work, America!

CHAPTER 5

ORGANIZATIONS DO GROW

Nearly all organizations start small but they are not meant to remain forever small. They just have to grow just as human beings do. Towards the end of the last chapter, we saw how organizations ensure that the ideals of their founders live on. This is basically achieved through growth. So, in this chapter, attempt shall be made at identifying, as well as discussing, some of those factors that are responsible for the growth, development, and sustainability of organizations. Why do some organizations last for several centuries while others are struggling to survive the first few months of their existence? This subject is very critical considering the overwhelming statistics on the failure rate of new businesses in the United States and around the world. It is one thing to start an organization and it is another thing to make it last.

I believe that no individual starts on enterprise with the hope that it will either remain small or die away. There is always the hope that someday the enterprise will grow bigger. Growth is, therefore, one of the main purposes of every enterprise, whether the initiators express it or not. We experience this growth as we see the number of organizational members increase based on the increased activities stemming from increased patronage of its products and services. As organizations effectively meet the needs of their customers, more and more customers are attracted. This consequently increases demand.

As the organization works to meet the new demand, more workers are hired, more equipment purchased, more raw materials ordered, large warehouses needed, factory space expanded, new branches opened and so on. So, the only way organizations grow is when their customer base expands. The big question becomes 'how should organizations work to expand their customer base?' The answer to this question shall be discussed below as the factors that lead to the growth of organizations.

Ten factors that contribute to the growth of organizations have been identified and they are listed below and discussed thereafter.

- a) Offering great products that satisfy customers' needs
- b) Having an effective management team that provides true leadership
- c) Operating ahead of the competition
- d) Diversifying operations to reach new markets
- e) Innovating for excellence
- f) Initiating customer-focused marketing programs
- g) Establishing a long-term plan
- h) Monitoring the environment constantly to avert threats and to exploit opportunities
- i) Establishing a culture of Corporate Social Responsibility
- j) Developing new leadership through structured mentoring

Offering great products that satisfy customers' needs

Organizations are established with the objective of meeting an existing need - the need for products, services, or ideas. Organizations can only grow when they produce good products and provide excellent services to their customers. Experience has shown that the organizations that last are the ones that continue to satisfy the needs of their customers with high quality products. Those that deal on inferior goods or provide low quality services soon go into extension as their customer base dwindles over time. No matter how cheap an item is, the customer still expects it to meet the need for which it was purchased. Those enterprises which offer inferior products at a reduced price are doing themselves more harm than good. You can't deceive all the people all the time. If customers discover that it takes up to four pieces of an inferior product to meet the need that one quality product meets, and that the combined price of those four is more than the price of unit of the quality brand, you have lost the market. When people purchase low priced products, they equally want to gain value for their money. So, if an organization sacrifices quality in a bid to offer a low price, that organization is neither helping itself nor its customers. The best option is for organizations to offer quality products at competitive prices. There can be no alternative to quality products. Once quality is compromised, satisfaction is sacrificed. And once satisfaction is not guaranteed, long-term patronage is jeopardized.

The need to provide the customers with high quality products cannot be over emphasized. Let us take a hypothetical example from the health/medical sector. Company A produces drugs that you need to take at least 20 pills for a period of 5 days (2 in the morning and 2 in the evening) that cost $4.00, in order to get well while Company B produces similar but stronger drugs of 2 pills that cost $6.00 and need to be taken just once to get well. Which of the two companies' brands do you think more customers would patronize? The answer is very simple! No sane person wants to lie on the sick bed for 5 days when extra $2.00 can get him or her out of it in 24 hours. Those who understand the value of time know what they can gain in 4 days of healthy and active life. As a result, Company B is going to get the most patronage. People are still going to patronize Company A but those who truly understand the importance of time and health to their daily success will not. Those who sought to gain $2.00 actually lost their 4 days income which can amount to hundreds, thousands, and, sometimes, millions of dollars. When more and more people truly understand these two scenarios, Company A would end up with less and less loyal customers while Company B will have more and more.

Let us take another example from the food sector. Company Y offers its products at $2 per unit that expires 5 days after the initial purchase. Company Z offers a similar product at $2.50 per unit that expires 15 days after the initial purchase. Which of the companies would customers patronize the most? Patronizing company Y means you have to visit the store more often and also use its products immediately after purchase to avoid expiration and total loss of your money. You can't afford to eat expired food because it would make you sick and sometimes lead to hospitalization or untimely death of a family member, especially the children and the aged. Patronizing Company Z means you have an additional 10 days to use the food product for a fee of $0.50 only. This is a good deal but those who are price conscious will not notice it until they start throwing away expired products from company Y and losing their health and wealth as well.

Low price attracts customers but high quality sustains them. An organization that intends to achieve a sustainable growth must continue to offer quality products and provide superior services. The average customer does not usually bother so much about what he or she spent on a product but what he or she lost to get the satisfaction he or she needs. They are always comparing what they paid with what others paid to get similar satisfaction. To pay a little more to get a higher quality is never a loss but to spend less to get no quality at all is a huge loss indeed because you have to spend all over again. So, those who go for low-price-low-quality products end up spending more. The day this group of people realize their mistake is the day their supplier goes out of business!

Having an effective management team that provides true leadership

Nothing grows an organization like effective management. You will recall that chapter two of this book highlights the role of management in advancing the course of an organization as well as in actualizing its objective. Management plays a critical role in determining what the objective of the organization is, the nature of resources needed, and the processes and procedures required to actualize the objective.

The fact remains that when an organization fails, it is its management that failed and when an organization succeeds, it is also its management that did a great job. The reason for this is that management literally holds all the authority it takes to make decisions about organizational resources, processes, procedures, strategies, and responses. Failure to get the right human, material, financial, and other resources needed to operate the organization effectively is, therefore, seen as management inefficiency. Failure to establish the right processes and procedures needed to operate the organization successfully is known as management deficiency. Failure to make the right responses to environmental opportunities and threats is what is referred to as management ineffectiveness.

An effective management team must provide true leadership to an organization. The difference between management and leadership is exactly the difference between information and inspiration. As managers utilize information to maintain the status quo in their organization, leaders use inspiration to explore new frontiers for the organization. Nothing happens until someone makes it happen. If you place the wrong people in management position, the organization will continue to suffer losses. The worst scenario is a situation where friends and family members, who have no idea of what management is all about, are placed in management positions. Instead of running the organization, they end up ruining it. Management can simply be described as the process of utilizing available resources for the attainment of organization's objectives. Every manager must have a deep understanding of what the objectives of the organization are, what the needed resources are, what the processes are (i.e. the system of converting inputs into desired outputs), what the opportunities are, and what the threats are. Every manager must also understand the critical role of human resources in getting things done. If you hire less qualified people just to save cost, it will show up in delays and bad jobs. If you use inferior materials in production, it will show up as defective and substandard products. If you install a wrong process or engage a wrong procedure in your operations, it will show up in customer complaints, employee frustration, poor customer review, and negative public image for the organization. If you keep having lost time because of machine breakdowns and employee absenteeism, it will show up in the organization's inability to meet production quotas, customer orders, and consumer demands. This situation not only leads to loss of income and reduction in profits but creates an opportunity for competitors to take advantage of.

Management must be consistent in implementing existing policies while working to ensure that better policies are put in place. Management must focus its attention towards meeting the organization's objectives while working to ensure that better objectives are put in place. Management must see the workers as partners in progress while ensuring that they are provided with all the tools they need to perform their duties more effectively. Management must place each worker in positions based on their skills, strengths and experience while working to train them to handle higher tasks in the organization. Management must respond to environmental challenges while working to avert them. Management must seize existing environmental opportunities while working to create them. Management must understand the areas of the organization's strength and build on it while working hard to reduce its areas of weaknesses. Management must continue to find ways to upgrade the processes and procedures in a bid to take advantage of new technological breakthroughs in providing long term customer satisfaction required to ensure long term profitability. Management must continue to improve its effectiveness by engaging in training events and attending management development programs. Management must have a means of getting current information about the industry of its operation, while not forgetting to pay attention to the economic, legal, and political environment which equally influence the success or failure of their organization. Effective management is what is required to grow an organization.

The whole essence of management is the improvement of operational efficiency for greater productivity and better profitability. Management is a process of utilizing available resources in such a way as to achieve the set objective of an organization. Management determines what the objective is, what the resources are, the processes of converting the inputs into outputs, the timing of production, the physical layout of the factory, the number of people to be engaged, what each individual will perform, and the remuneration for the job. Management also determines the policies and procedures that would guide operations and interactions within the organization. Management was born out of the desire to improve the production and profitability of the organization. Even if an organization renders services such as transportation, it takes management to determine what nature of transportation to offer, that is, either air, road, water or rail; ascertain the materials needed, say airplanes, buses/trucks, ships, or trains; establish the human resources requirement; find out the cost of the entire operation; and determine which routes to operate as well as the type of passengers to attend to. The management literally creates the image of the organization and ensures that its daily actions reflect that image.

Operating ahead of the competition

Competition originated from the word compete and the Websters All-In-One Dictionary and Thesaurus gives the best definition of the word. It states that 'compete' is to seek or strive for something, such as a position, possession, or reward, for which others are also contending. So, competition among organizations is almost a battle of who will get the best position, possession, or reward in the marketplace. This is huge! It is a battle for who will get the best market position (highest market share), possess the best resources (human, financial, material, etc.), and have the best economic reward (increased sales, increased profitability).

Organizations that offer similar products and/or services are, therefore, in direct competition among themselves. Organizations that offer alternative products or services are in indirect competition. There is also a general competition among all products and services for the customer's attention because the more a customer spends on a particular item, say bread, the less the amount that will be available for him to spend on all other items, say sugar, salt, cake, milk, egg, chocolate, etc.

Industrial competition is the most intense. This is the competition that involves organizations producing similar products, say, evaporated milk, or providing similar services, say, air transportation. Any customer that wishes to purchase evaporated milk has a lot of brands to choose from. Assume we have brands A, B, C, D, and E. The more of brand A the customers purchase, the less of brands B, C, D, and E that would be sold. Assume also we have airlines V, W, X, Y, and Z. The more customers fly airline V, the less of the tickets belonging to airlines W, X, Y, and Z that would be sold. The reason we see series of advertisements through our radios, televisions, newspapers, magazines, and billboards is that companies are spending tons of cash aimed at aggressive brand promotion. Other marketing programs are engaged by firms in a bid to outwit each other and attract more patronage to their brand. In fact, most of the operating cost of organizations goes into marketing effort either to increase the customer base or to sustain the existing customer base. The marketing strategies include price reduction campaigns, award of prizes to loyal customers including sponsorship of anniversary vacations and sponsorship of special projects selected by customers, etc.

Operating ahead of the competition is to anticipate where the market is heading and putting together plans to get there before other competitors do. Organizations that wish to grow their customer base must continue to be customer-oriented in their planning, execution, monitoring, communication, and response. Every member of the organization must communicate the same message and provide the same response to the demands of their customers. If the GM (the general manager) states on TV that the organization is committed to treating the customer as the King, the other GM (the gate man) should also convey a similar message when customers approach him at the gate. When your competitors do for your customers what you are reluctant to do, you simply lose them. When your competitors adopt the new technology that improves production processes and increase product quality and you cannot, you start losing your customers. When your competitors offer better employee packages to take away some of your best staff, your customers go away with them. When your competitors succeed in buying off your sources of supply, you will be forced to shut down operations and lose your customers permanently.

Organizations that cannot operate ahead of the competition are always at the mercy of their competitors. Such organizations never grow but keep crawling from behind. One of the ways an organization can grow is to identify its real competitors, know their strengths and weaknesses, study the nature of the market it is operating in, and then devise a strategy to make it remain relevant both at the present and in the future. Growth is a process, and a process is a series of activities. Those organizations that continue to take relevant and consistent actions for a sustainable growth are the ones that actually grow. There is no other way!

Diversifying operations to reach new markets

To diversify means to make different or various sizes, shapes, and qualities of an item. It also means expanding your product line or service range to provide more options for different categories of customers or segments of the market. It can also mean venturing into new areas of operation for which the organization has strategic advantage based on its access to new technology, skilled manpower, and financial resources.

It has already been established that the only way organizations grow is when their loyal customers grow. It has also been highlighted that competition seeks to shrink the customer base of any organization. However, one of the sure ways to overcome competition and grow an organization's customer base is to diversify. This entails the introduction of new products or services that target new customers while working hard to retain the existing customers. When an organization is the first to produce certain products or provide certain services, it enjoys monopoly; a situation where one firm supplies a certain product to the entire market. At that point, the monopolistic organization determines quality, size, and price with little or no contribution from the customers. Soon, other people begin to see this as a business opportunity. They secretly study the product, processes, and procedures of the existing organization, apply for operational licenses, and introduce similar products to compete with the original supplier. The new entrants usually supply at a lower price to attract customer patronage. Noticing a cheaper alternative, some customers shift to the new supplier and the prize war begins.

In a free market economy, the only way to reap the harvest of a monopolistic market is to be the first to introduce a new product or an improved alternative of an existing product or service. For example, introducing dual service, energy saving electronic gadget can be a plus to an engineering firm. A television with an inbuilt DVD is a diversification. A computer system with an inbuilt Internet decoder is a diversification. A television with inbuilt cable service is a diversification. A car with an inbuilt GPS is a diversification. A car that can use both solar and petroleum energy to function is diversification. A boat that can run on the water and drive on the road is a diversification. A photocopying machine that can print and scan documents is a diversification. Introducing airplanes that can land safely on the water during an emergency is a form of diversification. Cell phones that can record full video and audio messages, take pictures and connect to the Internet and other applications, is a diversification. A gas stove that can also operate on electric energy is a form of diversification. A gas turbine that can also operate as a wind turbine to produce electricity is a form of diversification. A doorbell that serves as a video recorder is a form of diversification. Introducing domestic electricity-generating machines that use water as its fuel is a form of diversification. This innovation will drastically reduce cost of maintenance as well as the danger of fire and smoke disaster. Introducing a microwave machine that can heat, boil, grill, bake, or roast is a form of diversification.

When an organization diversifies, it increases the use for its products by altering the product's features to attract new set of customers. When an organization diversifies, it develops new ways to use the same products in a bid to expand its customer base. When an organization diversifies, it simply alters the size, shape, or quality of its products in a bid to appeal to the needs of different segments of the market. Diversification helps to grow an organization.

Diversification also enables an organization to create entirely new product lines or service groups for new markets, using its current process or an adjustment of it. For example, when a car manufacturing firm starts producing buses, pickups, and trucks, it is diversifying. When a radio manufacturer starts producing televisions and DVD players, it is diversifying. Also, when a traditional retail store goes into online retailing, it is diversifying. When a publishing company specialized in publishing fictions decides to venture into non-fictions, it is diversifying. Diversification aims at expanding the market as it targets both new and existing customers with new products but also increases the use of old products by existing customers. For example, certain television screens can now be used as writing boards for training programs. Also, certain vacuum cleaners can now be used to mop the floor as well as wash the rug carpet. These are forms of diversification. Successful organizations must continue to find new uses for their products and new products for new customers. As products reach their decline stage in the product life cycle, organizations must seek for new uses for those products or create new products to replace them. This is how organizations are grown and sustained.

Innovating for excellence

To innovate is to introduce new ideas or make remarkable changes for improvement in the value of an item, a system, or a process. When organizations innovate, they make necessary changes to improve their processes or upgrade their systems so that their products are better and their services second to none.

In a market where every supplier does the same thing the same way, the customers will settle for the nearest supplier. But where a particular supplier distinguishes him- or herself by doing things differently, such as offering better products at the same prize or a little higher price, customers will rush to that particular supplier. Introducing major changes in the production process can improve the nature of the product and its appeal to the customers. No organization can grow its market share by doing exactly what other organizations are doing. Certain things must be done differently if new results are to be expected.

Sometimes the introduction of new machines in the production system can improve the production process, increase volume of production, and ultimately reduce the unit cost of the product. In fact, the first organization to introduce an improved system of production has a way of dominating the market. Most customers are looking for 'a great product at a good price' not necessarily 'a poor product at a low price.' If your product is great you can then negotiate price but if your product is poor, you have nothing to negotiate about. Organizations must, therefore, continue to seek ways to improve upon their production system so that their product offerings will rank among the best in the market.

For example, an organization that manufactures auto batteries that do not last more than 12 months cannot attract more customers than the one which batteries last at least 36 months guaranteed, even if the first manufacturer sells at half the price of the second manufacturer. A bad battery can spoil a driver's day. I'm quite sure that no driver would like to make this sort of mistake the second time. Innovating may be costly to an organization but if the organization compares its losses (in sales and profitability) for not innovating, to innovate becomes a better option. Things are changing so fast in the society and these changes affect consumer tastes and customer preferences. Any organization that expects to remain relevant in today's market must consider these changes and then design its offerings to suit the current needs of the market.

Innovation may not just be in terms of the core product but in its size, packaging, storage, mode of transportation or handling so that the customer gets greater value for his or her money. For example, if a current health research shows that plastic containers are not good packaging materials for dairy products, the first dairy products producer to switch to a recommended packaging material clears the market. Remember that there is a difference between the product and its packaging but if the packaging begins to negatively affect the core product, it becomes a major issue and any organization that is unable to switch to a better packaging material loses out big time in the market. Another scenario will help us understand better how innovation can improve the performance and growth of an organization. If a health research suddenly discovers that glass bottles are not good materials for packaging wine products, what do you think would happen to wine producers who fail to switch to a better packaging as soon as possible? They would be forced out of the market by those who do.

Series of innovations in the electronics industry is improving the quality of products and increasing patronage to the organizations that are at the forefront of these innovations. Right now, the heavy-weight box television has given way to the light-weight flat screen or LCD television. It used to take at least two able bodied men to lift a 36-inch television set but now a 10-year-old can confidently carry a 50-inch television set from downstairs to upstairs. This is a good example of innovation. The rate at which our dumpsters are filled with the old television sets, which are still functional, is a clarion call for organizations to try to be the initiators rather than the imitators of innovation in their industry. Those who fail to innovate often look around to realize that the market they once led has not only slipped out of their hands but has also disappeared from their sight. Innovating for excellence can greatly enhance the growth and long-term survival of an organization.

Initiating customer-focused marketing programs

One of the ways to grow an organization is through marketing. Good marketing programs not only deliver the right information about an organization or its offerings but also offer valuable education on the uniqueness of its products, in comparison with other organizations' products, while eliciting patronage from the customers at the same time. The goal of every good marketing program is to position an organization ahead of others in the same market. Marketing is a business function that involves activities aimed at speeding up the exchange process by researching and creating the right products or services as well as pricing, promoting and distributing them in such a way that they add the desired value to the customer by meeting his basic need for satisfaction. Marketing should be holistic in that it must aim at creating quality products at reasonable prices, conveying the right information about the organization's offerings, and delivering the products through channels that are within the reach of the customers.

The promotion aspect of marketing involves advertising, sales promotion, publicity, as well as personal selling. An organization must use all these marketing activities to pass across a compelling message to its customers. Advertising is the art of calling public attention to your organization aimed at selling your products or services. It involves information about your organization, its products, value of the products to the customers, and why customers should settle for that product among others. It also includes information about the nearest location where the product can be purchased. It can be in the form of a blog on a website, an audio message through the radio waves, a video message through the television network or a message through the social media. Most advertising jingles, as they are often called, last between 30 to 60 seconds and must convey a comprehensive and convincing message within this limited time frame as not to lose the money spent to put it together. Professional advertisers or celebrities are often engaged for advertising endorsements. Corporate entities across the globe spend billions of dollars annually in advertising campaigns because this is the only way potential customers will know that those organizations exist in the first place. Beyond that, it also helps customers to discover what a particular organization does and how that relates to their individual needs. An organization that wishes to serve customers beyond its immediate location must send its message far and wide. This means an extra expenditure. Also, new organizations must announce their entry into existing industries if they are to successfully penetrate the market and make the desired impact.

Apart from advertising, organizations also engage in sales promotional campaigns. These include corporate sponsorship of individual or community projects, funding of charity organizations as well as establishing foundations for scholarships or research efforts aimed at making the world a better place for us all. Sales promotion also entails organizing bonanzas where loyal customers can win valuable prizes at certain periods of the year. As the name implies, all sales promotional activities are aimed at promoting sales. Price reduction is also a form of sales promotion just as the buy-one-get-one-free sales events. During a sales promotional campaign, the organization is prepared to let go of certain value in the short run in a bid to gain a greater value in the long run. Sales promotion helps to build long term customer loyalty just as it appreciates loyal customers, solves problems in local communities, funds laudable projects, and promotes corporate social responsibility. In the United States alone, corporate sponsorship runs into tens of billions of dollars annually.

Publicity or public relations is another aspect of marketing operation. Publicity is always basically aimed at promoting and sustaining a positive public image for the organization. Fact is, competitors are always looking for ways to tarnish the image of a rival organization for their own benefit. Press conferences and media chats should be held from time to time to keep the press and the public abreast of what an organization is doing or not doing. Every negative information about the organization must be addressed with a counter narrative while at the same time promoting a positive image. Customer complaints, employee grievances, regulatory expectations, community demands, and stockholders' concerns are issues that cannot be swept under the carpet by any organization that seeks to grow and glow. One negative review by an unsatisfied customer or a demeaning comment by an aggrieved employee can have a ripple effect that can paint an organization in a bad light and reduce the number of its customers overnight. It does not cost so much to publicize an organization or maintain good public relations. Every organization must learn to tell its own story by itself instead of letting someone else do it. Someone else always ends up doing it badly.

The last but not the least marketing program that can be engaged in promoting a business organization is personal selling or one-on-one contact with customers. This exercise is becoming more and more extinct due to the greater value today's society attaches to personal safety and home security. Personal selling is especially important when a new product, that requires expert knowledge to operate, is introduced into the market. Most personal selling activities are done on phone these days; the exercise that still eliminates the one-on-one contact between sellers and their customers. However, retail outlets now have technical units or customer service departments that help to address the concerns of customers for more information on how to use certain new products. Big retail enterprises also allow their shop floors and parking lots to be used by certain marketers for personal selling activities.

Every marketing program must be customer-oriented. It must be aimed at sustaining your current customers as well as attracting new patronage. An organization that loses touch with its customers is bound to regret at the end of the day. Customers are sometimes hard to attract but very easy to lose. An organization that seeks to retain its customers must continue to introduce daily deliberate programs that inform, educate, disabuse, and empower its customers and the public to have confidence in its products and services.

Establishing a long-term plan

No organization exists without a plan and no organization grows without a plan. Unfortunately, any organization that does not have a plan of what to do in ten years does not really believe it will last up to the next ten years. So, if you desire your organization to grow and last up to the next 50 years, you must have a 50-year plan on the ground. There is always room for adjustments. No good thing happens without proper planning. Planning simply means taking decisions today about future actions and expected results. This means deciding today what will be done in the future by predicting and speculating what conditions you foresee in the future based on the realities of today. No one can really say for sure what is going to happen in the far future, but one can reasonably forecast what would likely happen based on available facts and figures. This is called long term planning.

An organization that wants to grow into the future must establish a long-term plan. This plan must include the position the organization wants to occupy in the industry, the kind of market it wants to serve, the products or services to focus on, the production process to adopt, the kind of workers it would need, the location that would suit the operations, which aspect of the functions to outsource, and how to raise new funds for the expected growth. These are critical decisions that determine the continuous survival of any organization. However, these long-term decisions must be reviewed and updated from time to time as conditions change and as new facts emerge.

There is this saying that 'when people fail to plan, they have planned to fail.' An organization can be described as a complex system that requires many units coming together to achieve a certain objective or group of objectives. If things are not planned, nothing can be achieved. Through planning, we set limits on individual behavior, place controls on the use of resources, establish checks on the exercise of authority, and determine the direction we want the organization to go. Proper planning helps in the establishment of policies and procedures required to form an organization's culture. Everyone knows what is expected and the lines not to cross. Relationship codes, dress codes, time codes, compensation codes, hiring codes, training codes, promotion codes, termination codes, succession methods, and general work ethics are established through planning. All these activities sound so simple in words but are very demanding in practice. So many conditions must be taken into consideration before establishing the right codes for these organizational practices.

The entire life of an organization depends on the effectiveness of its planning process. Planning involves determining the mission and establishing the vision for an organization. Vision is the long-term objective of an organization. It includes where the organization intends to be in the future and the unique strengths it has with which to get there. An organization without a vision has no place in the future. Organizations must continue to evolve by developing new ways to set realistic long-term goals which enable them to be relevant in the future marketplace. Once the operations of an organization are not in alignment with the expectations of the market, the organization can go into extinction. The market keeps evolving, customer needs keep changing, competitors keep adapting, and customers keep switching sides. Any organization that desires to grow into the future must develop a long-term plan which addresses current realities and anticipates future challenges. The tools that provided today's solution may not assist in taking care of tomorrow's challenges. So, forward-looking organizations must continue to develop plans that address today's issues as well as prepare for tomorrow's threats. Anything less can be catastrophic.

Monitoring the environment constantly to avert threats and to exploit opportunities

This is very critical to the growth and success of organizations. All organizations operate within the environment and every environment poses a series of threats just as it provides numerous opportunities. Organizational growth is a function of environmental variables. If environmental conditions are favorable to an organization, it grows and prospers but if environmental conditions are unfavorable to an organization, it shrinks and disappears. If organizations decide to wait and watch events unfold, the unfavorable situation might overwhelm and overtake them. So, the best way to go is to constantly monitor the environment to avert the unfavorable situation or threats, as well as to take advantage of the favorable conditions, which create opportunities for growth and success.

Environmental threats are those external conditions which decrease the growth potential of an organization. Some of them show up as limited supply of needed human resources, unavailability of needed material resources, paucity of funds, activities of competitors, poor economic conditions, lack of market, natural disasters, adverse weather conditions, negative government policies and programs, lack of space for expansion, scarcity of public infrastructure such as steady electricity, roads, railways, airports, seaports, etc., and lack of access to modern technology. Though these conditions are external, an organization can do at least three things aimed at averting them or reducing their effect. The three things include avoiding the threats, adapting to them, or fighting them head on.

For example, an organization can adopt the avoidance strategy by relocating its operations to an environment with little or no incidences of natural disaster or adverse weather conditions. It can also relocate to areas where there is less competition, etc. On the other hand, an organization can adopt the adaptation strategy by adjusting its operations to fit into the existing adverse condition. By extending scholarship offers to students undertaking studies in its core areas of operation, an organization can ensure the continuous availability of the right human resources for its current and future operations. By sponsoring research efforts, an organization can continue to set the pace in new product development in its area of operation. These are adaptation strategies aimed at reducing or eliminating adverse environmental conditions. As part of the adaptation strategy, an organization can also establish its own farm for raw materials or operate its own materials processing factory through backward vertical integration. Organizations can also avert the adverse conditions by fighting them head on. For instance, an organization can mobilize a legal team to challenge a government regulatory policy that has negative effect on its success. When the government arbitrarily and unilaterally raises corporate taxes, an organization can challenge it in court. When competitors engage in industrial espionage, an organization can also take them up in the court of law. Organizations must be prepared to fight to secure a conducive environment necessary for their continued successful operation and long-term survival.

Apart from averting environmental threats, organizations also explore and exploit environmental opportunities to increase their chances of growth and success. Environmental opportunities are those set of external conditions which increase an organization's chances of growth and profitability. They include increased demand for an existing product of the organization, market demand for a new product, exit of a major competitor from the market, introduction of a new technology that improves product quality and enhances production speed, and a piece of government legislation which improves general economic conditions and encourages greater customer patronage. One of the best ways for an organization to grow is to position or reposition itself to continue to take advantage of environmental opportunities long before competitors get hold of them or to continue to do things better than their competitors would.

For example, when traditional retail companies started shutting down some of their stores across the United States, the online marketing giant, Amazon, started opening traditional retail stores. What other companies saw as a threat to their overall success, Amazon saw as an opportunity for its growth and development. An organization must be wary of what it considers a threat and plans to avoid because it might be just an opportunity for a forward-looking competitor to take over the market. Organizations must engage the services of independent business consultants to help them analyze environmental conditions before taking major decisions that can either make them or mar them.

Establishing a culture of Corporate Social Responsibility

Organizations are established by a group of individuals for the provision of certain services, production of certain products, or processing of certain information. As far as organizations achieve these objectives in line with existing laws, they are said to be doing well. However, great organizations go above and beyond the letters of the law to perform certain activities that contribute to the well-being of the society in which they operate. They strive to become ethically and socially responsible. By seeking to be socially responsible, organizations make choices, take decisions, and execute actions that contribute to the general welfare and overall interest of the society while performing their legal obligations and implementing their corporate policies.

These days, the society is going beyond the need for organizations to provide quality goods and deliver excellent services to their customers at a fair price to demanding that they exhibit a very high ethical standard and social behavior towards their employees, competitors, communities, investors, regulators, and the environment by operating with a high moral standard that is based on truth, honesty, sincerity, and utmost good faith. For example, organizations are required not to send out false information about their products just to attract customers or beat competition. Whatever information organizations display on their product labels must not be deceptive in any way but a true reflection of the nature of the product. If you report that a certain food product contains 250 calories, it must be 250 calories and nothing less. If you report that 28% of the product is made up of protein materials, it must be so and nothing else. If a certain product expires in 60 days after the date of manufacture, it must be reported in a conspicuous manner so that the customer is fully aware before purchasing the item. If a highly profitable organization informs its employees that business is not doing well just to avoid increasing their pay, this is unethical and socially irresponsible. If an organization falsely reports high profitability, just to attract investors, it is an unethical practice and a form of social irresponsibility.

In the past few decades, organizations are being pressured to preserve the environment and support the communities in which they operate. Environmental Impact Assessment (EIA) has become a normal practice for organizations that operate within areas of human habitation. If your organization emits a certain gas or releases certain chemical waste, the impact on the immediate environment must be ascertained to reduce or eradicate health and safety implications. Liquid and solid wastes have a way of filtering into our streams and rivers from where public water supplies are sourced. We have had many incidences of water poisoning due to industrial activities and the health implication on the citizenry is quite huge. Organizations, therefore, have a greater social responsibility of properly disposing their waste materials to avoid environmental pollution and contamination. Those organizations that slaughter animals and fell trees as part of their raw materials must consider the implication of their actions on the environment. Automobile companies as well as oil and gas firms have been constantly asked to reduce the amount of carbon monoxide emitting from automobile exhaust pipes and the amount of hydrocarbons and oil spills resulting from oil and gas operations, respectively. If organizations fail to protect and preserve the environment today, their future operations might be jeopardized. We must realize that every organization is a part and parcel of the environment.

Finally, organizations must support and promote the welfare of the communities in which they operate. People from local communities should be given employment opportunities. Organizations should sponsor events that promote community peace and welfare. Things that bother host communities should also bother the organization. Organizations should support such initiatives as the Cancer Society, cultural societies, children education societies, etc. Organizations should also participate in philanthropic efforts with financial donations and staff volunteer activities for local needs and national challenges like the Feeding America initiative, The Red Cross Society, Wounded Warriors project, etc. Great organizations also go as far as providing scholarship funds to members of the communities in which they operate. They also support general education development by funding school districts for the proper training of their teachers and equipping of the classrooms. Organizations should also get involved in sponsoring youth development and career advancement programs so that young people in the communities of their operation are better qualified for job opportunities or empowered to go into private businesses in the areas of technical practices and commercial services. The fact remains that as organizations work to improve the society in which they operate, they are inadvertently creating a future for their continued growth and development.

Developing new leadership through structured mentoring

Leadership is one of the core ingredients for organizational growth and development. Leadership is the ability to exert influence on other organizational members which causes them to voluntarily take actions in line with meeting the objectives of the organization. Leadership provides guidance and direction to the organization and ensures members are highly motivated to take the journey towards organizational success. Without the right leadership, it will be difficult for organizations to attain their desire for growth and development.

The need for leadership in organizations cannot be over emphasized. We live in a world of constant change and the only way an organization will survive is to continue to have the right kind of leadership that would help it successfully navigate the ever-changing environment. These environmental changes not only affect the organization's bottom line, but they also affect employee morale, investor reaction, and public perception of the organization. Failure to have the right kind of leadership at any point in the life of an organization can be very devastating, if not catastrophic. It is important to note that an organization can only have one leader at a time; even though it has plenty of managers all the time. The Chief Executive Officer, also referred to as the President, General Manager, or Group Managing Director, is the leader of the organization. The leader must be someone who can recognize current environmental threats, anticipate potential challenges, and create a response program. The response must achieve one of two things: adapt the organization's operations to the expected environmental changes or alter the challenges to the ultimate advantage of his or her organization. The leader must also be someone who recognizes the potentials in his managers and employees, develops those potentials into strengths, and deploys them into relevant areas of need in the organization. Remember, it is the employees that would carry out organizational policies and strategies, and it is employees that would interact with the customers on a continuous basis. Successful change happens when motivated employees devote their time, energy, skill, and experience towards reaching new goals which might involve a certain level of sacrifice. Anyone that cannot influence his or her employees to willingly make the sacrifice necessary for organizational survival has failed as a leader.

The need for a structured mentoring program that will continue to produce new leadership in an organization cannot be over emphasized. The sudden death, resignation, or retirement of a good CEO due to health or other reasons can spell doom for an organization if there is no ready replacement within. Bringing in an outsider to replace an outgoing successful leader can also be a problem. The best time to bring in an outsider to lead an organization is when there is a need for a total overhaul of the systems, structures, and strategies to chart a new direction for the organization. It is also necessary when the organization wants to diversify into new areas of operation. A successful leader in ABC organization may not necessarily be as successful in XYZ organization. Every organization is different based on its original philosophy, existing culture, environment of operation, as well as the nature and duration of its operation. So, the best way to ensure the continuous existence of the right kind of leaders for an organization is to put in place an internal mentoring program that identifies managers with sterling leadership qualities and develops them into becoming the next set of leaders needed for successful future operations.

One of the best ways to develop the leadership potentials of the next CEO is to delegate to him or her assignments that cut across departments, regions, and products/services. The person must be granted unlimited access to the current CEO to observe and to learn how issues are handled and how decisions are reached. The person should also be trained on crisis management as well as how to manage change in organizations to prepare him or her for similar challenges ahead. Great organizations do not thrive on assumptions neither do they survive on presumptions. Organizations that fail to plan for their next leader are often the ones that do not grow into the future. Great organizational leaders are not born, they are made. An organization that desires to have a great leader must make one.

CHAPTER 6

ORGANIZATIONS DO DIE

In chapter 5, We discussed the factors that contribute to the growth and expansion of organizations. We observed that all those factors ultimately lead to the expansion of the customer base of an organization. In contrast, the factors which we shall be discussing in this chapter are those that shrink the customer base and ultimately lead to the decline or death of an organization.

We have already established that an organization is an extension of an individual but it is also necessary to note that organizations do last beyond the individuals that initiated them. This is based on the extent to which the management of such organizations are able to harness available resources to attract and sustain the customer base needed for the organization's growth and success. Failure to do this can be catastrophic in the sense that the organization can die while the initiator is still alive or shortly after his demise. The question now is 'what are those factors that can lead to the decline or eventual death of an organization and how can we avoid them?'

To further discuss these factors, I have made an attempt to differentiate between the factors that lead to the failure of new businesses on one hand and those that lead to the failure of established organizations on the other. This helps organizations at various stages of operation to appreciate those common factors that can adversely affect their growth and success and eventually lead to their decline and extinction.

A) The major factors that lead to the failure of a new business enterprise include the following:

1. Insufficient working capital

One of the major factors leading to the failure of new businesses is insufficient working capital. Available statistics show that about 80% of new businesses close shops within the first five years of their existence. One of the main reasons for this high rate of business failure is insufficient capital. Business capital is that amount of money needed to run all the affairs of the business. It will be used to purchase needed materials for operations, rent or lease the office space, get needed equipment, hire workers, buy raw materials for production, pay bills, provide transportation and storage, provide furniture and fittings, as well as provide for cash at hand for other unforeseen expenses. It is not enough to conceive an idea, put up a business plan, gather some money and then rush into a startup wishing to attract 'angel investors' soon enough. If your business is not up and running for at least two years, no investor would risk putting his or her money into that venture. Angel investors usually provide funds for business expansion not for business survival. Avoid using credit cards or commercial bank loans with outrageous interest rates. Starting a business with a high debt profile is never a good idea. Do not fall into that trap except where it becomes necessary as the last resort.

Before getting your business off the ground, you must be sure that you have all the funds needed to take care of the business needs for at least one year and six months whether or not the business makes an income. Do not jump into the business with the sole intention that revenue from sales will cover the cost of operation from day one. This is not usually the case 95% of the time. It is always better to wait a little longer to raise the required amount of capital than to bear the pain of business failure after investing the little cash in your hands. You may have a fantastic business idea but a good idea without the right funding soon amounts to frustration and filing for bankruptcy.

Most times getting the required capital will entail partnering with someone else. A lot of entrepreneurs are usually afraid to share their ideas with someone else thereby closing the door for raising the proper funding. There is always someone somewhere who has the money but lacks the idea and there is always someone else who has the idea but lacks the money. Partnership bridges the gap and provides the capital required to nurture the idea into a profitable venture while providing a great opportunity for future investors. You will always need other people to make it great in this life. So, look for that individual or group of individuals who value your ideas, have the funds to contribute, and are willing to partner with you for the successful execution of the idea.

There are also government initiatives aimed at providing funds for startups. You must conduct a thorough research to find out which ones that would suit the nature of your business. Also, visit the Small Business Administration website for detailed information on business funding. Knowledge is power so get all the information you need before starting your business. Ask questions to those who are already well established in that kind of business and make sure their answers adequately address your needs. As much as possible, try to minimize your financial obligation in the early part of the business. Lease instead of buy, rent instead of own, engage outside contractors for non-routine jobs instead of hiring full time staff, etc. These actions would drastically reduce the amount of capital needed to start, as well as run the business. If your new business is up and running for at least 18 months, and has the potential for success, investors will come knocking at your door. At that point you would have the power to negotiate to your own advantage. Starting a business with insufficient capital is like taking poison and wishing that you live long.

2. Little or no technical knowledge of the business

Another major factor that leads to the failure of new businesses is lack of technical knowledge of the business by the entrepreneur. Every business has its secrets. You must get as much information as possible about the nature of the business you wish to engage in. The entrepreneurial stage of every business requires that the entrepreneur possesses the knowledge-base needed for innovation and survival in the new business. He or she cannot depend on someone outside the business to provide the knowledge required to operate the business successfully. If the business is technology based, the entrepreneur must be technology savvy to take the business off the ground and running. If the business is logistics based, the entrepreneur must be knowledgeable in logistics to be successful in the business.

The entrepreneur lays the foundation for the initial survival, growth, and sustainability of the business. This foundation is based on his or her knowledge of the business dynamics. For example, anyone desiring to go into hotel business must have full knowledge of the hospitality industry and how it operates. He or she must know the various levels of hotels that exist: 5-star, 4-star, 3-star, etc. He or she must also know the features of each level and the sources of critical resources such as food, furniture, personnel, security, transportation, music, and such basic amenities as portable water, access roads and constant electricity supply. All these will ultimately determine the best location for the hotel and its availability and accessibility to potential guests. You cannot site a 5-star hotel in a place that is not close to an international airport, commercial city or tourist center. Doing that would amount to a total disaster! People do not leave their homes to check into a hotel on the next street. Those who make use of hotels are either on vacation in a faraway city or on a business trip outside their base. As a result, the ideal hotel must provide basic amenities as a home away from home. The safety and security of the life and property of guests is of paramount importance. The next is the water, food, general hygiene, security, and other side attractions such as live music, wine bars, swimming pool, car park, flower garden, casino, gymnasium, and emergency medical care. A hotel that does not provide all of the above services cannot attract the right kind of guests required to sustain the operations of the business for a long time.

Most of the business failures that happen are as a result of limited technical knowledge of the business by the entrepreneur. Experience shows that some people just observe that others are making money in certain businesses and they decide to raise little funds and then rush into that kind of business without first gathering enough information required to operate the business successfully. All they want is to make good money without any concrete plan to provide the kind of service required to make the money. The average consumer wants to get the most value for his money and you cannot provide such value without having basic knowledge in the business you are operating. Depending on others to provide the knowledge required to operate a business raises the operational cost of the business because those people have to be paid for their services. No good entrepreneur should let this happen. You cannot depend on your employees to provide all the technical knowledge required to operate the business. They are looking up to you for information and direction and you cannot afford to turn to them for the same. You cannot afford to lead from behind! The moment your employees realize that you solely depend on them for the survival and growth of the business is the moment they start asking for indiscriminate raises. If you do not grant the raises they leave and if you grant the raises the operational cost of the business goes over the roof. This is not a good place to be as an entrepreneur.

If you have the funds to start a business but lack the technical knowledge in that line of business, you have to partner with someone who does. Knowledge is power! When you provide the funds and partner with someone who has the technical knowledge about the business, the sky would be your beginning. Funds without knowledge amounts to waste of resources. How can you prepare a realistic business plan without good knowledge of the business? How do you know the capital requirement of the business? How do you know the best location for that business? How do you know the source of human and material resources for the business? The truth is no one succeeds in a business he knows little or nothing about. Your business success is often a function of your knowledge base.

3. Lack of managerial ability

Every business is an organization and every organization requires proper management to be successful. As a management professional, I have come to realize that management is everything to business success. Effective management is what is required to take the business beyond the entrepreneurial stage and launch it into the growth stage. Management helps to provide the structure and system required to run the organization as more and more people join and as more and more operations are undertaken.

As the business begins to expand by serving more more customers, more employees are hired, more equipment engaged, and more funds needed. These requirements challenge the capacity of the entrepreneur and if he or she is not a management professional or has not received any form of management development training, he or she will begin to falter in decisions and actions. This situation adversely affects the growth and development of the business as well as threaten its very survival.

At the entrepreneurial stage, the entrepreneur probably handled most aspects of the business all by himself or with the assistance of a few employees. When the enterprise starts growing, the entrepreneur will not be able to do all that by himself. He will need someone else to handle the marketing, the human resources, the finances as well as the production/operations jobs of the enterprise while he handles the general administration as the chief executive officer. If the entrepreneur lacks the managerial ability to act as a CEO and to determine the right time to hand over various aspects of the business to more competent staff or partners, the business will begin to suffer and might even begin to struggle for survival. The reality is that it is usually very difficult for entrepreneurs to hands off certain aspects of their business either for lack of trust or fear of losing control. When delegation, one of the main principles of management, is difficult to practice, the long term growth of the business is jeopardized. If the entrepreneur, who is now the CEO, wants to handle every aspect of the business and to determine what happens in every unit of its operation, without given opportunity to other members of the organization to contribute to its growth and development, the business begins to fumble and crumble. Employee turnover increases, absenteeism begins, and machine breakdowns, down times and material waste become the order of the day. All these are natural reactions to bad management. Soon, the above experience will lead to increased customer complaints owing to delayed orders, substandard products or services, and increased costs. When major customers begin to complain about your business lapses, patronage will begin to decrease and a competitor could cash in on the opportunity by offering a better service at a better price; leading to your business failure.

No matter your profession, if you want to do well in business you should go for a business management training. You will never regret the amount of money and time spent on this sort of training. More businesses will survive and the American economy will be more sustainable if more and more entrepreneurs have some sort of training in business management. If you know that you do not have what it takes to effectively manage your business, then you have to hire professional managers and give them the free hand to do what they know best. Management is the process of determining the objectives of an organization, ascertaining the resources required to achieve them, and performing all other functions required to ensure that those objectives are effectively and efficiently realized for the benefit of the owners of the organization as well as the good of the society. This is the best definition I have ever given about management. Management must not only focus on the organization but also on the society or environment that sustains it.

Lack of managerial ability on the part of entrepreneurs has scuttled the growth, and led to the death, of businesses with often great growth potentials. If your business must grow and have departments and branches, you need to let go of the archaic mentality that you are the only one that can make the business survive. Until and unless your business gets to the point where it can operate without your physical presence or incessant zoom calls, I'm afraid you have no business!

4. Insufficient knowledge of market dynamics

Not everyone that has an idea for a product or service knows how to prepare a business plan. Every business plan has an aspect that assesses the market potential for the new business. Here, you are required to present valid data on the amount of potential customers for your new business by identifying the number of similar businesses within and around the location and the estimated total amount of customers to be served. When you divide the total amount of customers in that area with the number of suppliers, including yourself, that gives you an idea of the average potential market availability for your new business.

There is hardly any business success without customer patronage. There is no need to start a business if there is no identifiable need to be met by that business. What provides a business opportunity is the 'presence of a need' that is not being met satisfactorily. If there is no marketing gap, that is, a noticeable difference between growing demand and available supply, any new business is bound to fail for lack of patronage. This is a major reason for most business failures.

If you cannot prepare a business plan, you need to pay an expert to prepare one for you. The business plan gives you an idea of the success or failure of your new business based on available economic indices. You don't just assume that everybody in the neighborhood will abandon their current supplier to patronize your new business when you are offering exactly the same type of products or services at the same price. Any business that is started on assumption, presumption or speculation, will definitely end up with low patronage and will go into extinction over time. It is also pertinent to note that once you start a new business that offers distinct products or provides better services, existing competitors will adjust their strategies by copying you while new entrants will also flood the market as well. To mitigate the effects of this situation, you must register and obtain applicable licenses for your new products, services or ideas so that it becomes illegal for others to copy within the duration of your patent right.

The success of a new business is determined not by how great its products or services are but by its market acceptability. If your business cannot generate enough patronage required to sustain its annual operations, its failure is guaranteed. How I wish there is a softer way to present this! The number of new businesses which go into extinction every year is a testimony to the fact that entrepreneurs need to do more if their businesses must survive and thrive. Not every reasonable business idea is profitable. If your idea is not profitable enough, there is no need to convert it into a business. A business that has no potential for profit is a walking dead. For example, if an entrepreneur decides to site a grocery store in an area with seven hundred households and six existing grocery stores, he has an average of 100 potential households to serve. Will these hundred households generate enough patronage that would sustain its operations every year? If the answer is 'no' then there is no need to site the business in that location. Even if the new entrepreneur decides to lower the price of his items, only a few more customers will be attracted and this could lead to a price warfare which is not a very good idea for any of the businesses. Price warfare benefits only the customers and it is never sustainable. The moment you revert to the market price in a bid to make profits is the day most of your customers would run back to their former suppliers. This makes you a double loser. First, you lost your profits due to price reduction and, second, you lost patronage due to 'mobile' customers.

Every entrepreneur must have an in depth knowledge of the market he or she wants to operate in before venturing into business. Business failure is real and the only way to avoid it is to have an understanding of market dynamics and how to maneuver it. Knowledge is not cheap. You have to invest in good business books or engage the services of a reputable business consultant who will help you navigate the rough waters of business startups. Don't just assume that good products make great businesses. Get as much information as you possibly can about the nature of the business you wish to engage in and its market potential. You can't afford to waste your life savings or borrowed funds in an investment that is bound to fail. There is nothing smart about that. Successful entrepreneurs are not just those who have great ideas, good products or excellent services to offer but those who understand that market availability plays a vital role in the profitability and sustainability of their new businesses. Those who cannot afford to obtain the necessary information about the market usually end up paying a greater price simply known as business failure!

5. Choosing wrong partners

Earlier in this chapter, I stressed on the need for an entrepreneur to have a partner who will make up for his or her lapses in the areas of technology, finance, management, and marketing, etc. No man is an island of knowledge. When an entrepreneur engages a partner, he or she complements and completes himself or herself with the needed skill set to make the enterprise more successful in its operations. The idea is not just to pick a partner but to pick one that has what you lack. This means that choosing a wrong partner can adversely affect the success and growth of the business. Good partners can become great assets whereas bad partners are gross liabilities to any business. The choice of a partner requires great care and caution.

Before deciding to engage a partner, an entrepreneur must find out what the new business needs to survive and thrive. This entails the level of skills required, the nature of experience needed, the amount of financial resources needed, and the managerial capability required. The entrepreneur then realistically articulates his personal ability as it relates to the requirements of the business, determines what is needed to make up for his lapses, and then sets out to look for someone, a group of individuals or a corporation that can bring in those needed technical skills, operational experiences, financial resources, and managerial abilities. An entrepreneur that cannot realistically determine the needs of his or her business before take-off will end up believing that he has the ability to perform all the roles required for business success. This takes us back to the business plan. You cannot determine the actual needs of the new business until you have prepared a comprehensive business plan. There is an aspect of the business plan that highlights the manpower requirements of the new business. If this section is not properly articulated, the entrepreneur will continue to operate under unnecessary pressure. The critical question is 'how many entrepreneurs can prepare a good business plan?'

It will be necessary to state that there is a huge difference between a partner and an employee. A partner is part of the ownership of the business while an employee is just a worker who is there to help. Partners are entitled to the profit of the business whereas employees are entitled to wages or salaries. An employee cannot be engaged in an aspect that is very critical to the survival of the new business. The day the employee realizes how important he or she is to the overall success of the business is the day the business will start dying. The reason is that he or she will start asking for all manner of unrealistic raises and if the requests are not met, he or she would threaten to quit. The best decision at this moment will be to convert the employee into a partner or bring in a partner that would play such a role and perform such a task. This saves your business from going down in the early stages.

Having the right skill mix is not just enough reason when choosing a business partner. You must select someone who shares your vision, passion and aspiration concerning the new business. Never ever consider someone who is there just for the money because once he makes as much money as possible, he will check out and leave you in the cold. Always consider someone who is ready to go the long distance with you and make the necessary sacrifice for the survival and growth of the new business. Always consider someone who is willing to put in extra hours of hard labor, available to be contacted whenever needed, and ready to move to wherever his or her presence is needed. Entrepreneurship is not bread and butter; it is more like pregnancy. If a pregnant woman is required to make certain sacrifices to ensure that she delivers a lively and healthy baby in due time, likewise an entrepreneur must make certain sacrifices to ensure that he or she establishes a lively and healthy business over time. And every partner in a new business is a co-entrepreneur. You must engage a partner who exhibits similar burning desire for the long-term survival of the business and not just the short-term benefits of the owners.

Choosing the wrong partner is one of the factors that lead to the death of new businesses in America and around the world. Most family owned businesses are often affected by this factor. When a man decides to partner with his spouse to run a family business, he must ensure that she possesses what he lacks which is needed for the survival of the business. When the father decides to partner with his son to start a family business, he must ensure that his son has what he, the father, lacks which is needed for the survival of the business. Failure of the entre-preneur to make the right choice of partners has ruined many businesses with great potential.

B) The major factors that lead to the failure of an established business organization include the following:

1. Overgrowing its managerial capability

The importance of management to the overall success of an organization cannot be over-emphasized. Every organization is established to fulfill a certain purpose. To do this, the organization needs certain amount of resources namely human, material, financial, information, technology, and time. In a bid to use the available resources to achieve the set objective, an individual or group of individuals, often referred to as the 'management' has to be actively engaged to ensure that the objectives are realistic and that the resources are in the right proportion. Management also ensures that the right knowledge (intellectual capacity) is available, and that decisions are made and actions taken at the right time in order to deliver needed solutions to the right people at the right time and at the right price. It is the duty of management to ensure that everything is right. This is the reason why the coach is usually fired when a team starts losing, commanders are changed once the army starts displaying lack of discipline, a president is removed when the nation starts drifting, a CEO is sacked when the corporation starts faltering, a principal is replaced once the students start failing, a pastor is transferred when the church stops growing, and the chief medical officer is fired once the hospital starts losing its patient population. I can go on and on to highlight areas where the importance of management is so glaring yet many people do not give the management profession all the credit it deserves.

An organization can actually overgrow or outgrow the managerial capability of its management team. Growth is a good thing but when it happens faster and bigger than the current management can handle, it becomes catastrophic. A management team that can handle an organization with five hundred employees may not be able to handle an organization of 5000 staff. Organization expansion is a fantastic idea but it must be handled with much caution else it can spell doom for the organization. Everybody is not trained to manage and everybody is not meant to manage. Management involves a whole lot of things and cannot be left for the uninitiated. Because management entails the exercise of authority over the use of resources for the attainment of group goals, every member of an organization often desires to climb to the management position without realizing that it also poses a whole lot of challenges both to the informed and even a lot more to the uninformed.

As the driver is to a vehicle, so is the manager to an organization. Hand over the best car to an amateur driver and you will regret the journey. Just as the ability of the driver determines the performance of the automobile, so also does the capability of the management influence the operations of the organization. It would amount to a disaster to hire a medical professional who does not understand the meaning of organizational system or structure to become the chief medical officer and CEO of a world class hospital. At that level of the organizational hierarchy, his medical profession and experience play less role than the managerial experience and training he has gained over the years. As the CEO, he or she is no longer required to conduct surgery or offer prescription to patients. He or she simply makes decisions and takes actions that ensure that the medical facility has the right quality and quantity of medical and other staff at all times, that staff welfare is taken care of in a timely manner, that the right funding is available at all times, that a cordial relationship is maintained between the hospital, the community, and the government at all times, that needed materials such as drugs, syringes, beds, sheets, toilet papers, microscopes, medical scanners and X Ray machines are available in the right quantity, and that the staff are well motivated to do their jobs to the best of their ability under existing corporate, professional, legal, and regulatory policies, procedures and principles. Some of the things I just mentioned are hardly taught in most medical schools but rather in all business schools. So, if you place the best neurosurgeon in the world, who has no managerial training or experience, in the position of Chief Medical Officer and CEO of a cancer treatment center, that institution might collapse. His or her success as a surgeon cannot automatically translate into success in his new position as the Chief Medical Officer and CEO.

In every failed organization, there is usually an element of 'management's failure to do the right thing at the right time with the right resources.' When an organization starts expanding, the capacity of its management team should also be critically analyzed to see if it can sustain the organization at its next level. To assume that today's management team is capable of effectively and efficiently operating the organization at a new level is to assume that someone who is used to driving a four wheel personal car can successfully drive an 18-wheeler truck filled with merchandise. This amounts to building a castle in the air! Management must continue to seek ways to update the system as well as upgrade the structure of the organization to guarantee an effective and successful operation. When an organization fails, it is the management that failed. Management must, therefore, be well positioned to provide direction to the organization and ensure total control of its activities in a bid to continue to achieve the set objectives.

2. Fierce competition

Fierce competition can destroy an organization. As a result of competition, organizations operating in the same industry are often faced with the challenge of retaining their current customers, creating more customers, or snatching their rival's customers. There are so many marketing strategies involved in these. What determines the general success of an organization is its ability to maintain a high level of 'loyal' customers; that is, those who will never switch sides no matter what. This is not always easy since there are other organizations within the same location offering similar products or services who equally want to maintain a large volume of loyal customers.

Retaining current customers is not as easy as it sounds. I have classified current customers of an organization to include loyal customers, mobile customers, and occasional customers. It is much easier to retain your loyal customers. If you maintain your policies, improve staff courtesy, guarantee good shop layout and security, and ensure that needed products and services are always available at a fair price, your loyal customers will always be there. Even if there are slight price increases, an explanation is all you need to retain your loyal customers.

Mobile customers, on the other hand, are usually hard to retain because they are 'price conscious.' They are the swingers looking for as much as one cent in price difference without considering how much gas it takes to move from one store to another. They complain about everything and are never satisfied over anything. There is nothing you can do to retain them except sell at the lowest price; even if it means selling at a loss. They do not really care about your business success as much as they do about their personal savings. The worst scenario is 'even if your shop shuts down due to losses, they will still complain on why you choose to shut down in that neighborhood.' Price competition is the worst strategy an organization can adopt because it seeks to satisfy a group of customers that can never be satisfied. This is why I call them mobile customers. The only time you see them is if your price is the lowest or if other shops are closed. Striving to please such customers can give you a heart attack. Since the overall success of your business does not depend on them, you do not have to concentrate most of your efforts in trying to please them.

Occasional customers are those who are either on vacation in town, or came on an official visit or to provide some sort of services within the neighborhood. For example, a building contractor that moves to a different city to provide technical services, needs a local store where he can purchase building materials to execute the contract. This makes him an occasional customer to a nearby Home Depot store because it might be the only time he would patronize that store in his lifetime or for a long time. You cannot do much to retain occasional customers. If you are the only organization that offers the products or services they need within the area, they will have no choice but patronize you.

Creating more customers in an already saturated market is not an easy task. Remember, as I stated earlier in this book, that there is a minimum number of customers required to operate a business successfully and profitably and if you do not have this number of customers, your business cannot survive. The mistake retail organizations usually make is to site their branches in the same location where other retail organizations seem to be operating successfully without considering if the number of customers in that area will be adequate for the survival of all the stores. You cannot create more customers where there are no extra human beings. This leads to snatching of customers which is usually targeted at mobile customers and done through price warfare. Price warfare comes in different forms: general price reduction, buy-2-and-get-1-free, occasional seasonal percentage sales rebates, etc. All these strategies tend to reduce the revenue accruing to the business and negatively affect its bottom line. You cannot operate this strategy for so long and expect your business to be afloat for too long. Attempts to snatch competitor's customers can lead to spying or industrial espionage, paying more to buy over some of their key employees, hiring people to disrupt their operations, or paying people to adulterate their products, etc. These are mostly illegal, and immoral, actions that can ruin your reputation, lead to endless litigation, and ultimately ground your business. You can't afford to be involved in any of these.

Sometimes it is good to attack competitors head on but, as much as possible, avoid fierce competition and seek to operate in areas where you have a competitive advantage. Avoid the strategy of pushing others out of the market because that might be a costly strategy both to you and the society. Competition without consideration is an evil pill that does no one no good.

3. Environmental changes

Changes in the physical environment can adversely affect a business organization. Business is established to serve people by meeting their needs. Whatever disrupts the ecosystem of a particular location also has the ability to destroy a business organization in that area.

Natural disasters and climate changes can destroy a business organization in two ways: they can cause physical damage on the business itself or they can cause the relocation of the customers. Natural disasters come in the form of thunderstorms, hurricanes, tornadoes, wildfires, landslides, earthquakes, flooding, etc., and climate changes can come in the form of excessive rains, excessive snow falls, and ozone layer depletion with resultant cold and excessive heat, respectively. The implication of this is that you must be very knowledgeable about the location of your business and the prevalent climate conditions.

There are certain locations that are known for certain natural disasters. To site your business in such locations is to intentionally sign the death warrant of that business. Some parts of the State of California are known for annual wildfire disasters that claim scores of lives, and properties worth hundreds of millions of dollars. Successful business organizations or their branch locations have been gutted by fire along the way. This makes every business man or woman very skeptical about siting his or her business in such location where fire disasters are mostly certain to happen. Business can be insured against fire disasters but at a very high cost due to the high prevalence of such risk. Remember that the insurance company will rebuild the business in the same location where it was gutted by fire. Consider also the loss of patronage between the time of the fire disaster and when the business is rebuilt. What if most of the customers decide to relocate?

The states of Texas and Florida are known for hurricanes, rain storms and flooding at certain periods of the year. Business organizations have been destroyed as a result of such natural disasters and every business man or woman should be wary of siting his or her business in such locations that are prone to such disasters. The business can be insured against flooding no doubt, what about the loss of patronage encountered during such periods? Businesses that survive on daily sales, such as grocery stores and gas stations, can't afford to operate in locations that are prone to natural disasters. Your loyal customers may also relocate as a result of incessant disruption of their family life, career and health due to such natural disasters. Coincidentally, siting your business in these disaster-prone locations can result in high revenue and profitability due to less competition but that is only during periods when the natural disaster is yet to strike.

The state of Oklahoma, and its environs, is prone to severe tornado attacks at certain periods of the year. In such attacks, buildings are torn apart with deadly debris flying about, parked trucks with their contents are ripped apart, cars are flown to different directions, while huge trees are uprooted and relocated. Businesses are completely obliterated as the owners barely escape. It is a catastrophe that is better imagined than experienced. Any business which is located in such areas is never sure of its future. Tornado can strike when you least expect and even when there is a specific warning of a threat, there is nothing anybody can do about it. If you stand in its way, it will blow you away. If you try to stop it, it will succeed in stopping you. The best option is to stay out of its way and take your business elsewhere.

Areas that are prone to climate changes such as excessive snow and cold, excessive sun and heat, excessive rain and thunderstorm, and unpredictable temperature fluctuations can affect the operations of a business. For example, during severe snowstorms, airlines cancel flights and lose revenue while retaining and paying their staff. If such periods last longer than necessary, certain businesses will be completely grounded. In such periods also, delivery trucks and vans cannot make needed deliveries to meet customer needs. Perishable goods can also be lost due to severe weather conditions and any situation that increases operational costs for a business also decreases its profit potentials and takes it closer to extinction.

Environmental changes can pose a serious challenge to an existing business organization. The owners and managers of a business organization must make concerted efforts towards deciding whether to relocate their businesses and avoid business failures caused by environmental disasters or remain in their current locations and hope that such disasters never happen.

4. General economic downturn

Every business organization operates within the broad economic spectrum of the place where it is located; be it a city, state, region, nation or territory. The prevailing economic condition of your location, therefore, has a way of determining the success or otherwise of the business. The economic cycle generally has such conditions as recession (doom), recovery (zoom), and prosperity (boom). If the general economic condition of your location is that of recession, your business will be adversely affected. People need to work and make money before they can patronize your business. If there are no jobs and no household income, how do you expect your customers to patronize you? Selling on credit, and accumulating bad debts, is one of the factors that lead to the demise of many businesses. General economic downturn reduces the amount of patronage needed to sustain an existing business and makes it even more difficult for new businesses to be established. Economic downtown or recession is characterized by high rates of unemployment, high interest rate, low return on investment, low patronage of commercial activities, high cost of production, and higher price for products and services. Most of these conditions shrink demand and whatever reduces demand affects the revenue profile and profitability index of a business organization.

The main factor that drives economic development is production – agricultural and industrial production. This is why the economic cycle begins with production as shown below:

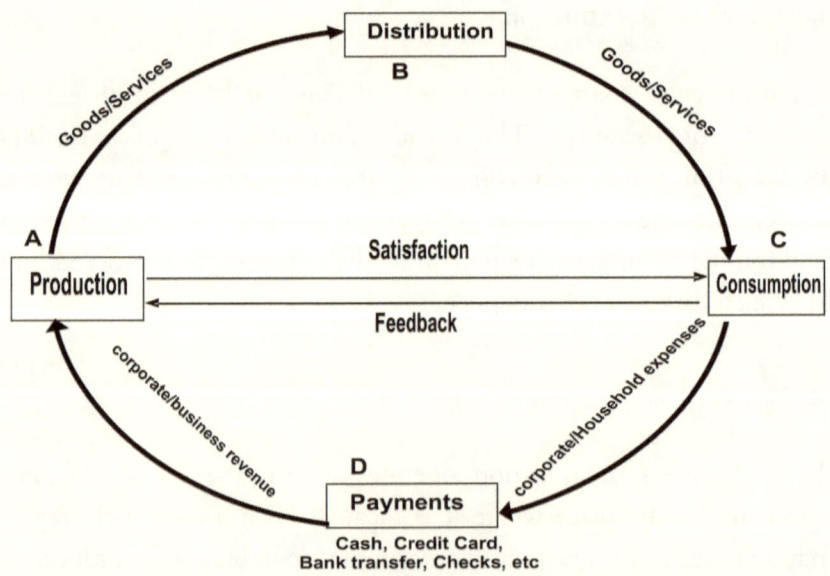

Production includes agro-production, food processing and preservation, energy production, raw material processing, power production, mineral processing, chemical production, auto manufacturing, aircraft manufacturing, pharmaceutical production, electronics manufacturing, arms and ammunition manufacturing, building and construction, furniture making, textile manufacturing, paper production, printing and publishing, etc. Whenever production happens, distribution is kick-started. Distribution involves all commercial activities that ensure that products or services get to the final consumers. These activities include transportation, banking, insurance, warehousing/storage, security, maintenance, wholesaling, retailing, marketing, advertising media, shipping, courier/postal services, internet services, administrative services, etc. All these and many more activities help to facilitate the movement of products and services from the point of production to the place of consumption and also ensure that the right revenue, through customer payments, accrue to the producer to sustain further production. From the feedback from consumers, research and development activities are conducted to improve existing products or introduce new ones to meet consumers' ever-changing tastes and desires.

The above analysis shows that whatever cripples production threatens economic development. There can be no jobs without production. So, if you want to create jobs and improve economic development you must first establish an environment that encourages production especially industrial production. Also, remember that there can be no meaningful industrial production without a robust agricultural production. The industrial sector is simply in the business of processing both agricultural produce and natural resources into industrial goods. I have also realized that industrial production is sustained by energy and power – fuel and electricity. It is also important to note that the supply of energy is what is driving most of the international trade that happens across the globe and that the price of petroleum products has an overriding influence on the price of other products and services. This is the reason why industrial nations are looking for alternatives to fossil fuel. I have also come to the conclusion that the difference between developed nations and underdeveloped ones is the amount of electricity supply available to each of them. Light or electricity drives production, improves preservation, and ensures that goods are moved from the area of production to the area of consumption in their proper form at the appropriate time. Electricity also ensures that productive activities take place both day and night to satisfy growing global demand. The current global hub for industrial production is China and this is leading to a noticeable economic development reflected in their increasing annual GDP. By implication, China's political influence is also growing at the international stage. The relocation of industrial production by American corporations, to places such as China, took away American jobs, economic development, and political influence.

Inability to attain energy independence also makes a nation economically vulnerable. When industrial production falls due to the scarcity of energy supply or diminishing power supply, jobs are lost, household incomes reduce, and demands for products and services plummet. This sparks off a general economic downturn which leads to the demise of certain businesses due to lack of patronage. Is there really anything a business organization can do to forestall a general economic downturn? Your guess is as good as mine!

5. Wrong choice of new leadership

This is one of the major factors leading to the death of well-established organizations. An organization can only have one leader at a time in the person of the Chief Executive Officer. The first CEO of an organization, usually the founder, grew the organization and himself through years of experience based on the principle of trial and error. The next CEO does not have the luxury of time to grow through similar conditions because the organization is already grown and, therefore, requires someone who already knows what leadership is all about to sustain its current position and prepare it for the next level. Failure to get the right candidate to succeed the current CEO can be catastrophic.

The current practice in the choice of a new CEO for family owned business organizations is for the founder of the corporation to appoint one of his kids, usually the first son, to replace him. This is not a bad idea especially if the young man observed and participated in the operations of the business with his father over the years. But if you appoint an unconcerned or a less-concerned observer, just because he happens to be the first son of the founder of the organization, calamity is not far from the reality. Leadership is not a simple task. A leader must have an idea of what it takes to move an organization from where it is to where it ought to be. More so, an organizational leader must learn and understand the principles of management as this is going to determine his or her success in the new position and the overall direction of the organization. He or she must also understand that organizations thrive on well defined systems and survive on well designed structures. He must also understand and have what it takes to harvest, harness, and galvanize the various talents, skills and experiences of all the members of the organization (managerial, supervisory and operational) as to sustain it's current growth as well as develop new strategies for its future growth and progress. As a strategic leader, the CEO must also have the skill required to face environmental threats, overcome internal challenges, and explore and exploit environmental opportunities for the overall benefit of the organization.

Every organization has its culture and politics. Every CEO must understand and fashion ways to manage these issues. Organizational culture involves the acceptable group behaviors and social practices built over the life of an organization. Most of them are positive while a few others can be negative to outsiders. A new CEO must build on the positive practices but also develop a plan to break the negative ones, if he intends to take the organization to a new height. Culture, as we know, is based on habit and habit is not easy to break. For example, an organization might have a culture of accepting 5 to 10 minutes lateness for employees but where this practice is seen to be negatively affecting the operations of the organization, the new CEO must be able to put a stop to it. This will require stepping on some sore toes, you know, but the job has to be done. There are other organizations that allow employees to make use of organizational resources for personal benefits such as telephone, stationery, copiers, scanners, vehicles, computers, printers, etc. If this 'acceptable' practice seems to be unnecessarily increasing the cost of operations, the CEO has the obligation to stop it. This might temporarily affect employee morale but will ultimately save the entire organization.

Organizational or office politics entails all the power plays that take place within an organization. It happens between regions or districts, departments, sections, units, and among individuals. Personality clashes among managers can affect the operations of the departments they head by creating silos. For example, if the Finance Manager has a conflict with the Marketing Manager on the way the later approves overtime pay for the sales staff, this might negatively influence relationships between the staff of the two departments and ultimately affect the operations and success of the entire organization. Another example will buttress this point. If the Assistant Production Manager in charge of products ABC discovers that the soon-to-retire overall production manager favors the assistant production manager in charge of products XYZ and will most likely recommend him or her to be the next production manager, this can create a serious crisis and a huge challenge to an inexperienced CEO. Every CEO must establish a succession plan or parameter based on the principles of fairness, performance, skill, and experience and not allow departmental managers influence such decisions based on favoritism, nepotism, or outright racism. These are the little things that destroy an organization and if a new CEO does not have what it takes to tackle and overcome them, a once-successful organization can go down the drains over a very short period of time. Wrong choice of new leadership can ruin as well as destroy an organization, not minding how big it currently is.

CHAPTER 7

ORGANIZATIONS CAN BE TRANSFORMED

(The challenges and opportunities of the 21st century organization)

In this last chapter of the book, we shall be looking at ways to strengthen, re-engineer and reposition an organization to actualize its objective amid daunting challenges. Is organizational transformation possible? If the answer is yes, what are the factors that can facilitate it?

First, we need to understand the true meaning of the word 'transformation.' It stems from the root word 'form' which means 'the nature of something.' Transformation, therefore, means 'changing the nature of something to make it better.' One of the ways organizations survive in the midst of daunting challenges is to change the nature of their operations in line with changes in the environment. Those who fail to change are often overtaken by change. The world is changing so fast and so are the options available to organizations which desire to survive and thrive. In this chapter, we shall be looking at the fundamental challenges of the 21st century organization as well as what can be done to convert these seeming challenges into opportunities for growth, advancement, and sustainability. In an era where workers are seeking increased wages, customers asking for low prices, suppliers expecting better deals, regulators demanding higher quality products, governments threatening to increase corporate taxes, environmentalists lobbying for cleaner energy sources and greener environment, shareholders calling for better return on their investments, and the entire society clamoring for improved corporate social responsibility, what can organizations do to survive?

We shall discuss the challenges of the 21st century organization and proffer possible solutions under the following headings:

a) Changes in information technology
b) Globalization of products and services
c) Unlimited improvement in production technology
d) Environmental concerns of industrial production
e) Over-consumption – threat to future generations
f) Redefining the core values of organizations – Focusing on what really matters
g) Effects of capitalism on international trade
h) The issue of collaboration and integration between organizations and the societies they serve
i) Running the corporate world on credit card – The credit-card-craze!
j) Leading the learning and changing organization

Changes in information technology

Knowledge, they say, is power; the power to create solutions to human challenges. It has also been established that knowledge appears in two forms: information and inspiration. Inspiration is a supernatural influence on the human intellect to receive ideas that are entirely new and sometimes strange but have the capacity to produce incredible results when put to productive use; especially if understood and properly developed. Information, on the other hand, is the documented facts about past and present events, discoveries, inventions, innovations, experiences, and observations meant for dissemination. Sources of information include books, newspapers, magazines, radio, television, sign boards, notice boards, billboards, and the Internet. All that we study in school are based on information about what other people had discovered, observed or experienced.

It has been observed that the invention (discovery and development) of the printing press brought about the industrial revolution of the 18th century because information about events in one part of the world was able to be documented in books and made available to other parts of the world to read, understand and apply. Remember also that the world does not speak the same language. So, the extent to which a particular part of the world adopts a new industrial method is dependent upon the speed with which they are able to learn and understand the foreign language or get someone to translate the information to their local language for local application. This is the reason why learning a foreign language has become so important.

The basis of the interactions that take place among the nations of the world is always economic in nature; the need to exchange what one has for what one needs. Nature endows different parts of the world differently so as to establish a relationship based on exchange and not exploitation. This is the reason why it is difficult for nations to relate socially or politically if they do not relate economically. Information helps to link areas of supply of certain economic resources with areas of deficit so as to establish a relationship of exchange. Advances in information technology has reduced the distance between the source of information and the use us of such information. Nowadays, with a touch on the screen of your cell phone or the click of a button on the computer keyboard, the information originated in one part of the world can become available in other parts of the world at the same time. This is what the Internet accomplishes. The international network of computers (INTERNET) is an advancement in information technology that has made the entire world look like one global community where there is unlimited interaction and unfettered communication between individuals, organizations, and nations resulting in improvements in socio-political relationships and culminating into better economic exchanges around the world.

The Internet has had a profound impact on the media sector more than any other industry. We now hear of such things as the social media, which is adversely affecting the operations of the traditional media, leading to the decline of once-famous and powerful media houses which failed to be transformed in line with global trends in information dissemination. These days, members of the society are not just consumers of information but producers of it as well. Armed with a smart phone that has a video recorder and is connected to the Internet, individuals now have the ability to record events real time and upload them to social media platforms for the global viewing audience. Just before the traditional media house gives a breaking news, the social media is already inundated with such news material. But unlike the traditional media, the social media sends out uncensored version of the news report which can often trigger unnecessary fear and pandemonium. That there are no well-defined and strictly-obeyed rules and regulations in the social media sub-sector is one of its major challenges.

As a result of improvements in information technology, terrorist organizations are now able to create confusion among the populace, threaten peace in the society, divert the attention of government, and recruit new members into their groups more than ever before. With a telephone set and a computer system, each individual actually has unrestricted access to the entire world at anytime of the day. Those who understand the power of today's information technology are using it either for good or for bad. Social mobilization is now a lot easier using the social media. Teaching and learning are now much easier using the computer system. Research is now less difficult because a huge array of resources are posted on the Internet on a daily basis. For example, the Wikipedia website has tons of resources for virtually any subject of interest under the sun and they are being updated daily by the individual contribution of users across the globe. The result of a scientific research conducted in India is now available to a student of Indiana State University at little or no charge. knowledge is now being transmitted from areas of conception to areas of consumption at the speed of light; making it possible for the world to operate as a global community.

As a result of the monumental changes in information technology, organizations operating in the 21st century era must have a means of tapping into the enormous information resources for their corporate improvement. In order to gain competitive advantage in the industry or location of their operation, organizations need a lot of correct and current information. Also, we now know that information is one of the resources of an organization and organizations which have access to superior information end up ahead of the competition. They also end up as market leaders. Through improvements in information technology, customers can now view company products online, compare prices and make their purchases online, make payments online, and report issues to the customer service unit online concerning returns and replacements. This means that customers outside the location of your branches can still purchase your products and enjoy your services. This is simply incredible! It entails that 21st century organizations must design, develop, and host interactive websites if they want to remain relevant in today's market. They must also recruit employees that are knowledgeable about the improvements in information technology, install state of the art equipment that interacts with a computer system on the Internet, and maintain and update the system regularly for optimum performance.

Improvements in information technology, by the use of the computer and the Internet, have helped to reduce the cost of paperwork in daily transactions within the organization as well as in the number of workers engaged to carry out certain functions. Financial accounting, stock audit, customer checkout, and shipping details are now made easier with the use of improved information technology. Certain computer applications or programs can now be installed to automatically update stock levels and financial balances while reducing customer checkout time and eliminating theft through the 'scan-pay-go' process. The P.O.S (Point-Of-Sales) terminals are also part of the improvements in information technology where credit/debit card purchases are processed directly into the organization's bank account with just a swipe. So, improvements in information technology have brought about improvements in virtually every other aspect of the society and any organization that desires to succeed in the 21st century environment must adopt all of these changes or avoid them and risk its survival and growth. The transformed organization is the organization that is sensitive to the changes within the environment of its operation, adaptive to the improvements within the environment, and prepared to take advantage of this position in providing products and services that satisfy the needs of the customers and meet the desires of the investors as well.

To transform an organization to be in sync with the demands of the 21st century environment can be very challenging but not impossible. Adapting to the changes in information technology is the first step. With the right information technology in place, it is easier to determine the type of organizational structure to be adopted and the nature of the employees to be hired. The free flow of information within an organization is also breaking the communication barriers often created by the traditional organizational structure, which often delays decision making and slows down operations. Changes in information technology is actually revolutionizing organizations and redefining the basic principles on which they once stood. Transformed organizations are indeed successful organizations.

Globalization of products and services

Globalization is the development of increasingly integrated global economy. It is the trend in international business which connotes the movement away from distinct national economic units toward a huge global market with a free flow of products and services from areas of production to areas of consumption. It discourages national barriers to economic activities and encourages nations to concentrate on major economic activities where they have absolute advantage while depending on others for the rest of their product and service needs.

I have earlier established the fact that the basis of international relationships is economic exchange. When one nation has an abundant supply of what another nation needs to survive, an economic relationship is established and with this comes other relationships, such as social and political, in a bid to sustain the economic relationship. For example, before attaining energy independence, the United States needed a lot of petroleum products for its industrial and commercial survival. To guarantee the continuous supply of the needed oil products, the US entered into social and political relationships with the nations that have abundant supply and reserve of crude oil, which Saudi Arabia happens to be number one. The United States knew that whatever directly affected the peace of Saudi Arabia and the its oil supply chain will indirectly affect the progress of the United States. To ensure that such does not happen, the United States assisted the government of Saudi Arabia in maintaining internal peace and stability so that it will continue to have unrestricted access to the supply of its crude oil needs. So, international politics is an extension of international economic exchanges.

Globalization tries to establish a new economic system where there is free flow of products and services across national boundaries so that each part of the globe gets what it needs, at the time it needs it, and at the price it can afford. We all know that technological advancement is not evenly distributed among the nations of the earth. Some nations have an abundant supply of natural resources but do not have the right technology with which to process them into finished and usable products while others have the technology but lack the natural resources. By the principle of absolute advantage, the nations that have the natural resources are supposed to acquire the technology with which to process their natural resources into final products for global distribution and consumption but this is not always the case. Those who develop new technologies are not always willing to give them away and those who have natural resources are not always willing to grant unlimited access to those who have the right technology with which to process them for fear of losing out in the game of economic exchange. This brings us to the need for compromise in the name of strategic partnerships, trade agreements, joint ventures, subsidiary operations, offshore operations, etc.

Globalization is basically leading us to two distinct scenarios: globalization of markets and globalization of production. Globalization of markets connotes the movement away from an economic system in which national markets are distinct entities, isolated by trade barriers and barriers of distance, time, and culture, and toward a system in which national markets are merging into one global market. Globalization of production, on the other hand, denotes a trend by individual firms to disperse parts of their productive processes to different locations around the globe to take advantage of differences in cost and quality of factors of production. From the ongoing, it is very clear that the nations that are expected to benefit most from globalization are those that have developed the right technology for production. You cannot seek access into the global market if you do not have products to offer and you cannot disperse parts of your productive processes to gain competitive advantage across the globe if you do not possess the right technology. So, advanced production technology is what drives globalization and the firms or nations that do not possess it cannot reasonably benefit from globalization.

Globalization of markets implies that local firms are now in direct competition with foreign firms and if foreign firms have better technology that lowers unit cost and increases quality, local firms can be sent out of the market; creating unemployment for the local people and loss of tax revenue for local communities. Globalization of markets actually means to open up the US borders so that automobiles manufactured at a lower cost in South Korea are imported to compete with automobiles produced at a higher cost in the US. This does not happen! Local firms can't afford to let the government implement such a policy which tends to stifle national economic growth. What grows an economy is production. It creates jobs, produces products, provides services, guarantees household income, grants tax revenue to the government, and ensures return on investment to investors, which encourages further investment. When imported cheaper products are allowed to compete which local products, local firms struggle to survive and so does the local economy. On the other hand, globalization of production benefits the firms more than the nation. When firms are allowed to move different parts of their production processes outside the shores of the parent nation to areas where the cost of factors of production is cheaper, only to bring in these products as finished goods or parts of a product to be assembled and sold to local customers, the local economy is in shambles. Jobs are lost and household income gone. The big question becomes, 'with which income will local consumers purchase these imported products since they have no jobs?' They have to fall back to the government for unemployment benefits and other welfare and economic stimulus packages thereby placing greater burden on the government that has also lost substantial parts of its income tax revenue. This is exactly what is happening in the United States.

Globalization tends to favor well established firms that have access to funds as well as advanced technology with which to disperse parts of their production process to different locations in a bid to take advantage of low costs of production and then move their final products to markets where prices and profits are higher. This is the reason why US firms site their factories outside of the US soil, manufacture there at a lower cost and then send the products back into the United States to sell at a higher price. This practice is negatively affecting the US economy with rising number of unemployed and underemployed. For local economies to grow, certain trade barriers become necessary! Cheaper imported products with local alternatives kill production and hurt the economy. What boosts economic development is production and not distribution. Production leads to value addition while distribution simply makes goods available for human consumption. It is the area where production takes place that economic development is guaranteed. This is the reason why China's GDP is trailing that of the United Stated even though this does not improve its per capita income due to huge population. Products made in China are sold all over the world thereby creating more employment opportunities for the Chinese and placing plenty of Yuan into the hands of the Chinese Communist Party with which it advances its political agenda in Africa and around the world. When production activities increase in a nation, economic growth becomes its natural result.

A lot of people argue that globalization will eventually benefit every nation as each nation concentrates in the economic activities where it has absolute advantage while depending on other nations for the rest of its product and service needs. When we talk about absolute advantage we should remember that the emphasis is on the cost of production. Now, what if it is cheaper to produce nearly everything in one location, does it mean that the entire world will site all production activities in that area and then distribute the products to the rest of the world? With the low cost of labor, a major factor of production, in hugely populated countries such as China and India, it is becoming increasingly more profitable for industrial production to be located in these two Asian countries. It is also becoming increasingly profitable for certain commercial activities to be handled in this two countries through what is known as outsourcing or offshoring. Air ticketing, mass shipping, hotel booking, typing of voluminous documents, tax preparation, medical billing, digital designs, software production, web designing and hosting, telephone answering, and a host of clerical activities originating from the United States are now handled by virtual and independent workers in India, China, Mexico and some south American countries where it is cheaper compared to the 'high' labor cost in the United States.

However, the above scenario presents two major challenges. One, the presence of one supplier often leads to monopoly. China is fast becoming a monopolistic nation in terms of certain industrial production such as textile, shoes, bags, clothing, kitchen utensils, paper products, electronic parts, auto spare parts, home care products, fashion and beauty products, plastics, porcelain and ceramic products, arts and craft materials, digital CD's and DVD players, toys and computer accessories to name just a few. The world now depends on China for the supply of most of these products. If anything happens to China right now, the rest of the world will have nowhere to fall back to. Recall what happened during the holiday seasons of 2021 where gift items ordered from retail stores could not be delivered either because the products were still on the way from China or yet to be cleared at American ports. This is a dangerous economic trend. If China decides to introduce a certain tax or increase current taxes to cause a slight increase in the price of these products, it is the rest of the world that would pay for it while China benefits. It is pertinent to note that the United States is fast losing its position as the largest economy in the world and with the loss of economic power comes the loss of political influence. The second challenge is that unemployment rate is increasing in other parts of the world because of their relocation of most industrial production to China. Coupled with the high unemployment rate is the fact that residents of a place such as the United States are now forced to patronize made-in-China products when they have no jobs to raise income. And, if government decides to impose higher import taxes on these products, it is still the final consumer that bears the burden of increased prices. So, the only nation that actually grows in this exercise is China while the people that gain are the industrialists that produce in one 'cheap' location and then sell to the rest of the world for a greater profit.

As I earlier stated, international business should be about exchange and not exploitation. It amounts to exploitation when a particular nation or group of nations tend to exert control over certain economic activities at the detriment of the rest of the world. Economic resources or factors of production are dispersed across the globe in such a way that there is no particular resource that is found only in one location. And, when you have more that one supplier of a resource, competition sets in to help improve the quality of the product offering at a fair enough price.

Therefore, concentrating or localizing industrial production in a certain area all in the name of globalization is not only counterproductive to international trade but also dangerous to global economic growth and development. As the emerging global economy creates opportunities for certain businesses and nations across the globe, it also presents serious threats to other businesses and nations. Local firms now face the challenge of foreign competition and whether or not to extend their products or operations into foreign markets. Extending into foreign markets may seem very profitable but firms should also remember that there are barriers in terms of language, currency, general lifestyle, and regulatory requirements when deciding to make the move. Transformed organizations must be re-positioned to take advantage of market opportunities, local or global, to increase their profitability while adding greater value to their home countries and the world at large. Transformed organizations do not destroy the very society they are meant to serve.

Behind the subject of globalization is the World Trade Organization (WTO); the arm of the United Nations Organization responsible for global commerce and the monitoring of inter-national policies on trade and tariffs. Due to the clandestine and non-inclusive nature of the decision-making process of the WTO over the years, such things as public health, environmental protection, democratic principles, national sovereignty, and cultural values are being undermined at the expense of trade benefits. A few powerful multinational corporations and their supporting nations, under the umbrella of WTO, cannot continue to hold the entire world hostage by initiating and implementing global trade policies that do not only violate environmental safety, but also pose danger to the health and life of seven billion human beings around the world today. Any organization that promotes economic gains over and above human and environmental safety is dangerous to the survival of the human race. It is important to note that no organization exists outside of the human race.

The activities of WTO have continued to widen the gap between the economies of developed nations and that of the developing nations in such a way that while the developed nations are getting stronger, the developing nations are getting weaker. The WTO must, therefore, be transparent, all-inclusive and democratic in its operations so as to eliminate exploitation, avoid manipulation and ultimately encourage real economic exchange among the nations of the world. It does not make sense for the UN to be preaching democracy while WTO is busy practicing dictatorship. Both developing and underdeveloped nations can no longer be coerced into signing trade agreements that bring them economic doom all in the name of globalization.

Globalization, which facilitates global free market enterprise and greater access to the global market by multinational corporations, has only succeeded in achieving greater profitability to the corporations involved and a great wealth to few individuals who are major investors in those corporations. However, it has also succeeded in impoverishing the rest of the world including developing nations in Africa, South America and Asia as well as the working class in developed nations, by eliminating employment opportunities for the unemployed and at the same time reducing wages for those who are employed. By moving production activities to low labor cost areas of the world, corporations involved in globalization are producing at a lower cost, selling at a higher price, and making all the money while the rest of the world is getting poorer and poorer. If something drastic does not happen to correct this seeming imbalance, the world will soon experience an economic crisis that will be nothing compared to what we have experienced in the entire history of mankind.

Globalization, the new trend in international business led by the World Trade Organization, has succeeded in making a few corporations, and by extension their individual investors, super rich while the rest of the world is getting super poor. If this ugly trend is not checked immediately, there will be another industrial revolution; this time a radical change from the use of well-advanced digital technology in industrial production, to the long-abandoned manual means of subsistence production. Frustrated industrial workers around the world may soon take their freedom back by reverting to working for themselves in their family farms or personal workshops instead of going to work in industrial factories and warehouses. When this happens, it would be catastrophic to both global production and progress!

Unlimited improvements in Production Technology

Technology can simply be described as a scientific technique applied in production or operations. We have manual technique, mechanical technique, and electronic technique. Manual technique entails the use of basically human hands in production. For example, where you use your hands, sticks, hoes, spades, knives, sickles, ladders, wheelbarrows, and other tools and domestic animals to plant seeds, water the crops, and harvest the fruits, vegetables and other food materials for consumption. Mechanical technique entails the use of machines and tractors, with substantial human involvement, in planting, caring, harvesting and processing of food and other materials for human use and consumption. We can observe that the mechanical technique is an improvement of the manual technique. It also gets more job done with the involvement of less human labor. The application of electronic technique in production entails the use of electronic or electric-driven equipment, with less human involvement, in planting, caring, harvesting, transporting, storing, processing, and preserving of food and related materials for human use and consumption. Apart from food and related materials, natural resources such as air, soil, water, salt, timber, copper, iron ore, tin ore, aluminum ore, coal, sand, stone, natural gas, cobalt, diamond, silver, gold, uranium, and crude oil, etc., can be electronically processed for greater benefit. There is agricultural equipment that can plant seeds, water the farms, harvest the crops, process and transfer them to areas of storage with little or no involvement of human labor. These are done by a set of specialized computer programs installed in that piece of equipment. Industrial production is an extension of the electronic technique in production. In most industrial and certain parts of the service sector, robots are being installed to perform what used to be human functions. The electronic technique is an improvement of the mechanical technique and it makes use of less and less human labor to produce more and more products and services for human consumption. The advent of the electronic technique, which drives industrial production, is largely responsible for differences in economic development among nations. The nations with massive industrial production are more economically developed than those with minimal industrial production because, with the aid of electric-driven equipment, five persons are able to produce the food meant to serve five thousand people in a space of one hour. This is why I had earlier concluded that the main reason for the huge difference in the economic development of developed and underdeveloped nations is electricity. With adequate electricity supply, different nations of the world can produce their own food and have more than enough to consume. They will then store their surplus against periods of scarcity or for exchange with other nations undergoing scarcity due to natural disasters or other reasons such as poor harvest or lack of preservation facilities.

The electronic technique of production has undergone several transformations leading to improved methods of production and each new method tends to render previous methods obsolete, thereby, making organizations to operate in constant fear of obsolescence in their current process of production. Unlimited improvements in production technology seems to be one of the major threats to organizations engaged in industrial production because each improvement has its own cost, speed, quality, and adaptability implication on current operations as well as market expectations. An organization that uses a device which produces a thousand outputs per day at a total unit cost of $5 cannot comfortably compete with another organization that uses a modern device which produces a million units of output a day at a total unit cost of $3. The second company can afford to lower its price to sell more and make more profit than the first company. By the time the first company is struggling to adapt to the new technology, the second company would have eaten deep into its market share. It should, however, be noted that improvement in technology on its own does not determine success; it only facilitates the success of a thriving organization. Producing the wrong product at a higher speed and lower costs does not lead to success. So, adopting a new technology that produces what the market does not need is a colossal waste on its own and a perfect example of management myopia. Before a new technology is acquired, an organization must be sure that the new technology will assist in accelerating its success, not in creating it.

Technology keeps changing and if your main objective is to adopt every new technology in town your future is not guaranteed. Every piece of new technology you acquire increases your fixed cost and alters your current operational procedure. Continuous improvement in production technology arms new entrants with better, faster and sometimes cheaper ways of carrying out their operations while putting pressure on existing firms to either adopt the new technology or suffer from competitive disadvantage. We must understand that those who invent new technologies are also in business and will do everything possible to influence operators to patronize them. It is, therefore, left for each enterprise to determine how the new technology affects its existing situation, how it fits into its anticipated operations as well as how it enhances the pursuit of its core values. If the new technology does not help the organization fulfill it's reason for existence then it is not worth adopting. New technology does not drive growth; it only enhances the operations of the organization to achieve growth. An organization that does not have a comprehensive plan and strategy for growth cannot achieve growth by mere introduction of a modern technology in its operations.

To remain competitive in an industry where new entrants seem to have new production technology that guarantees a lower unit cost of products, an existing organization can engage in other measures to reduce its unit cost. Example, identifying cheaper sources of raw materials, shutting down unnecessary sections of the organization that drain the corporate purse while adding little or nothing to it, contracting out non critical services, and maintaining a satisfied and motivated workforce that delivers expected results at all times. New technology on its own does not guarantee success. What guarantees success is the capacity of management to initiate policies, establish procedures and put in place processes that require the new technology in meeting the core values of the organization while satisfying the needs of its customers. Therefore, organizations should no longer see the existence of new production technology as a threat to their existence but a test of their strength to survive in an ever changing business environment. New, and sometimes better, production technology will continue to emerge but what is more important is how organizations adapt to the challenge this situation presents and not necessarily if they will adopt the new technology. Those organizations who seek to adopt every new technology in town will soon discover that there can never be an end to it. New technologies not only disrupt current operational procedure but also render the workforce helpless as it grapples with the need to adapt to the new way of doing things or face loss of job as well as household income. This situation leads to serious management-labor crisis and adversely affects industrial harmony which is needed for the success of the organization.

Organizations must weigh the options and their implications before acquiring new production technology so that the aim for acquiring the new technology will not be defeated long before its actual installation. The critical question here is, 'do we need the new technology to enhance operations or do we need it to be ahead of competition or at par with the competition?' If the new technology does not help to improve our operational capacity in line with fulfilling our core values for being in existence, then we do not need it. Technologies come and go but great organizations remain strong. For example, selling your products through the online store is a new technology in marketing. Amazon has remained the big player in global online marketing; raking in billions of dollars through the warehousing and sale of other organizations' products. This success is now forcing uncountable retail companies into online marketing. Let's not forget that Amazon embarked on online marketing because it could not compete head on with well established retail companies such as Walmart, Giant Eagle, Kroger, Macy's, Sears, J. C. Penny, Best Buy, etc., who already had chains of traditional retail stores across the United States and beyond. Today, Amazon is acquiring retail stores and opening up new retail branches while mega retail companies are busy shutting down most of their branches to go online. Amazon's founder and CEO, Jeff Bezos, simply used the online marketing technology to break into the retail industry where he has always dreamed of being a major player. Technology did not drive Amazon's success; strategy did. Technology only enhanced Amazon's strategy and made it possible for it to become a major player in the retail industry of the 21st century.

When new technologies emerge in the market, forward looking organizations must not rush to acquire them but rather take their time to evaluate the situation based on their current operations, future needs as well as how the new technology relates to the pursuit of their core values for existence. New technology is good but if it is acquired at the wrong time and for the wrong reasons, it can lead to disaster for an organization.

Environmental concerns of industrial production

Environmentalists have often warned of the adverse effect of industrial production on the human environment. Industrial wastes such as harmful chemicals, contaminated water, poisonous gas, etc., often find their way into the environment. Some leak into sources of public water supply while others are dumped on the ground or released into the air; causing serious health hazards to unsuspecting members of the public. There are plenty reported cases of lead poisoning in our public water supply systems, gas flaring and oil spillage in the oil producing regions of the world and other chemical wastes that do adversely affect aquatic life and devastate our farmlands. These are some of the environmental concerns owing to industrial operations and the list goes on and on.

When industrial operations begin to pose a threat to environmental well being, the whole essence of value addition becomes questionable.

Industrial production involves the processing of natural raw materials and agricultural produce into higher forms as food for direct human consumption or as raw materials for use in further production. For example, converting fresh tomato fruits into canned tomato paste is industrial production; converting sugar cane into sugar cubes is industrial production; converting logs of wood into pulp and paper is a form of industrial production; and converting corn flour into loaves of bread is another form of industrial production. Every form of industrial production generates some kinds of waste: some so harmful and others not so harmful. Both the harmful and not so harmful will find their way into the environment to cause health hazards or create an ugly scenery. These conditions are unacceptable. So, what should a forward-looking organization do to reduce the amount of harmful waste products it releases into the environment and its effect on human, animal, and aquatic lives so as to maintain the desired balance in the ecosystem?

Air pollution, water pollution, and land pollution have become common experience in our urban cities and rural communities because of industrial production. The amount of carbon monoxide emitted by combustion engines of factories and exhaust pipes of automobiles combine to deplete the ozone layer and expose the human race to an excessive heat from direct sun rays on a daily basis. The current debate is whether industrial production should stop in order to preserve the environment or whether the environment should continue to be devastated by continuous industrial production. However, the big question remains, "can we allow uncontrolled industrial production while seeking to enjoy a decent environment devoid of pollution?" How can we reduce the negative effect of industrial production on our environment? Can new production processes be introduced that pose lesser threat to the environment? What would be the real cost of such innovation? Will the final consumer be able to pay the price for products from the new production process? These are critical questions that beg for answers. The truth, however, is that any industrial operation that devastates the environment is not sustainable. If we destroy our environment today, where will we operate tomorrow?

The greatest form of environmental pollution is from our source of energy supply. Energy from fossil fuel has for over a century remained the major and less expensive form of energy for industrial and transportation operations. It has also remained the major source of environmental degradation. The exploration and exploitation of oil resources have continued to devastate environments in the host communities; causing health, economic and other hazards to the people, and creating social disharmony among communities, their governments and the corporate organizations operating in those areas. Some of the organizations involved in oil prospecting activities care less about the effect of their operations in their host communities. Oil spills on the land and water are often left unattended for months and even years. Gas flaring has become the norm instead of the exception. Heat from combustion chambers continue to threaten agricultural and aquatic life while slowly destroying the people's health. Abandoned oil wells continue to pose a danger to host communities who live in fear of sudden explosion. Oil pipelines that lack regular maintenance might explode and cause fire outbreaks that destroy homes, farmlands, economic trees, and electric poles, erase animal habitat, and sometimes claim the lives of innocent citizens. Worthy of mention is the carbon monoxide which is constantly released into the air and its health implication on human beings as well as animals. This is the main reason why governments of developed nations of the world are leading and funding the research for alternative sources of energy. Already, there are electric cars that do not need petroleum products to function and there are electricity plants that make use of wind mills, solar panels and hydro turbines to generate clean energy for the industrial, commercial, and residential needs of the society.

One of the requirements of corporate social responsibility must include the efficient disposal of industrial wastes so as to reduce or eliminate the health effects of poisonous substances on our environment. The need for greater profit should not dwarf the need for better health. Health is wealth and if health is abandoned in pursuit of wealth, the two can be lost. Environmentalists have continued to harp on the need to preserve our environment from the hands of desperate industrialists who care for nothing else than the economic benefits they derive from industrial activities often at the expense of the health and general well being of the society in which they operate. If we fell all the trees to produce pulp and paper, from where will the oxygen required to sustain human and animal life come? If we tear down all the forest to build roads, railways, pipelines, airports, factories, and nuclear stations, where will the animals live and breed? If we poison our rivers with chemical wastes from industrial operations, where will the fishes live and breed? Industrial organizations must begin to fashion out ways to do things differently or risk being labeled as environmental terrorists by those who fully understand the devastating nature of their operations on the human environment and the entire ecosystem of the universe.

There have also been occasions where industrial wastes are shipped out and dumped in the third world countries. This is an unacceptable practice. We must not fail to understand that what goes around always comes around. Some parts of the world cannot be made to suffer from the result of industrial operations while others are busy enjoying the benefits. All lives matter. The right to life is a fundamental human right and must be preserved at all times. Stakeholders must come together to find acceptable solution to the problem of industrial pollution and the best time to do it is now. If we continue to delay action in this direction, we might wake up one day and realize that our world has become too toxic to sustain life. Certain dangerous industrial activities have to be stopped while some archaic industrial practices have to give way to more acceptable and environmentally friendly methods. This world can be a much better place for us all if antiquated and hazardous industrial operations give way to healthy and environmentally friendly industrial practices.

One action which is becoming increasingly relevant to the reduction of the impact of industrial waste on the environment is that of recycling. Recycling is the process of converting waste materials into raw materials for further production. Plastic, glass, rubber, steel, tin, aluminum, copper, bronze, gold, silver, paper, concrete, ceramic, and other materials can be recycled. This singular exercise will help to reduce the amount of physical waste products which find their way into our environment, especially our water and land. A visit to garbage dumpsters will reveal that most of the wastes found there are predominantly paper, plastic, glass and metal materials and if we make concerted efforts to recycle these materials, the issue of physical wastes will reduced drastically. Developed nations, such as the United States, have already reduced the amount of physical wastes on the environment by as much as 50% to 75% while developing nations are still battling with the problem as though it has no solution. Recently, the government of Ethiopia, in East Africa, installed a power plant which converts waste to electricity. This is a laudable initiative to tackle the menace of environmental pollution.

However, there is an alarming rate of electronic waste from televisions, personal computers, laptops, I-Pads, Tablets, smart phones, lithium batteries, digital cameras, computer games, radio sets, DVD players, refrigerators, air conditioners, etc., that may not be easily recycled. These materials are toxic and non bio-degradable and do find their way into our environment in large quantities on a daily basis. They destroy the portion of land upon which they are dumped and begin to emit poisonous gas into the air over a period of time. If these materials accidentally find their way into our rivers, the health implication can be quite devastating, to say the least. Government agencies which are saddled with the responsibility of regulating business operations must ensure that manufacturing organizations are discouraged from using materials that pose greater danger to the environment than the benefits they seem to provide. Forward looking organizations do not need to wait for the regulatory agencies before making the right decisions and embarking on the right actions necessary to safeguard today's environment for our tomorrow and for the enjoyment of future generations.

ORGANIZATIONS CAN BE TRANSFORMED

Over-consumption: threat to future generations

Consumption is believed to be the end of the economic cycle. Recall that it is the need for consumption that begins the entire economic cycle in the first place. There can be no production if there is no need for consumption. Since production cannot take place in the absence of consumption, over-consumption, therefore, is the reason for overproduction as we see it today. What then is over-consumption? Over-consumption can simply be described as consuming more than what we need as well as consuming what we do not need. Needs on the other hand are necessities of life that we cannot do without. Basic needs include food, clothing, shelter. Other needs are safety, security, transportation, education, medicare, relationships, communication, and entertainment, etc. The biggest challenge we have in our society today is that instead of people consuming to meet their needs, they seem to be consuming to satisfy their greed and inordinate desires. This is the reason why the economist often distinguishes between needs and wants.

Transportation involves the movement of men and materials from one location to another. The need to move men and materials much faster and more conveniently from one location to another has led to the invention and use of automobiles, trains, ships, airplanes and pipelines as against the use of our legs and the camels. Over-consumption takes place when an individual decides to purchase a new sedan car every year instead of using one for at least five years. Over-consumption takes place when another individual decides to own three sedan cars at the same time when he needs just one for basic transportation. Over-consumption takes place when yet another individual decides to own a sedan, an SUV, a mini-van, and a truck at the same time. These days it is no longer the individual that decides to own more vehicles than he needs for basic transportation; it is the car dealership that pressures you into trading in your 12-month-old car to pick up a current model just because the auto manufacturer produced more in anticipation of demand. A visit to the auto dealerships these days reveals the presence of an array of used vehicles traded in for newer models. Who is going to buy these used vehicles? How do these auto dealers and manufacturers break-even and make profit? These are the questions that disturb my mind each time I drive past an auto dealership. Each and every year auto manufacturers churn out new models of existing vehicles with little or no modification from the previous models and they expect consumers to come patronize them. Instead of using automobiles for basic transportation, auto manufacturers now produce cars that double as luxury materials or symbols of social status. Now we have started producing vehicles that do not need drivers. How has this improved the life of an average member of the society? I hope the driver-less cars will still operate during severe tornado attacks or when the streets are heavily flooded. When we start manufacturing commercial air crafts that do not need pilots in their cockpits, we are simply displacing the human being from the society he is trying to build.

Advancement in technology now happens on a daily basis and producers and marketers are taking advantage of this to inundate the market with limitless items that consumers do not necessarily need, just to make more money. Functional and serviceable electronic products are being rendered obsolete every year just to make room for new models or slight modification of same product. Box televisions are being replaced with flat televisions while flat screens are being replaced by curved screens. Android phones are taking over from other mobile phones while new models of Android phones are released every year to render previous models obsolete. This is getting ridiculous just as it is getting disgusting! Parents are the ones that bear the full brunt of this 'new electronics madness' as their teenage kids bombard them daily with demands for latest models of I-Phones, headsets, television sets, laptops, I-Pods, tablets, video games, virtual video devices, DVD players, wristwatches, and home security systems. In our greed, we sometimes consume the products and technology meant for the next generation and are not even bothered about it. The aggressive competition among manufacturers for the first to bring in the latest and most sophisticated item to the market has put all of us on the edge. We no longer consume what we need; we simply buy whatever they bring. This is catastrophic! Instead of demand to drive supply, supply is now driving demand. Our world has become a crazy place. Doing business in today's world is becoming like fighting a war and only those who are better prepared will win in the battle. As long-established businesses are crashing out due to the intensity of the competition, new ones are replacing them without any assurance of survival. Business organizations are busy destroying each other while trying so hard to deliver to the consumer what he does not even need in the first place. This madness has got to stop!

Over-consumption is a threat to the welfare of future generations. Over-consumption leads to over-production. When we over produce automobiles, we use more steel materials than we actually need thereby reducing the raw material requirement for the next generation. When we add the amount of petroleum products needed to operate the automobiles, the situation becomes even more frightening. When we over-produce clothing materials, we use more cotton than we need thereby reducing the raw material requirement for the next generation. When we over-produce books, newspapers and magazines, we use more pulp and paper materials than we need thereby reducing the raw materials available for the next generation. When we over-produce air crafts, we use more aluminum materials than we actually need thereby reducing the raw materials available for the next generation, and when we over-produce houses, we use more wood, tiles, concretes, cement, pipes, rugs, carpets, plastics, glasses, metals, ceramics, and paint than we need thereby reducing the raw material requirements for the next generation's housing needs. Basic economics tells us that there is limited supply of every factor of production. Even if there is unlimited supply of certain raw materials, their overuse or abuse can create momentous scarcity which would negatively impact the next generation. For example, if we fell all the available trees to produce timber, or pulp and paper, it will take years before newly planted trees can grow into maturity and ready for harvest. When we make use of more resources for today's over-consumption, we create an unnecessary scarcity for tomorrow's real needs.

Available statistics show that Americans consume at least 30% of the world's resources annually whereas its population is less than 5% of global population. This means that most of the products produced in different parts of the world such as China, India, Japan, South Korea, Canada, Mexico, Brazil, Italy, Germany, France, Australia, Middle East and Africa, etc., find their way into the United States. The average American family lives like a King compared to what is obtainable in other parts of the world yet complains more than anyone else in the world. Americans make use of latest toys, mobile phones, television sets, laptops, and I-Pads; drive the latest sedans, SUVs, trucks, and minivans; and operate the latest video games, drones, guns, etc. It is a good thing that America's quest for something more is what drives technological advancements (inventions and innovations) to the next level but we should also be very careful to introduce checks and balances so that we do not end up using tomorrow's technology today or consuming tomorrow's products today thereby jeopardizing the welfare and comfort of the next generation.

Over-consumption of the wrong type of food and the inability to burn off excess food calories, are part of the main reasons for the high level of obesity and other related health challenges that plague us as a nation. That Americans are the most obese people in the world is no longer news. What is news is that Americans spend billions of dollars annually to treat cases related to obesity. Take a visit to the gymnasiums and physical fitness centers and you will see Americans sweating it out and burning off excess fat which they often gain soon after because they keep going back to the same lifestyle that gave them the excess fat in the first place. Our kids now eat fruits that have been genetically modified or re-engineered and beef and chicken that are treated and bloated with steroids while still consuming predominantly processed, bleached and canned food preserved with toxic chemical components that do not belong to the human body. Cancer cases are on the increase while medical facilities and personnel battle to treat them with medicines that are no longer effective or with procedures that no longer produce desired results. People are getting sick not as a result of their personal mistakes but because of consuming what is available in the market. Organic or natural fruits and vegetables now cost so much more than the modified, processed, and canned alternatives because it is much easier and more profitable to grow, process, preserve and store the modified food materials. They also last a longer time in our local stores and are easily made available for sale in locations far away from production sites. Business organizations must continue to abide by the basic regulatory ethic of not producing items that are harmful to the body or deploying materials that endanger the environment. Forward-looking organizations cannot afford to be operating to increase their corporate profitability while working to undermine our collective humanity.

Redefining the core values of organizations: focusing on what really matters

As new organizations emerge daily, quite a good number of them are not able to survive the harsh realities of the business environment. In the recent past, some notable organizations have had to go down the drains while a host of others simply declared bankruptcy or received government bailout just to stay afloat. But at the same time, a few organizations have continued to navigate the rough waters and are able to overcome the realities of today's market situation. What could they be doing differently? Can other organizations learn from them?

Organizations that survive and thrive are those that have and maintain certain core values. Core values are those fundamental principles of an organization upon which all its operations are anchored. It can also be described as the main reason for being in business and is often reflected in the corporate mission statement. The mission statement of a typical manufacturing organization may sound like this: "To produce high quality products in a safe environment, with the application of state-of-the-art technology and the use of highly skilled and motivated workforce, for the satisfaction of our esteemed customers around the world while maintaining a balanced competitive environment and delivering a modest return on investment."

From the above mission statement, we can deduce the core values as:

1. quality products,
2. safe environment,
3. skilled and motivated workforce,
4. best technology,
5. customer satisfaction,
6. global orientation,
7. balanced competition, and
8. modest return on investment

Each of the above eight core values will be discussed in details but before then it is important to state that any organization that does not have core values, or that has long abandoned them, will not survive, not to talk of thrive, in today's corporate environment. You cannot jettison your reason for existence and still believe that you will survive. The core values of an organization are like the oxygen of the organization and when the oxygen is gone, life itself is gone.

Quality products: the core value of every organization must include the production of quality products or provision of quality services. Consumers must receive something of commensurate value to the money they are willing to release to your organization. An organization cannot produce substandard products and expect to receive substantial patronage. Today's consumers are getting wiser by the day due to an unlimited access to information. Regulators now require products that carry detailed description of all the ingredients included in their production, the quality and quantity of each ingredient, the known side effects of these ingredients, the amount of calories contained in the (food) product, the actual expiry date, and the category of persons that cannot use such products. Any organization that desires to survive in the 21st century cannot afford to compromise on the quality of its offerings. Let the consumers know you for the quality of your products and services and you will never lack patronage. Your price may be a little higher than the competition due to your insistence on quality. So, let the customers know the real reason for the difference in price and they will willingly pay for it. Nothing is as disgusting as going home with a substandard product, even if you got it for free. Today's consumer is getting smarter and low prices can no longer compensate for low quality. The American Management Association describes quality as 'the totality of the features, characteristics, and traits that encompass the functionality and appearance of a product or service and its ability to satisfy the customers need as intended.'[16] When you use substandard materials to produce a product, the product itself will be substandard. When you use substandard steel materials to produce vehicle parts, the end product will be a substandard car which cannot guarantee the safe arrival of commuters to their destination; the major reason for buying the car in the first place.

Safe environment: Industrial safety is becoming a serious issue for organizations that desire to survive and thrive in today's business world. Failure to provide a safe environment for operations can lead to an injury that might result to a legal action which can ground the entire organization. Every organization must strive to provide a safe working environment where its staff will carry out their assignments without fear of minor accident, major injury or death. No employee needs to lose his or her fingers while at work and every employee deserves to go back alive to his or her family at the end of the day's activities. The production layout must be free of impediments so that employees can easily evacuate in times of emergency. Machine operators and the maintenance crew must be provided with safety gadgets and made to use them. Comprehensive safety training must be provided for all employees of an organization and evacuation drills conducted from time to time in preparation for real emergencies. Excessive heat, noise, dust, and smoke must be avoided since each has a serious health implication. Workers should not be exposed to chemicals and materials that cause harm to them remotely such as asbestos, chlorine, ammonia, sulfur, fluoride, nitrogen, etc. High quality personal protective equipment (PPE) must be provided to staff who come in contact with harmful materials or work in environments where they are stored. Toxic materials should also be stored far away from production lines especially where the organization produces foods and drugs. Industrial waste must also be properly disposed so that it does not cause harm to the immediate environment or filter into a river that is the source of drinking water for the next community. The warehouse for the storage of raw materials and finished products should also be properly secured to avoid rats, rodents, insects and unauthorized persons from gaining access and introducing a foreign material that can cause harm to the final consumers. The issue of safety is so broad and affects every aspect of the organization's operations. The factory where manufacturing takes place must be well organized so that there will be a free flow of the entire production process from the introduction of raw materials to the release of finished products for storage. The production lines must be safe enough for the workers to work on while the production floor must be free enough for emergency evacuation or lights out. Emergency exits must be well marked and easily identified and fire alarm systems put in place to alert employees of possible evacuation.

Skilled and motivated workforce: The difference between the strength of an organization and that of its rivals is usually in the nature of its workforce. When an organization has a pool of better workforce, its operations are better organized, and its objectives well achieved. Therefore, the ability of an organization to attract and retain a highly skilled manpower determines, to a large extent, it's competitive advantage in its industry of operation. Better staff means better ideas, better understanding, better application, and greater results in terms of productivity and profitability.

No two organizations are exactly the same. Even though the organizations might be operating in the same industry, there are bound to be differences in terms of management ability, operational capacity, staff quality, place of location, availability of funds, organizational culture and core values, etc. Therefore, 'stealing the best employees' from your competitor may not guarantee that you will have the best workforce. The only thing that guarantees that is 'training and retraining.' Organizations that seek to attract and retain highly skilled manpower must be prepared to spend quality funds and time to continuously train, develop, update and upgrade their employees to meet the current operational demands as well as future needs of the organization. Things are changing every day and so are the expectations of the customers. When a new technology is introduced, which enhances product quality, the market responds by patronizing the organization with the latest technology in town. This is the current experience in the auto industry. Acquiring and switching to new technology will definitely pose a serious challenge to an organization with unskilled workforce.

Successful organizations do not just have highly skilled manpower; they equally have highly motivated workforce. Motivation is a function of so many variables which include recognition, compensation, training, nature of environment, level of management-labor relationship, opportunities for career advancement, etc. Having skilled but unmotivated workforce does not guarantee success for any organization. If you cannot properly motivate your workers, you lose them. Nobody wants to stay in an environment where his or her contributions are not well appreciated nor his skills adequately compensated. It takes highly skilled and well motivated workforce to contribute meaningfully to the success story of an organization. If an organization desires to gain a competitive advantage in its industry of operation, one of its core values must be to maintain a pool of highly skilled and motivated workforce. They are the ones that will run the machines, answer the phones, operate the computers, type the letters, monitor operations, supervise units or sections, attend to the customers, drive the delivery trucks, secure the premises, store finished products, receive raw materials, repair the machines, and represent the organization to the outside world. If you expect the best from your people, you must be prepared to offer them the best as well.

Best technology: The issue of technology cannot be overemphasized. Technology is simply the scientific way and manner in which production and operational activities are carried out. We have manual, mechanical, and electronic technology. Electronic technology is an improvement of the mechanical technology and has enhanced production in terms of speed, quality, safety, and unit cost on the long run. The reality, however, is that technology keeps changing and if an organization wants to keep up with the changes in technology, it might end up incurring unnecessary fixed costs, which increases its total cost and reduces its profitability.

Every organization desires to have the best technology in its industry of operation. But if the technology does not improve operations as well as contribute to your bottom line, it becomes useless. The corporations that are introducing the new technology are equally in business to make profit and they will do everything possible to convince you that your organization cannot do without the new technology. You don't have to believe everything they say. I once worked in a food processing and packaging organization. One day we saw a machine the grabs the sausage and places it on the sandwiches as they moved along the production line on a conveyor belt. Normally, it takes just two employees to comfortably place the sausage on the sandwich. With the new technology, someone has to dump the sausages in the machine while another person still has to replace the sausages missed by the machine. Meanwhile the floor is littered with sausages which accidentally dropped on the floor. "I called it technology madness." If you consider what it would take to acquire and maintain the machine, and what it costs to pay the two staff members that assist the machine in doing the job, you will realize that introducing the technology was a mere waste of resources. It has not improved production in any way. Even if it does improve speed, it now costs the organization so much more. Who told you that machines must take over all the jobs meant for human beings? As for the new machine, you don't need to ask me what happened to it. It was sent back to wherever it came from with speed.

Don't get me wrong. Having the latest technology in town is never a bad idea. But where it does not in any way enhance productivity, improve operations or boost profitability, it becomes a bad idea. Spending a huge amount of money to acquire a new technology which adds no meaningful value to your operational capacity is a bad management decision, to say the least. If the main objective of an organization is to acquire every new technology in town, it should be prepared to spend the money it will never recover in the course of its lifespan. New technology does not necessarily mean best technology. What an organization needs is the best technology for its operations and once you have identified and acquired it, look the other way. What an average consumer needs is not new technology but quality products at an affordable price. Whatever technology that offers these two advantages is the best technology.

Customer satisfaction: Customer satisfaction is a relative term because it varies from one customer to another. Some customers get satisfaction from price while others get their own satisfaction from things like quality, proximity, convenient to use, environmentally friendly, long lasting, etc. It should, however, be noted that customer satisfaction is what leads to repeat purchase, without which an organization cannot be profitable. Customer satisfaction is what brings about customer loyalty. It has already been established in an earlier part of this book that the amount of loyal customers an organization has is what determines its profitability as well as its sustainability. If your customers are not satisfied with your offerings, you are not in business. One of the things that attract new entrants into an industry is the presence of unsatisfied needs and unsatisfactory customers. Every organization must identify the real needs of its customers as to plan and package the right products and services that would meet those needs at a profit.

Customer satisfaction has been described as the degree to which customer expectations of a product or service are met or exceeded so that customers return to the same products or services to meet their future needs. If an organization has customer satisfaction as one of its core values for being in business, then it must prepare to offer products and services that meet or exceed customer expectations with regards to quality, price, proximity, durability, adaptability, convenience, environment, etc. Products which satisfy both basic and generic needs tend to appeal more to customers than other products which do not. Basic needs are the primary needs for the product while generic needs are some other additional needs which the product meets. For example, the home paint which comes in a plastic container not only meets the color needs of a home (basic need) but the plastic container can also be used as a storage material or as a flower pot (generic need). The container can also be recycled as a raw material for future plastic production. Packaging paints in a container other than the plastic container might lower its appeal to customers and reduce patronage even when the basic need of adding color to our homes is still being met while the paint is stored in a non-plastic container.

Global orientation: It is no longer fashionable for an organization to be a local champion but a global charlatan. In this era of globalization, organizations can no longer afford to ignore the activities of similar organizations operating in other parts of the world. By removing national boundaries and making it easier for the movement of products, services, investments, ideas, and skills across the globe, globalization has forced an organization operating in the state of Indiana to now be in direct competition with a similar company operating in faraway India. Therefore, every organization must aim global or risk being swept away by global competition.

Having a global orientation from inception makes an organization more sensitive to happenings in other parts of the world to avoid being overtaken by cheaper alternative products. Cost of production differs in different locations of the world because the costs of the factors of production (such as land, labor, capital and entrepreneurship) are not the same. If you operate in an environment where your cost of labor is higher than others, due largely to high cost of living or other factors, that places you in a disadvantaged position. If something is not done really fast, cheap imported products can deal a deadly blow on your organization and jeopardize its very survival. However, relocating your operations is usually not the best solution.

These days, most thriving organizations are being sustained by the profits they make from their oversea operations as local operations are no longer as profitable as they used to be due to certain conditions such as excessive governmental regulation, activities of environmental advocates, demands of labor unions, and expectations of other social activists and political lobbyists. It should be clearly stated that global orientation does not mean relocating your organization to nations where you cut corners by bribing local public officials to flout existing constitutional provisions and international protocols, devastate the environment, pay the workers peanuts and subject them to inhuman treatments in a bid to maximize your bottom line. The United States government has a way of holding organizations accountable for illegal and unethical activities in their places of offshore operations. For example, you cannot use child labor to mine diamond or cobalt in Congo and then expect Americans to patronize your business. Going global also means being ethical in your operations.

Balanced competition: Competition should never be seen as a do-or-die affair. Companies are beginning to learn how to cooperate in a bid to profitably serve their customers. When rival companies engage in price warfare, it is the customers that ultimately benefit. But if they agree on a fair price for similar products, everyone benefits. Competitors gain more not by reducing price to sell more but by reducing costs wherever possible. If organizations work hard to reduce operational costs and internal wastes resulting from poor storage, lost production time due to machine breakdowns or absenteeism, costly raw materials, high overheads, unnecessary paper works, poor customer service, use of company materials for personal benefits, and introducing unnecessary positions that do not add any meaningful value to the organization, their profit levels will rise astronomically.

Competition is a situation where companies producing similar products and providing similar services try to gain business from the same potential customers. The problem with competition is that companies fight over a few 'mobile' customers by engaging in various activities such as price reduction, special advertisement, sales promotions, sponsorship programs, scholarships, celebrity endorsements, etc. Each of these activities costs a substantial amount of money. Organizations compete for customers because the more a customer patronizes one organization, the less he will patronize others. Just as similar products are in competition, all products are also in competition because the more of an item a customer purchases, the less of other items he will purchase. The reason is that the customer always has a limited amount of income with which to purchase all the items he or she needs at any point in time.

Competition is more intense in industries or areas where demand cannot expand. For example, where you have five major retail stores operating in an area with 1000 households only, it means that each store has an average of 200 households to serve. If any store wants more patronage, it has to engage in certain practices to 'steal' customers from the other four stores which are also trying to do exactly the same thing. If each of the five stores needs to serve more than 200 households to survive, survival becomes very difficult, if not impossible. The only way to have a balanced competition is for organizations to operate in areas or industries where current demand surpasses supply. Anything else is wishful thinking!

Modest return on investment: Return on investment is the bottom line for being in business. Every organization strives to maximize its return on investment by engaging in various activities which include increasing sales revenue, reducing operational costs, introducing new products or services, improving production processes, enhancing corporate policies and operational procedures, training and motivating employees to put in their very best, and ensuring that suppliers deliver best materials at least cost. Return on investment is the profit of a company expressed as a percentage of the capital employed. If capital is $10 million (i.e. fixed assets + current assets - current liabilities) and the profit before taxes and interests is $1 million, then the return on investment (ROI) is 10%.

Return on investment is a reflection of how well the organization is doing per unit of investment and usually assists in attracting new investors who bring in needed funds to boost the current operational capacity of the organization as well as guarantee its future expansion needs. Return on investment also helps to determine how well an organization is performing in comparison to other organizations. However, excessive return on investment usually attracts new entrants into the industry and sparks off intense industrial competition. This is the reason why modest return on investment is ideal. Modest return on investment shows that an organization is not exploiting the market by charging excessive prices on its products or services. It also helps to keep government away from increasing corporate taxation or introducing new regulatory policies that impede the success of the organization.

Every organization should aim at having a consistently modest return on investment as to make current investors happy, make potential investors eager, discourage new entrants, and maintain good relationship with its customers and the government. As a core value of an organization, consistent modest return on investment guarantees the predictable success and long term existence of the organization. Fluctuating return on investment brings about confusion and renders the organization unpredictable. This makes investors skeptical about the continued success of the organization as well as the security of their investments. Fluctuating return on investment raises hope at certain periods and then dashes it at other periods. Modest return on investment ensures continuity even as it guarantees stability for the organization.

Effects of capitalism on international trade

It was earlier stated that international trade came into effect as nations figured out ways to exchange what they have in abundance with what they lack at the present. International trade guarantees that each nation has access to what it needs, through exchange in cash or kind, for items which are being produced outside of its national boundaries. It should be noted that the basis of all international relationships is economic exchange. This means that if nations do not relate economically, it may be difficult for them to relate politically. Every nation operates its own economic system which determines how factors of production are owned and used in ensuring that the society has all the products and services it needs to survive and thrive.

Capitalism is an economic system in which the means of production are owned by private individuals and where markets and prizes are used to direct and coordinate all economic activities. What this means is that the price mechanism determines market demand and supply. Other economic systems are socialism and communism often grouped as command systems. Command economy is an economic system in which the means of production are publicly owned and the government uses central economic planning to direct and coordinate economic activities. In command economies, Socialist or Communist, the public owns the means of production but the government controls these resources through central administration to determine their allocation to productive activities and the distribution of products according to individual needs. Capitalism sometimes tends to 'exploit' the poor to sustain the rich whereas socialism tends to exploit the rich to sustain the poor. No nation practices extreme capitalism or extreme socialism/communism but a combination of both. A nation is however referred to as a capitalist nation when its production activities predominantly tend towards pure capitalism.

Capitalism would have been the best economic system in the world because it promotes individual efforts and rewards personal hard work. But the truth is that it is bedeviled with greed. Greed is selfish desire for wealth and position. When we amass the wealth that we do not really need, to feed the greed that we breed, we end up as greedy and needy monkeys. It was the great Mahatma Gandhi who said,

> "Earth provides enough to satisfy every man's needs, but not every man's greed."[16]

Greed is the origin of economic exploitation, environmental degradation, social devastation, and individual deprivation. I make bold to say that 'unbridled capitalism is the bane of global patriotism.' When greedy individuals own and control the means of production, the society is usually the worst for it. This is why regulation becomes imperative. When government fails to regulate in a predominantly capitalist economy, the capitalist gains at the expense of the society; prices are arbitrarily increased, products unnecessarily hoarded, and product sizes, quality and quantity intentionally reduced in a bid to make excessive profits. Where regulation fails, government takeover becomes inevitable. This is the reason why the United States government introduced the Affordable Care Act alias Obamacare to take care of the medical insurance needs of millions of citizens who are unable or unqualified to enroll in the health insurance programs offered by the private sector. It is also the reason why the American government manages the Social Security Administration instead of leaving it in the hands of private operators.

Capitalism on its own is not a bad idea but when greedy and selfish individuals operate it, its good intentions are often defeated. The average capitalist seeks to maximize his or her profits and the easiest way to achieve this is to exploit the market. The desire to produce in a low cost area to serve a high priced area, without taking into cognizance the overall long term effect, is the average capitalist's approach to maximizing his or her profits. Importing and selling substandard and low-price products is another approach of the average capitalist at maximizing his or her profit. Devastating the ecosystem and polluting the environment to maximize profits is part of what the average capitalist does on a daily basis. Developing nations with enormous amount of natural resources, often suffer from environmental degradation and all its health implication just to supply industrialized nations with their raw materials needs. In Nigeria, for instance, oil is spilled, gas is flared, and pipelines often explode to the detriment of oil-rich host communities. As a result, aquatic life is destroyed, farmlands decimated, and the people's means of livelihood completely eradicated. In some places like diamond-rich Congo, kids are engaged, workers mortgaged, and host communities enraged. In other places, the elders are confounded while the youths feel frustrated over the level of neglect and decay in the communities where natural resources are taken while the organizations involved and the government of the day continue to make billions of dollars daily at their expense. When you add greed to capitalism, it results in modern-day slavery.

If capitalism is operated devoid of greed, it would have a positive effect on international trade but this is mostly not the case. Greedy capitalists have taken over international trade thereby robbing Peter to pay Paul. They engage in all sorts of sharp practices in their host communities in a bid to satisfy the needs of their home markets at a very profitable price. Sometimes they operate in nations where the government is not strong enough to regulate their activities or sanction them for flouting existing laws. Major multinational corporations have often been accused of interfering with the internal politics of their host nations. They always interfere to stop laws that can impede their operations or to delay policies that might negatively impact their profitability. To them it's always about money. While multinational corporations which explore, exploit and export natural resources from underdeveloped nations continue to enrich their foreign investors, those nations have remained neglected, dejected, and subjected to perpetual poverty and penury. This is the handwork of greedy capitalists whose stock in trade is the impoverishment of others to improve their own economic status.

The surprising discovery is that capitalist nations have also become greedy nations where 1% of the population often controls 75% to 85% of the resources. The United States alone consumes about 30% of global resources annually even though its population is about 5% of the global population. These days the average American is busy buying what he or she does not need with the money he or she does not have in order to impress the people who do not care. Most Americans do not even know why they do what they do. America has become more of a consuming nation than a producing one with the highest national debt in history currently put at twenty seven trillion dollars. The nation is spending more and more to satisfy its greed and not its need and the greedy capitalists are the ones whose wealth is increased at the end of the day. America now boasts of having more billionaires than the rest of the world combined while poverty rate among Americans suffers highest sharp rise in 50 years. All that the greedy capitalist cares about is money and more money even if it is at the expense of of the rest of the society.

International trade is best when it is devoid of exploitation. Organizations involved in inter-national business must avoid the temptation to exploit others in a bid to enrich themselves. Good money can still be made through genuine productive efforts and not through deliberate attempts at defrauding other people. The money we make while exploiting others is usually the cause of our pain towards the end of our lifetime. International business must be based on exchange not exploitation, mutual gain for everyone and not monumental pain for someone. A system that makes the rich richer and the poor poorer is not the best for the human race. We must create an enabling environment that makes some of the struggling poor among us to also become rich some day. If we continue to promote an atmosphere of exploitation, a day will come when all we will have will be chaos and confusion, anarchy and acrimony, and woes and wars. And the rich will also cry!

The issue of collaboration and integration between organizations and the societies they serve

Before now, organizations have always seen themselves as separate legal entities which provide solution to the many challenges of society through the provision of goods and services or creation of ideas. It has always been a case of 'the society has a problem and the organization has a solution' and never the other way round. Most times organizations fail to meet the real needs of the society because they provide what they believe is the solution without necessarily receiving an input from the members of the society. The leading cause of organizational failure is 'acting on assumption.' Some organizations commit huge resources in the research and development of products that do not ultimately add real value to the consumers. As major players in their industry, large organizations often think more of how to boost their reputation with new products than leveraging it on the ability to meet the current or potential needs of their customers.

The feedback unit of the organizational system is so important that it cannot be overemphasized. Organizations must establish distinct procedures through which to elicit response from the customers they serve. The information gathered becomes the basis for future decisions considering how best to serve the customers. This means that there must be collaboration and integration between organizations and the societies they serve. This is the reality of the 21st century organization which serves highly educated and highly informed set of the human race. The Internet and the social media have helped in establishing a linkage between organizations and the society so that information is shared, responses gathered, and concerns addressed. There is now more integration between organizations and their customers and this interaction helps to foster a higher level of transparency needed to guarantee continued cordial relationship. For example, through the online banking system, bank customers can now check their accounts at home or from any location, make transactions, cancel checks, review their bank statements, and alert their bank in cases of discrepancy or traces of fraudulent activities. This collaboration has helped the banks do a better job while letting the customers have a good night's sleep. This is a major improvement in financial service delivery. All other organizations now have online accounts for their customers ranging from electricity providers to loan providers, insurance providers, gas providers, Internet and cable providers, book publishers, retail stores, restaurants, barber shops, coffee joints, etc.

Looking at the flow chart of an organization in chapter 2 (Figure 2.1), you will see the feedback loop which connects the organization to the environment for the gathering of information both on its failures as well as its successes. An organization needs information on what it is doing well so that it can consolidate on those workable actions and decisions to achieve greater success. You do not relax just because you are making money. Other organizations want to make that money too. You must carry out actions that help secure your areas of success so that a hostile competitor does not capitalize on your laxity to wreck havoc on your bottom line. This has happened to many organizations. The best time to be extra careful is when you think you are doing great. An organization also needs information on its failures and the best source of that information is the customers. The customer knows what he wants as well as the difference between that and what your organization provides. The customer also has a fair idea of what similar organizations provide which might be a little better than yours. If an organization establishes a forum where customers can freely register their concerns, seek redress and have their needs met without necessarily driving down to the store to speak to a customer relations staff, that organization has done a great job. In the insurance industry, for instance, good customer relationship has been discovered as the major factor in determining the difference between success and failure.

The feedback unit of an organizational system serves to keep the organization in constant relationship with the society it serves. Most organizations now conduct customer surveys to ask critical questions and elicit honest responses from their customers. This is becoming the basic procedure for service organizations. When they provide a certain service to their clients they always request the customer to fill out a form detailing how satisfied he or she is with the service provided. This is a welcome development even though it can sometimes be very boring to the customer especially when it becomes time-consuming. Feedback has been described as information or opinion about the quality of products or services and the performance of employees obtained from customers, clients and associates and considered essential for evaluation, quality management, and continuous improvement. Organizations must be involved in continuous improvement if they want to remain relevant in today's market and meet the real needs of their customers. Feedback helps to gather the information necessary for organizational improvement and is, therefore, very fundamental to the success of an organization. Also, when an organization solicits information from its customers, it makes the customers feel they are highly valued and considered relevant to the success of the organization. That is, they are partners in progress. As a result, they begin to see themselves as major stake-holders. This turns them into loyal customers who are ever willing to contribute relevant information for the success of the organization. You will recall that the major factor determining the profitability of any organization is the number of loyal customers at its disposal.

Collaboration and integration between an organization and the society it serves has taken a new dimension. These days, organizations are not only seeking feedback from their customers for the purpose of continuous improvement, they now depend on the society for information on new processes, procedures, technology and inventions with which to perform their core duties and to remain relevant and profitable in a highly competitive and innovative environment of the 21st century. Individuals around the world are carrying out research on daily basis in private laboratories, college laboratories, and government laboratories. The only way to benefit from the successes of such research efforts is for organizations to collaborate with the society to test and commercialize the ideas that are being generated and developed. An organization may encounter a problem that seems insurmountable but when such information is freely shared through the various social media platforms, it may be surprising to discover that someone in one remote location of the world may already have a solution to that challenge and willing to trade it for cash. The reality is that the Internet and social media are fast developing a global community in which there is unfettered information flow from the Eastern hemisphere to the Western Hemisphere and from the north pole to the south pole. Organizations can no longer afford to build 'high walls' that isolate them from the society they serve. They must rather establish a lasting linkage to receive the information they need to serve their customers satisfactorily and to acquire the materials and technology they need to remain competitive in the industry of their operation.

What used to be considered as organizational secrets are now being displayed on their websites. Plant layout, production procedure, list of ingredients used, the quantity of each ingredient in a certain size of the product, the calorie of each food product, the potency and side effects of each health or drug product, the fuel consumption rate of an automobile, etc. Organizations that operate in secrecy are losing out while those that operate open systems that depend on continuous interaction with their environment are constantly gaining. Organizations are beginning to realize the need to depend on the environment for their survival. Apart from collaboration and integration with the environment, organizations are beginning to cooperate among themselves to fund new researches in their areas of operation, so as to reduce the average cost on each of them. For example, organizations within the auto industry can collectively sponsor a research for the development of 'intelligent' cars and water-powered vehicles. Also, organizations within the telecommunications industry can collectively fund a research effort for the development of a phone that uses solar energy in the daytime and stores it up for use at night time thereby eliminating the issue of batteries. Organizations in the building industry can also jointly sponsor a research effort for the development of materials that do not aid fire but the ones that actually make it difficult for fire to spread during home fire disasters. This will surely preserve lives and protect properties. Some of these research efforts will cost quite a fortune if one organization tries to sponsor and conduct them in its R&D department. But when several organizations come together to engage in such research efforts that expand the markets for their products and services, the average cost to each of them becomes quite manageable while the benefits are unimaginable.

Running the corporate world on credit card: the credit-card-craze!

One of the major sources of income, as well as needed capital, to an organization is the granting of credit by its suppliers. This entails that certain needed materials are supplied at specific times while the organization spreads the payment over a period of time. Distributors can also pay for products ahead of time to enable organizations purchase needed materials for production. Selling products on credit is one of the worst strategies an organization can adopt because it is usually fraught with bad debts, which do not help an organization in any way. The cost of going after bad debtors and the loss suffered, when it becomes practically impossible to collect the cash, is counter-productive to an organization that wishes to survive and thrive in the 21st century. Funny enough, the reality of the 21st century economy is that most organizations will not sell their products except they grant credit (or provide financing) to their customers. A good example is the auto industry.

How many Americans can afford to pay cash for a car worth $15,000? Your guess is as good as mine! As a result of this challenge, the financial sector comes in to bridge this gap by providing financing (credit) to the car customer by way of paying cash for the car while the customer enters into an agreement to pay monthly installments over a period of 36 to 72 months and at a specified interest rate. This condition is both an opportunity for the bank or the concerned corporation to make more profit as well as a risk for the bank or the concerned corporation to lose money. The reality of the transaction is that someone is owing and someone is being owed. In the auto industry, if the customer has a poor credit score or is entirely new to the process, the banks usually decline the financing request thereby forcing the auto company to provide financing to sell its own products. By this arrangement, the auto company pays the auto dealer and then enters into an agreement with the customer to pay monthly installments over a period of time and at a specified interest rate.

Apart from the auto industry, credit card companies, often funded by banks and other financial institutions, are busy providing credit to people in the form of plastic cards with which to shop at grocery stores, gas stations, airports, restaurants, coffee joints, barbing shops, as well as online stores based on an agreement to pay monthly installments over a period of time at a specific interest rate. The reality is that folks now have access to credit with which to purchase stuff anytime and anywhere whether or not they actually need those items. A lot of people are now trapped by this process because they have gotten huge credit card balances from different credit card companies that are now very difficult and almost impossible to settle. And when you have millions of people each owing thousands of dollars in credit cards, that amounts to several billions of dollars with serious economic implications. The truth is 'until people operate within the limits of their actual needs and earned income, real economic development cannot take place.' The average American spends the money he or she does not have to buy things he or she does not really need just to please people who do not care. The United States is now a nation operating with a huge debt profile. Remember also that some of the funds issued as credit cards by financial organizations are deposits from individuals and institutions and if they come demanding for their money at any time, American banks may not be able to pay. This is scary yet nothing is being done to stop the slide. When will Americans clear their credit card debts? Your guess is as good as mine!

Economic growth is a network of so many things and not an isolated scenario of a single action. Growth in one sector can be counterbalanced by lack of growth in another sector. This is the reason why per capita income, a strong indicator of economic growth, is calculated by dividing the GDP of a nation with its total population. For example, if the banking sector keeps recording losses while the auto insurance industry is recording gains, the overall economic growth will be a reflection of the average effect of the two scenario. If people borrow money from banks to make investments, that is a good thing, but when people borrow money to acquire stuff, that is a bad idea. The only way out is for people to stop using credit cards to pay for food, cigarette, gas, electricity, cable, Internet, phones, household items, gift items, rent, vacation expenses, sports tickets, movie tickets, and other personal conveniences. We must develop the attitude of 'earn before you spend' if we are to recover from this economic comatose.

The global economy cannot be sustained true debts. Organizations need money to pay bills, make purchases, settle wages, pay dividends and taxes, and expand operations. When customers owe organizations and organizations become incapacitated in meeting their daily obligations, they stop functioning. As I stated earlier, debt is one of the major things that destroy organizations within a short period of time. Most developed nations of the world now contribute to the failure of organizations by living big on credit cards. They not only spend the money they have not earned, they actually spend the money they may never earn. This puts credit card companies and other financial institutions in a situation where they can no longer afford to give out credit to people who need it for actual investments. This set of condition stalls economic growth and stifles national advancement. I can categorically say that people from the so-called third world nations are, surprisingly, the ones sustaining global economic developments because they pay cash for all their transactions. For example, most of the used cars from the developed nations find their way into third world nations and the people there pay cash to have them. The reality is, if they fail to purchase these used cars, the auto industry of the developed nations might collapse. Apart from cars, the people in third world nations pay school fees in cash, build their houses with cash, pay their rent in cash, start their businesses with saved earnings, buy groceries with cash, pay hospital bills out of their pockets, buy flight tickets with cash, pay for utilities in cash, pay for gas with cash, repair their vehicles with cash, buy prescription drugs with cash, marry wives with cash, celebrate birthdays with cash, organize funerals with cash, buy clothes with cash, and pay for movie and sports tickets in cash, etc. They pay cash because no organization would grant them credit or give them credit cards. They have, therefore, learned to discipline themselves to work, earn, save, and then spend. This might be one of the many things that people in the 'developed world' can learn from people in the 'underdeveloped world.'

Most of the time, the people that buy things on credit are being pressured by marketers to purchase today and pay later what they do not actually need. What you need is what you cannot do without. When you have the box TV, they tell you that you need to have the flat screen TV. When you get the flat screen TV, they now tell you that you need to have the curved screen TV; the latest innovation in television technology. Now we are going into 'screen-less' televisions that beam live TV images on a white wall or mobile screen in our living rooms for as large as we want them. When they make you purchase I-Phone 6, they now develop I-Phone 7 and still want you to upgrade. As soon as you upgrade, they will bring out I-Phone 8 and tell you that you can't survive a day without it because it has everything you need to survive in this fast paced world of the 21st century. Now we have I-phone 13. People no longer buy the things they need, they simply buy the things that are in vogue. This is the reason why the credit card debt has continued to soar to greater levels every year. Marketers do flood TV screens daily with 'new products' that we must order within the next hour or regret missing the 'low and often limited' promotional price. Those who are gullible continue to fall victim to these marketing gimmicks while accumulating credit card debts that they will never be able to pay back in their entire lifetime. The credit card companies are the ones left with a burden to go after their debtors or shut down by declaring bankruptcy. And when credit card companies or financial organizations declare bankruptcy, it is investors' funds that just disappeared with a devastating effect on the overall economy. But why do credit card companies continue to issue credit cards to people who already have huge credit card debts? Once again, your guess is as good as mine!

The 21st century corporate world cannot continue to be operated on credit cards. This is not sustainable. If you must use credit cards for certain transactions, ensure that you pay them off by month end. We must establish an environment that ensures that organizations provide what their customers actually need and that those customers are able to pay with cash or debit cards. We cannot continue to be spending the money we have not yet earned and wishing that the debt disappears someday. Excessive debts is one of the many factors that lead people into committing suicide. All these negatives can go away if only people begin to learn to live within their means. Less organizations will go bankrupt when we pay cash. More jobs will be created when we pay cash. More of our wants will be overlooked and our real needs met when we begin to pay in cash. Credit cards should be used for emergencies only and to be repaid immediately or within a period of 30 days. Anything more than this spells doom for corporate organizations and stalls real economic development.

Leading the learning and changing organization

The 21st century organization is ever-learning. Individuals acquire knowledge in a bid to improve their capacity to create solutions to the common needs of the society. So do organizations. Organizations continue to devise new ways of doing things even as they continuously adapt in response to the challenges within the environment of their operation. It has often been said that the only thing that is constant in life is change. Just as individuals change over the course of their lifetime, organizations also experience change from time to time in the course of their existence. Failure to change as at when due can be catastrophic to an organization. Learning and changing can only happen successfully in organizations that have the right kind of leadership to drive them. What kind of leader can pioneer the affairs of a learning and changing organization and what are the best strategies to adopt to successfully navigate the organization through each change process? These will form the basis of the discussion in this section of the book.

The role of leadership in transforming and repositioning organizations cannot be over-emphasized. The word 'change' comes in different forms such as transforming, reforming, restructuring, re-engineering, reshaping, reorganizing, repositioning, overhauling, etc. The objective of every change process is to put the organization in a proper shape in a bid to explore new environmental opportunities and to overcome current and potential threats that tend to undermine its growth and development. So, change does not just occur for the sake of change but as a tool for both survival and growth. When an organization reaches its saturation stage (along the market reality curve of its life-cycle) there is a need for a radical change in order to avoid degenerating into the decline stage. Failure to embark on a life-saving program can lead to the demise of such an organization. For example, in 2018 there was an advertisement by the new CEO of the Wells Fargo bank which states "Wells Fargo Bank established in 1852 and reestablished in 2018"[17] and then goes on to list some new policies, processes, programs and procedures aimed at repositioning the bank for strategic growth and greater relevance in its service to the customers. Faced with numerous scandals threatening to run the bank aground, the new Management Board, led by the CEO, had to do something differently or watch one of America's foremost financial institutions go into extinction.

Any organization that fails to change when the time to change is due, no matter how old or big that organization may seem, stands the risk of going out of business. When an organization no longer cares about the reaction of its customers over its own actions, its demise is around the corner. The customers are the reason for an organization's existence as well as the catalyst for its continued success and progress. Whenever an organization grows beyond the yearnings and aspirations of its customers, it has equally grown out of existence. If the volume of daily customer complaints is beyond what the customer relations section of the organization can handle, there is fire on the mountain. The volume of customer complaint is an indication of the level of customer dissatisfaction. When customer satisfaction is no longer the priority of an organization, its continued existence becomes seriously jeopardized. Customer satisfaction leads to repeat purchases which guarantees profitability. Industry competitors usually capitalize on the satisfaction gap to wreak havoc on the customer base of a rival organization. What makes American organizations unique is their ability to withstand challenges, adapt to change, and bounce back stronger than ever. In the heat of the 2008 Great Recession, a host of companies filed for bankruptcy while others struggled to survive, prompting massive government bailout. Fourteen years along the road, the story has changed for the better. Some might argue that bailing out private enterprises is not a very good idea but looking back one can say that it helped save a very bad situation. It kept American jobs, rescued American families, salvaged American companies, and saved the American economy from total collapse. What could be better than that? Also, the global COVID-19 pandemic of 2020/2021 sent American corporations crawling on the ground. Organizations were forced to shut down operations for several months; losing their staff, losing revenue, accumulating fixed costs, and hoping for the best. Till this moment, many organizations are still grappling with the losses sustained during those two years. Restaurants, airlines, movie theaters, music concerts, sports events and small businesses in general were worst hit. Once again, the American resilience and bravery will be needed to turn things around for the best.

Going through the process of change is usually not a very pleasant experience for an organization. So, to relax the process and enhance the experience becomes of paramount importance to any leader who seeks to reposition his or her organization for greater, as well as brighter, future. Those who seek to lead the learning and changing organization must themselves be ready to learn and change. The future belongs to organizations that are ready to learn and change in response to the ever changing customer needs, regulatory requirements, and environmental demands. Leaders of forward looking organizations must have vision and not illusion, build an organization not an empire, be a mentor not a tormentor, be realistic and honest, be a good example, be willing to delegate, be a talker, be appreciative, and show compassion when necessary.

- Leaders of forward-looking organizations must have vision. They must establish a distinct picture of the future they intend to capture. The critical question for every leadership should be 'where are you taking the organization to?' Any person that cannot answer this question with certainty has failed the litmus test of leadership. A leader that cannot define the future has lost the present. Though not all visions will be actualized but at least they should be conceptualized. A leader must have the ability to formulate ideas, plans and dreams that help shape the future and also have the ability to persuade team members to buy into those aspirations. It is the vision that guides all the actions of an organization. When an organization lacks a leader with a vision, it loses direction. No organization can succeed without a vision.

- Leaders must build an organization, not an empire. Whereas an organization is a structured corporate entity made up of individuals operating under defined rules, protocols, roles, policies, procedures, and responsibilities, with a stated goal or objective, an empire is a large estate or collection of estates under a single sovereignty, usually an emperor or King. In an empire, the King makes all the rules but is not bound by any of them. In an organization, everyone follows the same set of rules, policies and procedures to ensure uniformity, conformity, and continuity. You cannot ask your team members to do things that you cannot do and expect the organization to succeed. The leader must establish positive corporate culture for the organization where every member will have a sense of ownership that would engender the commitment and cooperation required to achieve desired results. Team members must see themselves as stakeholders, ready to defend the organization and willing to make personal sacrifices for the greater good of the organization and all that it represents. Let every member be trained to know what is acceptable and what is not. The leader must endeavor to develop a sense of responsibility and accountability among organizational members and do everything possible to sustain them.

- Leaders must learn to be mentors in their organization and not tormentors. They must be prepared to train the next generation of leaders for the organization. Selfish leaders never accept the reality that they won't last forever in the organization. Even if you are the founder of your organization, you cannot remain the CEO forever. You must vacate the seat someday either by retirement or by ill health or death. Good leaders know when to step aside but before they do they find time to prepare their replacement. Continuity in leadership is very important to an organization. There must be no noticeable gap between the departure of one leader and the ascension of another. A succession plan must be in place. One day without a leader can spell doom for a forward looking organization. Raising the next CEO from the organization is a good idea provided the organization is not undergoing turbulent time, which requires the injection of a new blood into the system. A good leader must be concerned about the future leadership of his organization.

- Leaders must be realistic. Excuses are not acceptable in leadership. A leader that keeps making excuses for his or her failure will not go far. Leaders must be prepared to take on new assignments with vigor and put in the required resources for its successful completion. There should be no abandoned projects. Before he or she commits the scarce resources of the organization into a project, the leader must perform due diligence. He or she must make a proper analysis of the project, it's economic and environmental impact, as well as the state of the organization to ascertain if the decision is the best at that point in time. A CEO who rushes into conclusion without having the relevant facts will surely plunge the entire organization into the stormy waters. A leader must ensure that his or her personal ego does not stand in the way as he or she carries out his or her duties. If the CEOs of other organizations are using limousines as their official cars, the good leader must weigh the cost-benefit effect before asking the Board of the organization to upgrade his official car to a limousine. Great leaders make necessary sacrifices for the general good of their organization.

- Honesty is one of the prerequisites of leadership. A leader must be honest and admit his mistake whenever it occurs. No one is above mistakes. However, we must work to minimize them and their effect on the organization we lead. A leader must accept his mistakes, apologize for them, learn from them, and move on. Honesty also requires accountability. A leader must learn not to convert corporate properties to personal use. Honesty also entails that a CEO does not use the corporate platform to pursue personal interests. When a CEO engages his or her spouse, close friends or family members as an independent contractor or supplier, there is bound to be a conflict of interest, which might compromise the standards of the organization along the way.
- The leader of a forward-looking organization must be prepared to live an exemplary lifestyle. You must not do what you never want others to do. Leadership by example is the best form of leadership. If you do not want your team members to come late to work, you must always come early. If you do not want your team members to dress shabbily to work, you should always dress smart. If you want to ensure that your workers are paid on time, make it a habit not to collect your salary until everyone else has been paid. If you believe that your team members do not deserve a raise in their salaries, do not ask for a raise for yourself. We have seen organizations where the CEO is paid millions of dollars annually while the least paid of the workers does not make up to $20,000 per year. This is unacceptable. If a CEO deserves a good welfare package, those employees who work their ass off to bring in the money deserve it too. If the CEO deserves a good office accommodation, the least of the staff also deserves it. A CEO who isolates and insulates himself from his team members cannot make a good leader.
- Leaders of forward looking organizations must be willing to delegate authority and share responsibility. Though the CEO has the responsibility for the overall success of the organization, he or she cannot perform all the functions alone. He or she

must, therefore, delegate authority to other people so that they can carry out their own part of the job with a sense of honor and fulfillment. Delegation of authority comes with an element of trust. The CEO must trust that other team members have what it takes to carry out their job functions effectively. They only need to be provided with the requisite tools and training to achieve stated results instead of taking the job away from them. The CEO might be an expert in marketing but he still needs to walk away and let the Director of Marketing do his job. He can only advise and direct but must not try to take over the responsibility himself. Trying to take over another person's job will lead to serious problems which can adversely affect the overall operations of the organization. The CEO can also delegate his responsibility to someone else. If the workload on the desk of the CEO is piling up, the good CEO should be able to ask one of the directors to assist him or her undertake some of the tasks before they become threats. CEOs who lack trust in their team members keep piling up important tasks that have a way of undermining the success of the organization at the end of the day. Some of those tasks that keep the CEO too busy on his desk should be delegated to other team members so that the CEO has enough space to provide needed leadership. The CEO needs to visit the production floor from time to time to have a firsthand experience of what production workers are going through. He also needs to pay surprise visit to the HR, marketing, finance, warehousing, and other departments of the organization to find out how things are going. Delegation of certain responsibilities frees up the CEO to perform his core function of providing leadership.

- The leader of a forward-looking organization must be a talker. Great communication is key in leadership. A leader must be able to communicate the policies and procedures of the organization in such a way that team members understand them and commit to applying them in their daily operations by way of projects and programs. He or she must establish an open communication channel with each of the team members, where practicable, as to elicit the kind of information and feedback he needs to be able to provide right leadership for the organization. There are usually some supervisors and managers who make it difficult for their subordinates to share vital information with them. The CEO can't afford to miss an important information which can save the organization some money or guarantee customer satisfaction. The CEO can't afford to hide or hoard vital information from team members. Whether the information is good, bad or ugly, the CEO should be able to spill it out provided it does not jeopardize the overall operations of the organization or erode the confidence of team members. We must understand that the right communication usually sparks off the right response.

- Leaders of forward-looking organizations must be appreciative. Every leader must learn to appreciate and compensate superior performance. Those team members who go out of their way to make sacrifices that lead to an improvement in operations, reduction in waste or averting of disaster, should be adequately rewarded. This encourages all the team members to do the same. There are some people that never appreciate other people no matter what they do. An employee that averts a fire disaster deserves an appreciation. A truck driver that maneuvers to avoid an accident deserves to be appreciated. An employee who recommends an idea that improves industrial safety, deserves to be appreciated. Appreciation may not necessarily be an award or a reward. It can be in the form of a pat on the back or a well drafted thank-you note from the CEO. Team workers who perform extraordinary tasks, or undertake certain risks to save the organization, need to be appreciated. When team members feel appreciated, they can do things that we never imagine.
- Leaders of great organizations must show compassion. Leaders must learn to show compassion on certain members of the organization who are currently performing below average and then guide them until they are better positioned to put in

their very best. This is called motivation. Every member of an organization has a specific responsibility for which he or she was employed. Sometimes the new environment, processes, culture, and leadership style might be overwhelming at first and lead to low performance on the part of a new employee. A good leader should be able to show compassion and then find out what the problem is. He or she should also be able to provide counseling or training to enable the new employee settle down in the organization. The people we call lazy employees today may help save the organization tomorrow. This, however, depends on the amount of encouragement we provide at the time they needed it most. Great leaders do not condemn people for low performance; they assist them become better employees and high-fliers so that the organization continues to have the needed manpower to carry out its operations both at the present and in the future. Right leadership helps to reposition organizations for greater relevance in the society they serve.

The three things that distinguish great organizations (The 3-S of great organizations)

There are three things that distinguish great organizations and give them competitive advantage:

1. Possession of superior **system**,
2. Establishment of superior **structure**, and
3. Adoption of superior **strategy**.

Organizational system

At the initial stage of the organization, the management puts in place a system which shows the process of converting organizational inputs (resources) into desired outputs (products, services, ideas, experiences, etc.) in a bid to actualize the set objectives (profit, growth, sustainability, public recognition and appreciation, better society, etc.)

of the organization. The system shows us how things are done on daily basis as we convert inputs into outputs. The system must be unique, adaptable, and transferable. This means that the system cannot be mistaken for that of the competitors (unique), can be adjusted to suit current realities (adaptable), and can be learned by new and future employees (transferable) so that predictable and uniform results are achieved all the time.

In the absence of a system, an organization is headed towards confusion, chaos, and catastrophe. Where there is no system, everybody does his or her own thing; creating endless second-guessing and disjointed operations. We cannot achieve organizational harmony where there is no system in place. An existing system helps to create uniformity among functional units, branch locations and offshore operations. The organizational system can be likened to the organizational culture. Any organization that possesses a superior system will remain the industry leader anytime, any day.

Organizational structure

To effectively operate a system as to achieve predictable and uniform results all the time, an organization must establish an internal structure known as organizational structure (or organogram). Organizational structure has been defined by the American Management Association[18] as the 'framework of responsibility and the chain of command in an organization to achieve optimum efficiency.' It can also be described as a framework of formal relationships existing among the functional positions and various units of an organization detailing authorities and responsibilities, outlining who does what, who supervises who, who reports to who, and who to approach for what, etc. You cannot effectively operate an organizational system without a well-established organizational structure. A system determines what should be done and how it should be done whereas a structure stipulates who does it, who tells him when to do it, who sees that it is done properly, and what next to do with the result. So, if you remove structure from an organization, there is no guarantee that results will be the same at all times.

Organizational structure ensures checks and balances within the organization. It establishes the minimum qualification requirement for all the positions in the organization so that whoever occupies any position will possess the right skill and experience to produce expected results all the time. No matter how superior an organizational system is, if there is no adequate structure in place, the organization will continue to fall short of expectation. Organizational structure is a reflection of organizational systems. This means that structures are not to be copied. Just as organizational systems are unique to an organization, organizational structure should also be unique. An Organization must establish the structure that best drives its system. Any job position or function that is not reflected in the organizational structure is a mistake. By looking at the organizational structure, every member of the organization can see where he or she belongs and how he or she is contributing to the overall success of the organization. The organizational structure also depicts career advancement within the organization. It helps all members of the organization to determine their future in the organization and to decide if that is a future they desire. Establishment of superior organizational structure gives a competitive advantage to an organization.

Organizational strategy

Strategy is what gives the organization an edge at the marketplace. A strategy is a course of action which the organization selects as part of its marketing campaign, among various alternatives, with which to reach a specific target market. Hitt, Ireland and Hockisson[19] defined strategy as 'an integrated and coordinated set of commitments and actions designed to exploit core competences and gain a competitive advantage.' It is the management of an organization that adopts a strategy with which to gain competitive advantage. Strategy is based on knowledge and knowledge, we know, is power. Any organization that has a superior strategy will always be ahead of others in terms of market reach, market share, patronage and profitability. Today's business environment is not for the weakling. Challenges emerge every day, making it more and more difficult for organizations to survive not to talk of thrive. Newer and better strategies are, therefore, required to combat the threats, reduce internal weakness, and exploit the opportunities in the environment. It is, however, worthy to note that adopting certain strategies may require an adjustment in the organizational structure. Successful organizations are the ones that maintain a plethora of competent human resources that constantly come up with the right strategies needed to win the war in the marketplace.

Why do organizations pay so much to 'steal hot brains' from competing firms? Why do organizations take the time to hunt for fresh and smart college graduates? Why do organizations seek the best candidates during recruitment exercises? The answer is very simple! Organizations with smart employees will continue to adopt better strategies with which to outwit rivals, maneuver competitors, and remain the market leader in their industry. This is the reason why Amazon is taking over the retail industry in the United States and JP Morgan Chase is taking over the banking industry in the world. Any organization without an effective marketing strategy will continue to be a follower while others take the lead. It will continue to pick up crumbs from the floor while others are busy eating at the table. Whenever market challengers take over from market leaders, you can be rest assured that the former has come up with better operational as well as marketing strategies. Organizational success is no longer a matter of size but a function of strategy. An organization with a superior strategy will continue to gain competitive advantage over those without it.

Typically, it is the duty of the organization's management team to determine the organizational system, design the organizational structure, and develop organizational strategies. Whenever there are challenges in the organization, the best way to address them is to critically analyze the current system, review the structure and evaluate the strategies to ascertain if they align with or add to the current operations or expected results. Most of the time, it is either the system is no longer good enough for the current or desired operation, the structure is no longer suitable to the current or desired operation, or that the strategies are no longer relevant to the current condition of the market or industrial environment.

So, the only way to develop or improve an organization is to review its current system, reexamine its current structure, or reevaluate its current strategies. One or two, or all, of them must be wrong for an organization to experience difficulties. It is either the current system is no longer producing desired and sustainable results, the current structure is no longer effective enough to deliver acceptable results, or that the current operational and marketing strategies are no longer effective enough to tackle the competitive or general environment and yield a positive bottom line. This condition leads to the need for an organization's improvement or development. As Cummings and Worley[20] rightly stated (with a slight adjustment by the author), "organization development is an organization-wide application and transfer of behavioral science knowledge to the planned development, improvement and reinforcement of the system, structure and strategies that lead to organization effectiveness."

When a management professional is conducting an organizational diagnosis, he or she is looking at the challenges posed by the current system, structure or strategies as to determine the possible solution that is both practicable and sustainable. However, discovering the actual problem depends on how much information the members of the organization are willing to share. It should be noted that the management professional is not there to indict anybody or any group of individuals but to assist in finding an effective solution to the current situation so as to help reposition the organization for sustainable growth and development for the benefit of all stakeholders. The organization development expert or management consultant may adopt the use of questionnaires to elicit needed data. Respondents must treat this exercise with every sense of responsibility as it might save the organization from going down the hill.

When an organization is drowning, it poses a huge challenge to the management to either provide a quick solution or be ready to go down with it. When an organization is growing, it poses a new challenge to the management to sustain the growth by critically reviewing and constantly adopting the system, structure, and strategies that continue to deliver desired results. Nothing good comes easy. Successful organizations must continue to possess superior systems, establish superior structures, and, above all, adopt superior strategies.

CONCLUSIONS

The global society has gone through different identifiable stages according to human history:

1. Segregation stage – the era of the early man characterized by fear of others, selfishness, and the desire to have more room for hunting and gathering to feed self and dependents.
2. Migration stage – the era of moving away from hostile environments to seek solace in a place that is unknown.
3. Integration stage – the era of settling down in new areas where you are accepted as a member of the existing group.
4. Cultural stage – the era of developing and adapting to group norms and mores that guide individual choices and actions.
5. Socialization stage – the era of learning to behave in a way that is acceptable to society through family observation, social interaction and informal education; passing relevant knowledge from generation to generation.
6. Civilization/Occupational stage – the era by which the human society reached an advanced stage of social, cultural, organizational and career development characterized by nationhood, formal education, organized farming, entrepreneurship, the guild system, skill acquisition, and improved means of livelihood.
7. Colonization/domination stage – the era where certain powerful nations dominated and colonized others and controlled their natural resources and means of livelihood.

8. Industrialization stage – the era of the development of industries on a wide scale; transforming the economy from primarily agrarian to one based on manufacturing of goods.
9. Urbanization/Modernization stage – the era of democratically structured governments and improved public infrastructure characterized by better housing, good transportation, water supply, electricity and energy supply, improved healthcare, education, fashion, public sanitation; leading to urban migration from rural areas to cities. Industrial and government jobs became available to city dwellers while farming was left to rural dwellers.
10. Competition stage – the era of industrial rivalry among nations; the era of rivalry between democracy and dictatorship; the era of rivalry between capitalism, socialism and communism; the era of 1st and 2nd World Wars; the era of rivalry for supremacy.
11. Cooperation stage – the era of working together towards a common goal based on improved information and communication among nations; the era of the establishment of the United Nations Organization, GATT, World Bank, IMF, OECD, etc.
12. Globalization stage – the era of unification at the global level characterized by internationalizing processes, influences, economies, trade, cultures, populations, education, solutions, products, markets, technologies, religions, and other social systems, etc.

Major corporations are leading the globalization stage. Corporations do provide solution to global challenges in the areas of science & technology, health & medicine, agriculture & food processing, fashion, arts & crafts, media, entertainment, and sports. In addition, corporations also do exert enormous political influence as they contribute to public policy formulation and its implementation. Corporations sometimes lobby the Congress to pass laws that provide them with a soft landing regardless of how that affects the masses. Corporations can also sponsor protests to dissuade government regulators from executing their full mandates.

Large corporations are becoming too strong to control. What started as an individual's idea has suddenly become a global force. However, leaders of huge corporations must continue to know that the organizations they lead were established to provide solutions rather than become problems. They must work hard to reduce the gap between corporate profits and societal well-being. You can't have one at the expense of the other. The corporation must continue to be a source of solution and inspiration to the society it serves.

Corporation = SOLUTION

S = Space; a corporation must have an operational location or base.

O = Objective; a corporation must have a clear short and long term obligation.

L = Leadership; a corporation must have someone to lead the entire team.

U = Unity of purpose; a corporation must have team spirit where everyone supports everyone.

T = Technology; a corporation must have a scientific process for converting inputs to outputs.

I = Idea; a corporation must have a unique idea that drives every member.

O = Optimism; a corporation must be hopeful that things will work out as anticipated.

N = Needs; a corporation must be sure of an existing market need for the solution it provides.

American corporations have come a long way in providing needed solution to the myriad of society's challenges. Talk about smart phones, smart watches, smart eye glasses, laptops, the social media, 3D printing, credit cards, online banking, Internet of things, Artificial Intelligence (AI),

Global Positioning System (GPS), COVID-19 vaccine, medical prosthetic, video games, self-driving vehicles, drones, electric-powered cars, GMOs, smart earbuds, Email, voice mail, Anti Lock Brakes, digital cameras, nicotine patch, etc. The list is endless of what American corporations have achieved in the past twenty five years alone. Don't forget that all these discoveries, inventions and innovations first came as an idea from an individual. One thing that is unique about the United States is that it has created a conducive environment that attracts and retains top talents from around the world who bring with them great ideas that promote America and transform the world. Great individual ideas lead to great corporations. When a nation lacks men and women of ideas, it is bound to depend on others for survival. When a nation ignores men and women of ideas, it is bound to remain at the bottom of the global strata.

I cannot conclude this book without showing and discussing the diagram below.

Figure 8.1: The wheel of life

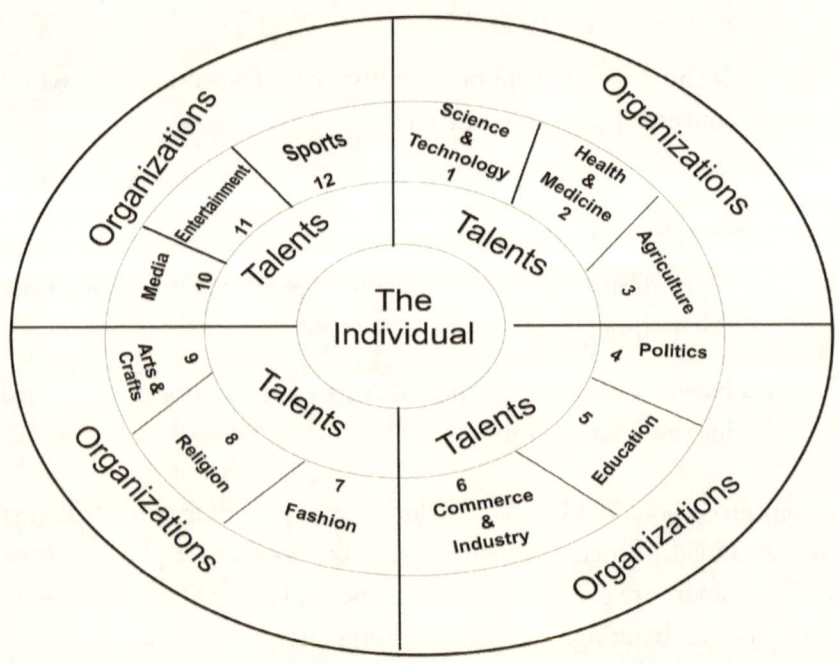

The above diagram describes the whole essence of this book: that organizations are extension of individuals. There is no organization without an individual. Someone must conceive the idea, develop the concept, draw up the plan, and then establish an organization. Every individual possesses natural talents which manifest in the twelve areas of human endeavor or systems of human faculty: Science & Technology, Health & Medicine, Agriculture, Politics, Education, Commerce & Industry, Fashion, Religion, Arts and Crafts, Media, Entertainment, and Sports.

Also note that all organizations revolve around these 12 systems of the world, which I choose to refer to as the '12 pillars of the earth.'[24] This is the reason why we have political organizations, media organizations, religious organizations, sports organizations, commercial and industrial organizations, entertainment organizations, scientific and technological organizations, health & medical organizations, educational organizations, agricultural organizations, arts and crafts organizations, as well as fashion organizations. There is no organization in the world that does not fall within one category of these twelve-tier organizational systems. Just define the main objective of each organization and you will find out where it rightly belongs.

This book has succeeded in demystifying the notion that there are a few 'special individuals' that can create great organizations. The fact is, anybody can establish a successful organization. The gift of entrepreneurship is universal but only a few make full use of it. If you are talented in the area of science and technology, you can go ahead and establish a scientific organization and if you are gifted in the area of health and medicine you can establish a health organization. Individuals are diversely talented and as a result they establish different forms of organizations. It is not just enough to establish organizations. The real challenge is on how to make them grow and develop into world class institutions that add greater value to humanity. Most of the renowned organizations around the world that we hear so much about were established by individuals like you and me. Examples include

Coca Cola, Adidas, Nike, Amazon, Walmart, KFC, McDonald's, Sony Corporation, Mary Kay, Procter and Gamble, Unilever, Pfizer, Johnson and Johnson, Shell Corporation, McMillan, McGraw Hill, Longman, Boeing, Microsoft, Google, Apple, Facebook, Gucci, Phillips, Kenwood, LG, Samsung, Frigidaire, Ford, Toyota, Honda, Mercedes, Kia, General Motors, General Electric, Mazda, Nissan, Dell, HP, Fox, Disney World, CNN, JP Morgan Chase, Bank of America, Citigroup, Wells Fargo, etc.

To grow and develop organizations that thrive and prosper is the responsibility of management. An organization without a strong management will surely falter until it finally falls. The strength of management is in the extent of its knowledge base. Until force is applied, advancement is denied. Knowledge is power. Knowledge is the force behind the strength of organizations. There is nothing you can do when you have no idea of what to do. Management failure is usually a result of limited knowledge of the environment of operation. Knowledge is the mother of twin babies - information and inspiration. As the managers spend their days in solving current problems, meeting current needs, and exploiting current opportunities, leaders spend theirs in anticipating future problems, providing for future needs, and creating future opportunities. This is the reason why there can be only one leader in an organization at any point in time. A boat can only have one captain at a time. As leadership pilots the entire ship by maneuvering through stormy weather and avoiding rocks and icebergs that have the capability of sinking the ship, management removes excess water from the ship, adds the needed fuel, checks the engine from time to time, maintains the electricity and cooling systems, gets needed supplies, and ensures crew members are paid when due, etc. Note that the management function keeps going on regardless of whether the ship is running fast or moving slow. To keep the ship afloat is the responsibility of management whereas to take the ship to its desired destination at the right speed is the duty of the leader, the CEO. The symbiotic relationship between the activities of the leader and those of the managers ensures that the boat does not sink either by hitting the rock, running into a storm, losing fuel in its engine, or taking up excess water. If the leader ignores the managers, the ship can capsize and if the managers ignore the leader, the ship can sink.

We must acknowledge that every organization is different whether they are operating in the same industry or at the same location. The reason is pretty simple. It is human beings that make up organizations and human beings are different. The factors that contribute to making human beings different is beyond the scope of this text. A good psychology textbook will help! So, if a new manager or employee happens to be coming from a similar organization across the street, he or she cannot be expected to have the same experience as is obtainable in the new organization. Organizational culture is people-based and varies from organization to organization because different people make up different organizations. When you move everybody in company A to Company B, and everybody in company B to company A, you also swap the organizational cultures. There is no culture without the people. When new CEOs emerge, cultures begin to change based on the new CEO's vision and aspiration aimed at taking the organization to a new level of activity, achievement, and attainment.

As we have seen in this book, organizations do have foundations and come in different shapes and forms. We also noted that organizations do grow and also die. Above all, we observed that organizations are very important to the society and can be transformed, re-positioned, restructured or re-engineered for better performance and greater impact. 21st century organizations will survive and thrive if they are able to articulate the real needs and challenges of the century, create the needed products and services, and operate in such a manner that does not devastate the environment or pose health challenges to their final consumers. The concept of globalization provides an ample opportunity to 21st century organizations even as it also poses a threat. As a result, there are no more local organizations but global enterprises which are operating in different locations. If your organization is not yet operating at a global level, it sure is being affected by the activities of organizations located in faraway countries. For example, if you are a furniture maker based in Cleveland, Ohio, you will one day realize that the activities of the wood feller based in Chittagong, Bangladesh, who supplies wood to a lumber company in the United States, affect the quality and price of your final products and determine the way your customers relate with you.

21st century organizations must realize that today's consumers have greater access to information about various alternative products as well as the organizations that produce them. As a result, corporate sincerity and accountability is the least that consumers expect from the producers of the products they buy and use. Organizations must, therefore, be sincere enough to report all information about the materials contained in their products and their effect on different kinds of consumers - the diabetic, the aged, the asthmatic, as well as patients with heart disease, cancer, blood disease, bone disease, eye disease, respiratory disease, etc. On the other hand, organizations must also be held accountable for any damage caused by their activities which include adverse health effects on the consumers, environmental degradation, and violation of existing regulatory provisions.

Today's organizations are not just commercial and industrial organizations but also governmental departments, political institutions, military formations, correctional facilities, educational institutions, nonprofit organizations, regulatory agencies, faith-based and charity societies, labor unions, social clubs, sporting groups, communities, counties, states, regions, nations, continents, and the entire world. Every organization has one or more objectives and needs a set of resources to attain those objectives. Having the right objective is one thing and having the right resources is another. Above all, what determines the success of the organization is the presence of the right management which utilizes the available resources in the right manner to actualize the set objectives. Having the right management is everything to an organization. Just as the management of a business organization determines its success, the management of a nation also determines its progress. No nation performs better than its management which in this case is referred to as 'government.' If the government of a nation is not effective, its development will be stalled. Ineffective government, which we also refer to as bad leadership, is the reason why nations fall behind in their developmental efforts and remain chronically underdeveloped. It is shocking when citizens willingly place the leadership of their nation into the hands of those who have nothing to offer and then turn around to blame God or others for their misfortune. When we talk about national leadership, we are talking about men and women who have the right solution to the challenges of the nation and not those who seek position for the sake of attracting fame or acquiring fortune. Leadership has a lot of sacrifices attached to it. Leadership without sacrifice equals building a castle in the air. Great nations are built by great leaders who see themselves as mere instruments for moving their nations from where they are to where they ought to be.

21st century organizations must continue to engage the services of seasoned management consultants who function as business advisors, executive trainers, corporate reformers, and organizational transformers. Management is a serious affair that cannot be left in the hands of quacks and amateurs. The management consultant, who doubles as an unbiased umpire, helps to reposition an organization by assessing its current condition viz-a-viz the market situation, and making recommendations on the best way out of the woods. The management consultant has access to information beyond the reach of a particular organization because he or she might be consulting for different firms doing similar businesses, though he has an ethical obligation to not disclose confidential information about one client to another. Due to the fact that management consultants are not under the same form of pressure faced by the management of the organization, they are better able to look at different options available so as to recommend the best course of action. Managers are constantly faced with the fear of failure and so are very skeptical about taking risks, even if they are viable risks. The recommendations of an external voice, in the person of a management consultant, can help boost the confidence of managers as they take daily actions in pursuit of the organization's objectives.

Management consultants may not have tangible products to offer but their professional recommendations can become an invaluable asset in the success of the organization. Just as we call on our doctors and explain the symptoms to them whenever we are sick, organizations facing challenges should also call on the management consultant and open up to him or her on the real issues and then give him or her the opportunity to provide professional advice and recommend practical steps. Organizations will do well when they have effective managers doing the right job. But organizations will do even better when they surround themselves with professionals who operate from outside but have the necessary skills and experience to make recommendations that help move the organization forward. No single individual can take credit for the success of an organization. Success in organizations is based on teamwork. Organizations are distinct entities with different individuals who come together to contribute ideas, time, experience and efforts towards the attainment of set objectives. Organizations are established for the purpose of creating solutions which are impossible for an individual working by himself.

All the Fortune 500 organizations, a list of the best 500 corporate organizations in the United States in terms of size of capital and annual revenue, were established by ordinary individuals who conceived an idea to produce products and offer services that create solution to existing needs within the society. An organization can be started in a neighbor's garage or a friend's kitchen. Provided the organization has a solution to a specific need within the community, where it was started is irrelevant. What is most important is having an idea or concept that creates solution to a problem in the society. As long as there is an effective management in place to attract the right resources, establish the right policies and procedures, carry out operations in an organized manner and monitor results, there is no limit to the growth and progress of an organization.

Finally, what makes America great is that it provides an endless opportunity for individuals to conceive ideas, develop those ideas and realize them without any fear of intimidation, incrimination, or confrontation by the government or its agencies. This results in huge new business start-ups on a daily basis even though, regrettably, a greater percentage of them do not last beyond 24 months after take-off. The American commercial and industrial base is second to none because it is a blend of democracy and capitalism. The current economic system being experimented by China can best be described as capitalist socialism of socialist capitalism. China is using the gains of capitalism to operate a government of socialism. Capitalism and control do not walk hand in hand. Capitalism without democracy entails robbing Peter to pay Paul. Democracy establishes good grounds for capitalism to thrive while capitalism provides the funds needed to sustain democracy. So, capitalism only survives in democracy. Democracy offers the freedom and capitalism provides the opportunity for individuals to unleash their talents, skills and strengths in pursuit of personal happiness and societal benefit. Without the combined power of democracy and capitalism, it is very difficult to create a progressive society on the long run.

Corporate America continues to flourish in an environment of freedom, justice, equality, and opportunity for all not minding differences in gender, race, religion and political affiliation; the unique characteristics of American democracy. However, the current form of American capitalism, bedeviled by greed, intimidation, and exploitation, must be contained before it gives rise to economic chaos and social anarchy. If fewer and fewer Americans continue to benefit from the huge gains of the American industrial and commercial sector, American capitalism, and by extension American democracy, will be continuously challenged. Entrepreneurs and investors must be allowed to enjoy the fruits of their labor, no doubt, but they should not be allowed to use existing loopholes in government policies to advance opportunities for themselves at the expense of the American public. Any time government fails to regulate properly, the society pays dearly for it. The main objective of government regulation is not to stifle industrial operations or fight against capitalists but to put in place a level-playing ground so that everybody has equal opportunity to participate as well as benefit from the wealth creation the free market economy offers be it as an entrepreneur, investor, manager or employee. Take away regulation and you will have exploitation. Unregulated capitalism breeds a new form of aristocracy while over-regulated capitalism is socialism in disguise. Unregulated capitalism can lead to monopoly due to the formation of cartels by related corporations that care less about its implication on public welfare. With proper regulation, competition will be fair and not a warfare. Corporations can still make billions of dollars without resorting to a nasty fight with each other or exploiting the employees as well as their customers. Corporate America can be properly transformed to reposition America for greater global relevance in the 21st century.

END NOTES

1. Walter E. Williams (1936 – 2020); An American economist, commentator, academic, columnist and author.
2. www.investopedia.com; Founded in 1999, Investopedia provides investment dictionaries, advice, reviews, ratings, and comparisons of financial products.
3. www.obamawhitehouse.archives.gov; The resolution of the 39th G8 summit held in Northern Ireland on June 17-18, 2013.
4. Genesis 1:28; 2:18, 21-24 is quoted from the Old King James Version of the Holy Bible.
5. ww.wikipedia.org; Wikipedia is a free online encyclopedia, created and edited by volunteers around the world and hosted by the Wikimedia Foundation.
6. Ralph Waldo Emerson (1803 – 1882); An American essayist, lecturer, philosopher, abolitionist, and poet who led the transcendentalist movement of the mid-19th century.
7. *Manifesting for Global Impact – Taking over the high places of the earth*; authored by Victor O. Okocha and published by Xulon Press, FL, USA. In 2013.
8. Norman Cousins (1915 – 1990); An American political journalist, author, professor, and world peace advocate.
9. Genesis 1:1-2 is quoted from the Old King James Version of the Holy Bible.
10. Genesis 1:3 is quoted from the Old King James Version of the Holy Bible.

11. Genesis 1:26-31 is quoted from the Old King James Version of the Holy Bible.
12. Hebrews 11:3 is quoted from the Old King James Version of the Holy Bible.
13. This is contained in Ecclesiastes 10:19 quoted from the Old King James Version of the Holy Bible.
14. www.returntonow.net; A Gallup global poll conducted in 2017
15. www.wikipedia.org; Wikipedia is a free online encyclopedia, created and edited by volunteers around the world and hosted by the Wikimedia Foundation.
16. Mahatma Gandhi (1869 - 1948); Indian nationalist leader, lawyer, anti-colonial nationalist, and politician who led non-violent campaign to gain India's independence from Great Britain.
17. www.latimes.com/business/la-fi-wells-fargo-ad-campaign-20180509-story.html
18. Kurian, George Thomas: *The AMA Dictionary of Business Management*; The American Management Association (AMACOM), New York, USA. 2013
19. Hitt, Michael A., Ireland, R. Duane, and Hoskisson, Robert E.: *Strategic Management – Competitiveness and Globalization (Concepts and Cases)*; South West (Thomson), OH, USA.2003. 5th Edition (page 9).
20. Cummings, Thomas G. and Worley, Christopher G.: *Organization Development & Change*; CENGAGE Learning, CT, USA. 2015. 10th Edition (page 2).

ACKNOWLEDGMENTS

I sincerely want to appreciate the opportunity of coming to America. Being in the United States of America has afforded me the opportunity to dream bigger, act smarter and expect greater. That is what they call the American dream! To live, work and study in the United States is a great privilege. America, as the melting point of the world, creates an atmosphere that smart guys can take advantage of to provide products, services or ideas that meet needs, solve problems and deliver solutions at local, regional and global levels.

When I conceived the idea to write this book, the initial challenge was on how to convince myself that I had what it takes to contribute to solving problems in America. The advancement in Corporate America is so overwhelming that anyone who desires to add value to it must better be damn sure of what they are talking about or shut the hell up! But then, obtaining an MBA in Global Management from Ashland University, Ashland, Ohio gave me the courage I needed to carry on.

So, I owe a lot of thanks to the faculty members of the Richard E. and Sandra J. Dauch College of Business and Economics at Ashland University, Ashland, Ohio (2019 to 2020) led by the marketing guru, the Dean, Dr. Elad Granot. Other faculty members include Dr. Sivakumar Venkataramany, Dr. Robert Stoll, and Dr. Debra Westerfelt. I will not forget to mention Dr. Ron Mickler, the Executive Director of MBA programs. These and many more people contributed immensely to my skill and experience in the field of management and organizational development.

Finally, I will also love to acknowledge the numerous women and men who played one role or another towards shaping and reshaping me for greater global relevance. You may not know how far your actions and in-actions contributed to my strength and resolve to be a voice in my generation.

www.ingramcontent.com/pod-product-compliance
Lightning Source LLC
LaVergne TN
LVHW041749060526
838201LV00046B/954